Diversity and Satire

Diversity and Satire

Laughing at Processes of Marginalization

By

Charisse L'Pree Corsbie-Massay

WILEY Blackwell

Copyright © 2023 by John Wiley & Sons, Inc. All rights reserved.

Published by John Wiley & Sons, Inc., Hoboken, New Jersey.

Published simultaneously in Canada.

No part of this publication may be reproduced, stored in a retrieval system, or transmitted in any form or by any means, electronic, mechanical, photocopying, recording, scanning, or otherwise, except as permitted under Section 107 or 108 of the 1976 United States Copyright Act, without either the prior written permission of the Publisher, or authorization through payment of the appropriate per-copy fee to the Copyright Clearance Center, Inc., 222 Rosewood Drive, Danvers, MA 01923, (978) 750-8400, fax (978) 750-4470, or on the web at www.copyright.com. Requests to the Publisher for permission should be addressed to the Permissions Department, John Wiley & Sons, Inc., 111 River Street, Hoboken, NJ 07030, (201) 748-6011, fax (201) 748-6008, or online at http://www.wiley.com/go/permission.

Trademarks: Wiley and the Wiley logo are trademarks or registered trademarks of John Wiley & Sons, Inc. and/or its affiliates in the United States and other countries and may not be used without written permission. All other trademarks are the property of their respective owners. John Wiley & Sons, Inc. is not associated with any product or vendor mentioned in this book.

Limit of Liability/Disclaimer of Warranty: While the publisher and author have used their best efforts in preparing this book, they make no representations or warranties with respect to the accuracy or completeness of the contents of this book and specifically disclaim any implied warranties of merchantability or fitness for a particular purpose. No warranty may be created or extended by sales representatives or written sales materials. The advice and strategies contained herein may not be suitable for your situation. You should consult with a professional where appropriate. Neither the publisher nor author shall be liable for any loss of profit or any other commercial damages, including but not limited to special, incidental, consequential, or other damages. Further, readers should be aware that websites listed in this work may have changed or disappeared between when this work was written and when it is read. Neither the publisher nor authors shall be liable for any loss of profit or any other commercial damages, including but not limited to special, incidental, consequential, or other damages.

For general information on our other products and services or for technical support, please contact our Customer Care Department within the United States at (800) 762-2974, outside the United States at (317) 572-3993 or fax (317) 572-4002.

Wiley also publishes its books in a variety of electronic formats. Some content that appears in print may not be available in electronic formats. For more information about Wiley products, visit our web site at www.wiley.com.

Library of Congress Cataloging-in-Publication Data
Names: Corsbie-Massay, Charisse L'Pree, 1981- author.
Title: Diversity and satire : laughing at processes of marginalization / Charisse L'Pree Corsbie-Massay.
Description: Hoboken, NJ : John Wiley & Sons, 2023. | Includes bibliographical references and index.
Identifiers: LCCN 2021061543 (print) | LCCN 2021061544 (ebook) | ISBN 9781119651970 (paperback) | ISBN 9781119652007 (pdf) | ISBN 9781119651963 (epub)
Subjects: LCSH: Satire--History and criticism. | Satire--Social aspects. | Cultural pluralism in mass media. | Marginality, Social.
Classification: LCC PN6149.S2 C67 2023 (print) | LCC PN6149.S2 (ebook) | DDC 809.7--dc23/eng/20220304
LC record available at https://lccn.loc.gov/2021061543
LC ebook record available at https://lccn.loc.gov/2021061544

Cover image: © sukrit3d/Shutterstock
Cover design: Wiley

Set in 9.5/12.5pt STIXTwoText by Integra Software Services Pvt. Ltd, Pondicherry, India
SKY10037138_102122

This book is dedicated to my husband, Jeremiah, who makes me laugh even when I want to cry.

Contents

Acknowledgements *ix*
Preface *x*

1 Defining Satire *1*
   What Is Satire? *1*
      Satirical Strategies *3*
   Satire and Power: The Power of Marginalization Satire *12*
      Hegemony, Ideology, and Discourse *13*
      Stereotypes, Prejudice, and Discrimination *16*
      Satire vs. Mocking: Issues of Directionality *18*
   The Inconsistent Effects of Marginalization Satire *20*
      Communication Process Model *22*
   Strategies for Satirical Literacy OR How to Read This Book *24*
      Is It Satire? *25*
      What Is Being Satirized and How? *26*
      How Does the Content Make You Feel? *27*
   Additional Activities *28*

2 Satirizing Socioeconomic Status (SES) and Class *32*
   Do Americans Dream of Class Mobility? Defining Socioeconomic Status (SES) and Class *32*
      The Intersectionality of the Self-Made Man *36*
   Pulling Yourself up by Your Bootstraps: Satirizing Stereotypes of Scarcity *39*
      The Pervasiveness of Poverty *41*
   Mo Money Mo Problems: Satirizing Wealth *44*
      Advantages for Some by Disadvantaging Others *46*
   What Is the Answer? Make Everyone Middle Class! *49*
   Laughing at SES and Class in the Twenty-First Century *53*
   Additional Activities *55*

3 Satirizing Gender *60*
   The Unbearable Binaries of Gender: Defining Sex and Gender *60*
   Real Men Wear Pink: Satirizing Masculinity *64*
      Intersectionality of Masculinity *67*

Beauty is Pain: Satirizing Femininity *69*
   Intersectionality of Femininity *74*
Satirizing Genderism: Beyond the Binary *76*
Feminism: Pushing Back on Genderism and Gendered Norms *80*
   Satirizing Anti-Feminists *82*
Laughing at Gender in the Twenty-First Century *86*
Additional Activities *87*

4 Satirizing Sexuality *91*
What's Love Got to Do with It? Defining Sexuality *91*
   Satirizing Heteronormativity *96*
Satirizing Individual Homophobia *100*
   Stereotypes of Sexuality *104*
Satirizing Anti-Gay Institutions *106*
Satirizing Erasure: What about the Ls and the Bs? *109*
Laughing at Sexuality in the Twenty-First Century *113*
Additional Activities *115*

5 Satirizing Race *120*
Black, White, Red, Yellow, Purple, Green: Defining Race *120*
   When Religion is Raced *125*
   "Racist" is an Adjective *127*
Satirizing Whiteness *130*
   Satirizing White Panic *135*
Colorblindness is a Medical Condition, Not a Solution for Racism *139*
   Assimilation vs. Appropriation *141*
Laughing at Race in the Twenty-First Century *144*
Additional Activities *146*

6 Satirizing Atrocities *150*
What are Social Atrocities? *150*
   Strategies for Satirizing Atrocities *152*
Satirizing Extreme Poverty and Homelessness *156*
Satirizing Sexual Violence *159*
Satirizing the HIV/AIDS Pandemic *162*
Satirizing Genocide and Slavery *166*
Satirizing Atrocities in the Twenty-First Century *170*
Additional Activities *172*

7 Epilogue *176*

Appendix A: Satirical Outlets/Artifacts *183*
Appendix B: 100+ Items of Privilege *185*
Glossary *189*
Index *197*

Acknowledgements

First and foremost, thank you to my students without whom none of this would be possible. Although I loved satire long before I worked as a professor, my students' experiences with satire inspired me to think – and elaborate – critically and deeply. As a professor, I learned to never assume anything is obvious.

Thank you to my parents, Dianne and Felix, and my grandparents, Elaine and Percy, whose lax oversight of my media consumption habits allowed me to consume a wide variety of – often age-inappropriate – content, from *You Can't Do That on Television* and *The Micky Mouse Club* to *In Living Color* and *Saturday Night Live*, from *The Little Mermaid* and *Animaniacs* to *The Color Purple* and *Goodfellas*. My media and satirical literacy emerged from a desire to understand jokes that were beyond my years.

Thank you to the friends, students, teachers, mentors, and collaborators who inspire me to think harder about the things that I laugh at, including Kiah Bennet, Joy Burton, Stacy Fernandez, Kandice Green, Joe Gibbons, Donny Jackson, Henry Jenkins, Akira Mizuta Lippit, Tara McPherson, Rae Ann Meriwether, Lynn Miller, Elizabeth Napp, Jeffery Ravel, Steve Read, Andrew Schrock, Patty Terhune, David Thorburn, Bob Thompson, Carrie Welch, and Larry Wilmore, as well as the brilliant people in my life whose satirical takes make me wish I was a better writer.

Even though I have never met them, thank you to the satirists that shaped me as a person and as a scholar, including Lucille Ball, Roseanne Barr, Mel Brooks, Brett Butler, Dave Chappelle and Neal Brennan, Margaret Cho, George Carlin, Tina Fey, Matt Groening (and every writer of *The Simpsons* ever), Bill Hicks, Aldous Huxley, Eddie Izzard, Gary Larson, John Leguizamo, Aaron McGruder, Trevor Noah, John Oliver, George Orwell, The Pythons, Joan Rivers, Jon Stewart, Matt Stone and Trey Parker, Maya Rudolph, Jennifer Saunders, Wanda Sykes, Keenan Thompson, Scott Thompson and The Kids in the Hall, Garry Trudeau, Aisha Tyler, Kurt Vonnegut, Keenan Ivory Wayans, Weird Al Yankovic, and Frank Zappa.

Finally, a special thank you to people who don't laugh at my jokes, especially my academic sibling, John Christensen. You taught me that the things that are funny in my head are not always funny when they come out of my mouth.

Preface

Satire (or the use of humor, irony, or exaggeration to expose and criticize social absurdities) has surged in the rapidly changing social and media environment of the twenty-first century. Satire can now be found in traditional media platforms such as television, film, music, and print, as well as via new digital media formats including memes, microblogging, and web videos shared via social media platforms. Furthermore, these digital formats allow individuals to easily post and share content that *they consider* satirical, regardless of its original meaning or intention.

In 2015, a student approached me distraught over something posted on a Whiteboard in their dorm. Someone had drawn a "Hangman" game with the clue, "People who annoy you" and the letters, "N _ G G E R S" (stacyfernandezb 2015). Rightfully outraged, the student brought it to my attention after classmates dismissed their concerns, citing that it was a joke from *South Park* and they should "get over it."

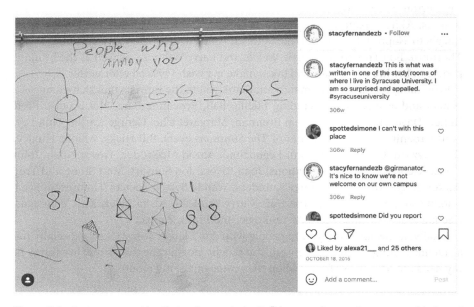

Figure 0.1 Instagram post by @stacyfernandezb of a "Hangman" game drawn on a whiteboard in a Syracuse University dorm (2015).

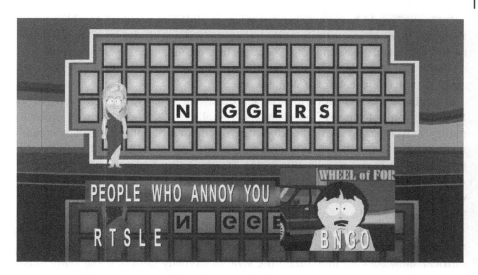

Figure 0.2 Randy Marsh finds himself in an awkward situation as a guest on Wheel of Fortune: shout out a racial epithet or lose $30,000. Still from "With Apologies to Jesse Jackson" (*South Park* 2007).

Their classmates were referring to a 2007 episode of *South Park* entitled, "With Apologies to Jesse Jackson." The episode begins with an inflammatory scene where Randy Marsh has a chance to win on *Wheel of Fortune* if he solves this same puzzle. When faced with this clue and word structure, Randy shouts out the racial epithet, only to find out that the answer is "NAGGERS." The rest of the episode follows Randy as he becomes a social pariah, widely regarded as "n*gg*r-guy;" he responds by reframing this social ostracism as a form of discrimination without a hint of irony. He performs at a spoken word contest expressing the dehumanizing effects of being labeled ("I'm a person. I'm a man. But no matter how I try, people just say 'Hey! There's that n*gg*r guy.'") and begs for recognition from an audience of Black people ("When people call me n*gg*r guy, they're bringing up a painful chapter of my history and all the negativity that went along with it. You just... you can't imagine how that feels.").

Eventually, Randy connects with Michael Richards and Mark Fuhrman, two other men whose careers were impacted by their use of the racial epithet, and they collectively decide to pursue political action. Randy goes before a congressional panel composed of 22 White men, two White women, and one Black man to argue that the term "n*gg*r-guy" should be made illegal.

> Senators, I know it is not normally considered "American" to ban words. But there is one slur that has caused so much damage that we believe it should finally be made illegal. I'm talking, of course, about the term "n*gg*r-guy" ... Two words which, by themselves, can be harmless but which together form a verbal missile of hate.

Ultimately, Randy convinces the senators that they, too, could be considered a n*gg*r-guy, to which a senator replies, "Hold on a second, are you suggesting that "n*gg*r-guy" could become a slur that refers to all White people?" At which point, the panel votes almost unanimously to ban the term, with the lone Black senator casting a shocked dissenting vote. The scene begs the audience to see the absurdity of a culture that willfully disregards how the word n*gg*r impacts Black people but is quick to protect the feelings of White people.

The episode was met with critical acclaim, boasting an 8.8/10 on IMDB, a 10/10 on IGN, and words of support from founders of Abolish the "N" Word, as well as public outrage at its repeated use of the word n*gg*r without recognition of the larger commentary. The contradictory reactions to this episode reveal how different people interpreted the same message differently. Moreover, the deployment of the first 90 seconds to make a "joke" eight years later in a dorm at a prestigious American university showcases how satire can be stripped of its context and ultimately used in a hurtful manner without accountability.

This was not the first or last time that Syracuse University dealt with issues resulting from bad satire. In 2005, university administrators pulled *Over the Hill*, a satirical show seeking to emulate the style of Comedy Central's *The Daily Show with Jon Stewart*, from the campus television station (Bowen 2005). Jokes intended as satirical appeared to positively frame the lynching of Black students, blame the fictional murder of sorority sisters on their promiscuity, and attribute the success of a White basketball player to cognitive disabilities.[1] Thirteen years later, videos showing a supposedly satirical sketch that featured racist, sexist, homophobic, anti-Semitic, and ableist jokes were leaked from an engineering fraternity on campus. The clips, recorded in the basement of Theta Tau, included an "oath" where an inductee states, "I solemnly swear to always have hatred in my heart for n*gg*rs, sp*cs, and k*kes" (i.e., epithets for Black people, people of Latin American descent, and Jewish people, respectively) and [imitates the] sexual assault of a man in wheelchair wearing a helmet who is unable to speak or move while brothers laugh in the background.

In both these instances, the students produced what they thought was satire. One of the producers of *Over The Hill* admitted that much of the show's fodder was "inside jokes" and that the show was not "smart enough" to get across the idea of playing with stereotypes (Bowen 2005). Similarly, the Theta Tau brothers argued that they were laughing at a "conservative Republican" brother by playing the part of a racist conservative Republican even though their brother was not a bigot (Selk 2018). They *claimed* to be laughing at people who believed bigoted things, but to an audience unaware of their inside jokes, they were simply laughing at disadvantaged and powerless groups who were often marginalized because of the exact content of the jokes (e.g., the institutional disregard for Black life, rape and sexual assault).

Satire can be a powerful form of social commentary, but its effectiveness is based on the audience's ability to understand the joke. User-generated content (i.e., content produced by non-professional users) has flourished with advances in digital media. With social media, almost anyone can publicly share any observation instantaneously, independent of industry stakeholders, standards, practices, critical feedback, and context. Without the collective production and distribution process, content can

---

[1] It was determined that a lack of faculty and staff oversight resulted in this content coming to air and the entire station was disbanded (Sajdak 2005).

Figure 0.3 In leaked videos from Theta Tau fraternity at Syracuse University, brothers appear to make fun of racial and ethnic minorities, people with disabilities, and sexual assault (2018).

be rationalized *as* satire if it *feels* like satire, a phenomenon similar to Stephen Colbert's *truthiness* where "...truth comes from the gut, not books" (The Colbert Report 2005).

Satire is more than cracking jokes or making humorous observations; satire specifically encourages audiences to see (and sometimes laugh at) the nonsensical aspects of real life. In doing so, the satirist highlights the flaws in institutions and norms that society has generally taken for granted, offers a unique way of processing difficult information, and fosters insight and critical thinking in the viewer. Marginalization satire focuses on the processes of marginalization (i.e., how groups become and continue to be excluded from full and equitable participation in society). Because marginalization satire focuses on long-standing stereotypes and prejudices that many have taken as truth, it can be uniquely difficult for audiences to "get" these jokes.

I frequently show a 2013 clip from *All In with Chris Hayes*, featuring Cord Jefferson discussing his article in Gawker entitled, "Video of Violent, Rioting Surfers Shows White Culture of Lawlessness" (Jefferson 2013). The two discuss riots in Huntington Beach, CA, during the World Cup of Surfing, where hundreds of young White men smashed cars, windows, and destroyed public property. To satirize how news outlets racialize stories about Black youth, Hayes and Jefferson contextualize the riots using White-on-White crime statistics, the problems of drug use at Ivy League colleges, and the lack of response from prominent leaders in the White community like Joe Biden, Justin Bieber, and Sean Hannity. Jefferson, who identifies as a person of color,

Figure 0.4 Disclaimer at the start of a satirical segment embedded within a traditional primetime news talk show. The subsequent segment flipped the frame, demonstrating how news outlets talk about violence in Black communites by applying the rhetoric to violence in White communities (*All In with Chris Hayes*, MSNBC July 30, 2013).

assures Hayes that his take on the event is not about his hatred of the White community.

> My best friend is White. My mother is actually White. My prom date in high school was a White woman. She was very White actually, she used to ride horses and that whole thing. I have very deep roots in the White community.

Many of the students laughed at the jokes but were unable to explain why. When asked what made them uncomfortable, one student said, "There were a lot of White stereotypes." Pressed further as to why they thought there were so many White stereotypes, they awkwardly suggested, "To make fun of White people?" It became evident that the satire was ineffective; simply showing satire was not enough to foster insight and critical thinking even though they were laughing at the appropriate moments. Mostly White, upper-income, traditional American college juniors and seniors at a top public communications school could not see that White stereotypes were being deployed to draw attention to how Black people were regularly framed in news media, especially around issues of violence. They were not recognizing institutional and social flaws; instead, they were just laughing in response to their discomfort.

These experiences revealed the need to critically engage with marginalization satire. We are living in an age of increasing social awareness as well as an age of satire; therefore, these two concepts must be explicity connected for generations that have come of age with satire as mainstream. This book is a diversity and inclusion textbook; it describes the past and present situations of social groups in the United States, with a focus on marginalized groups or groups that have been historically and systematically excluded from participating in society. This textbook is unique in that it is exclusively focused on the role of satire in conveying this information; diversity and inclusion topics are connected to satirical artifacts, and satirical artifacts are analyzed for their ability to promote diversity and inclusion to help readers appreciate and explain why something is *effective* satire with respect to issues of socioeconomic class, gender, sexuality, race, and atrocities extending from these processes of marginalization.

Note to Readers

Throughout the text, the word "we" is deployed to indicate attitudes, behaviors, or trends that are present in collective American culture. In teaching issues of diversity to students from diverse backgrounds, I have come to use this term to acknowledge and emphasize the role that we all play in these processes regardless of whether or not we have a direct hand in the marginalization or discrimination of certain populations. The term "we" is used to describe discrimination perpetrated by dominant segments of the American population and the American government including the genocide of Indigenous Americans and the enslavement of Black Americans even though my family did not immigrate to the United States until the second half of the twentieth century. However, anyone who lives in the United States benefits from stolen land and participates in institutions built on enslaved labor. Furthermore, it is important to avoid distancing oneself from pervasive discrimination regardless of its apparent magnitude. How *we* as Americans talk about different socioeconomic classes, genders, sexualities, and races has an impact on different socioeconomic classes, genders, sexualities, and races as well as ourselves.

There are dozens of satirical examples featured throughout this textbook from a wide array of platforms, including print articles, video, television, music, and social media posts. However, it is impossible to convey the full experience of many of these artifacts in text, so readers should search for the artifacts online to fully engage. In many cases, artifact descriptions are limited to the featured analysis and readers may glean additional observations from engaging with the artifact independently. In a world where content is widely and quickly available (Corsbie-Massay 2021), students should not rely solely on the examples as presented in the medium of print, where hyperlinks are impossible (or worse, broken!).

The four main chapters also feature essays from students enrolled in one of five "Struggle with Satire" classes held at Syracuse University in the fall semester of 2016 and 2019. These essays, which were submitted as repeated assignments, use critical analyses of marginalization processes to analyze the value of satirical artifacts and in some cases, offer suggestions to increase the effectiveness of the artifact. They were selected for the quality of their argumentation and relevance to the surrounding chapter content. Readers should consider these essays as additional examples of how to engage with and discuss issues of diversity and inclusion.

It is my hope that readers come away from this book with a keener eye for reading satire, a more dexterous tongue in describing processes of marginalization to others, and an innovative hand for create content that disrupts discourse. I look forward to everything you do.

References

Bowen, M. (2005). Your student fee...: HillTV's 'Over the Hill' prompts re-evaluation of programming. The Daily Orange.

Colbert, S. (17 October 2005). The word - Truthiness. The Colbert Report.

Corsbie-Massay, C. L. (2021). *20th Century Media and the American Psyche: A Strange Love*. New York: Routledge.

Jefferson, C. (29 July 2013). Video of violent, rioting surfers shows white culture of lawlessness. Gawker.

Sajdak, K. (23 October 2005). HillTV alumni react to disbandment. The Daily Orange. https://dailyorange.com/2005/10/hilltv-alumni-react-to-disbandment/ (accessed 5 May 2022).

Selk, A. (21 April 2018). Fraternity says oath pledging to hate blacks, Hispanics and Jews was satire — Of a Republican. The Washington Post.

stacyfernandezb. (18 October 2015). This is what was written in one of the study rooms of where I live in Syracuse University. I am so surprised and appalled. #syracuseuniversity. Instagram.

Trudeau, G. (2015). The abuse of Satire. The Atlantic (11 April).

1

Defining Satire

> *"Satire is a wrapping of exaggeration around a core of reality."*
> – Barbara W. Tuchman

We live in a satirical age unlike any other. There is an abundance of social absurdities to critique as well as a host of outlets through which to speak out. In the twenty-first century, satire is mainstream *and* avant-garde. Long-running network shows, like *Saturday Night Live* (1975–present) and *The Simpsons* (1989–present), cable television offerings like Comedy Central's *The Daily Show* (1996–present) and Cartoon Network's Adult Swim, and popular and critically acclaimed independent films like *Get Out* (2017) and *Parasite* (2019) keep satirical content at the center of today's entertainment industry. At the same time, social media has led to an explosion of user-generated satire that can be tailored to niche and intersectional audiences, especially those whose voices have not traditionally been embraced by and in mainstream media.

Regrettably, this flood of satirical content has exacerbated a long-standing issue for American audiences: The ability to distinguish and appreciate satire. This confusion is particularly troubling for satire that addresses issues related to marginalization, diversity, and inclusion. Even though discussions of social justice are prevalent in the public sphere, content that satirizes these processes is increasingly difficult to create and understand. This chapter will define satire as well as a set of satirical strategies before describing how satire serves to disrupt marginalization processes and the difficulties that satirists face in ensuring that their audiences understand their messages.

What Is Satire?

Satire is the use of humor, irony, exaggeration, or ridicule to expose and criticize social and individual absurdity or something that is ridiculous or wildly unreasonable. To satirize something is to reveal its inherent inconsistencies, thus inviting audiences to look - and laugh - at contradictions that have been passively accepted or actively concealed. Satire is more than cracking jokes or making humorous observations; it encourages the audience to see and make fun of the nonsensical aspects of life. In doing so, satire points out the flaws in institutions and norms that society has generally taken for granted. It demands that audiences see the world differently.

Diversity and Satire: Laughing at Processes of Marginalization, First Edition.
Charisse L'Pree Corsbie-Massay.
© 2023 John Wiley & Sons, Inc. Published 2023 by John Wiley & Sons, Inc.

Satire comes from the Greek word "satura," which means "medley" or "hotchpotch" (i.e., hodgepodge). As a form, it draws from different sources and may take many shapes. **Satirical artifacts**, or discrete pieces of satirical media content, include everything from books, articles, images, songs, television shows, films, tweets, and t-shirts. Regardless of the medium, content qualifies as satire when it exhibits "…a clear intent to promote critical thought…. If the program has an intention to stimulate critical thinking, what you have before you is satire" (McClennen and Maisel 2014, p. 111). Although satirical artifacts can be humorous, humor is secondary to their primary cultural objective of making audiences think.

Larry Wilmore at the White House Correspondents Dinner (2016)
At President Barack Obama's final White House Correspondents' Dinner in 2016, comedian Larry Wilmore was deeply critical of the president in his keynote address. In it, he exposed some of Barack Obama's inconsistent choices in the previous eight years:

- On Obama's comedic monologue: "Stay in your lane, man. You don't see me going around president-ing all the time, right? I don't go around passing health care, and signing executive orders, pardoning turkeys… *not* closing Guantanamo. Oh wait, maybe I did do that."
- On hanging out with two-time NBA most valuable player, Steph Curry: "You know it kinda makes sense, too, because both of you like raining down bombs on people from long distances, right?"

Each of these lines were grounded in truth. Obama refused to close Guantanamo despite campaign promises to do so and carried out over 500 drone strikes during his time in office, revealing a preference for killing rather than capturing enemy combatants. Although Wilmore delivers a series of **jokes**, lines that are designed to be funny or to get a laugh, his statements elicited shocked expressions, a few laughs, and plenty of groans from the crowd. He made the audience **cringe** or experience a visceral reaction to something embarrassing or awkward. Wilmore acknowledged this by saying, "Groans are good. Groans are good" (Transcript, May 1, 2016). In this case, audiences groaned because he was telling truths that were difficult to acknowledge, an important facet of effective satire.

Not all satire is "funny." Although colloquially we associate satire with humor, satire exposes and pokes fun at political, ideological, and societal foolishness, particularly through irony, parody, ridicule, wordplay, and exaggeration (McClennen 2011). According to Gilbert Highet, author of the foundational text, *Anatomy of Satire* (1962), satire (1) describes a painful, absurd situation or a foolish, wicked person, (2) shocks readers by making them see something they had missed or shunned, and (3) makes readers feel amusement and contempt. Therefore, satire may not make us laugh out loud. Instead, it may make us cringe by making the implicit explicit, refracting reality to center a marginalized viewpoint (Bennet 2022) and causing a painful awakening in the audience. As McClennen & Maisel describe, "The litmus test is intent, not how funny the bit is" (2014, p. 111). The way satire shocks us and makes us uncomfortable may not always make us laugh, but the discomfort it evokes should always makes us think.

The opposite of satire is **dispassionate commentary** or straightforward statements about the situation of life that do not deploy humor, irony, exaggeration, or ridicule. Consider the examples above. Wilmore could have stated explicitly, "Obama said that he was going to close Guantanamo but didn't" or "Obama carried out over 500 drone strikes while claiming to be a caring humanitarian," both of which were true and the crux of the jokes that were delivered. But these dispassionate statements are not satire: They are facts. Instead, Wilmore packages these facts in a way that obscures the contempt, making the audience and Obama himself laugh uncomfortably.

According to Highet, "...the satirist tries always to produce the unexpected, to keep [their] hearers and [their] readers guessing and gasping... in plot, in discourse, in emotional tone, in vocabulary, in sentence-structure and pattern of phrase" (Highet 1962, p. 18). Therefore, it can be easy to misinterpret their satire for dispassionate commentary. For example, a satirist may deliver a joke with a straight expression or deliver truth in a joking demeanor to highlight the seriousness of the issue and catch the audience off guard. Therefore, a working knowledge of the satirist's toolkit is essential for critically reading satire, including allegory, parody, magnification, flipping the frame, and juxtaposition.

Satirical Strategies

Strategy 1: Allegory

An **allegory** is a story, poem, or picture with a hidden moral or political meaning where fictional characters and narratives parallel real-world individuals and events. By turning a real-world event into a fictional one, allegories surreptitiously comment on power. Authors can always argue that their story is about something else until the parallels become inescapable.

Animal Farm (George Orwell 1945)

George Orwell's (1903–1950) penultimate book *Animal Farm* (1945) is a fable about farm animals that overtake and expel their human master, resulting in an ostensibly egalitarian community until the porcine leaders install themselves in positions of power, effectively replicating the class hierarchy that degrades the other animals not in positions of leadership. The story parallels the events of the Russian Revolution, wherein the imperial family was overthrown and the Bolshevik socialist government was installed, which quickly devolved into an autocratic regime led by Vladimir Lenin. Originally, the book was alternately subtitled *A Fairy Story* and *A Contemporary Satire*, but these subtitles have since been discarded. Orwell clearly intended for this allegorical story to be read as satire even if its political undercurrents may not be evident to the reader at first glance.

Similarly, many satirists deploy hypotheticals to create alternative timelines or fictional worlds as a special form of allegory. What if the world was different? What if some fantastical idea came to fruition? How would current social phenomena manifest in this hypothetical world? This strategy is common in contemporary satire, including *Idiocracy* (2006), *The Hunger Games* (2008, 2012), *The Handmaid's Tale* (1985, 2017–present), *The Underground Railroad* (2016, 2021), and *Sorry to Bother You* (2018). These hypothetical worlds reveal the inconsistencies within our own social structures and patterns that we do not question.

Gulliver's Travels (Johnathan Swift 1726)

Consider Johnathan Swift's classic novel *Gulliver's Travels* (1726). In it, he inverts demographic phenomena we take for granted (e.g., size, intelligence) thereby imploring readers to reconsider the things that they perceive as normal. Written as a parody of

Figure 1.1 The Servants Drive a Herd of Yahoos into the Field, from *Gulliver's Travels*. *Source*: Louis Rhead / Wikimedia Commons.

travel literature, the reader accompanies Lemuel Gulliver as he finds himself immersed in four fantastical worlds: (1) Lilliput, where the native people are tiny and Gulliver is a giant; (2) Brobdingnag, where the native people are giant and Gulliver is tiny; (3) the kingdom of Laputa, where knowledge is valued but not applied to social improvements; and (4) Houyhnhnms, where the native inhabitants are intelligent horses and the humans are uncivilized "Yahoos." Taken together, all four books reflect on the things that we take for granted. They enable our newfound ability to more clearly see the world in which we live by comparing it to other worlds. This approach was also embraced by *Rick and Morty* (2013-present), an animated show on Cartoon Network's Adult Swim.

Strategy 2: Parody
To **parody** is to imitate a particular writer, artist, or genre with deliberate exaggeration for comedic effect. Although not all parody is satire, parody rises to the level of satire when its observations address the inconsistences and ridiculousness of individuals and institutions. Furthermore, a satirist who deploys parody explicitly comments on the original (writer, artist, genre) while simultaneously revealing the norms of the original and using these norms as an ironic shield to detract from the seriousness of the satirist's message.

Party in the C.I.A. ("Weird Al" Yankovic 2011)
"Weird Al" Yankovic is a musician famous for his parodies of pop culture, but imitation alone does not make him a satirist. In fact, many of his songs draw their humor from relatable aspects of life that we can all find funny, e.g., "Fat," a 1988 parody of Michael Jackson's "Bad" that talks about a love of food; "The Saga Begins," a 1999 parody of Don McLean's "American Pie" retelling the story of *Star Wars*; "Tacky," a 2014 parody of Pharrell Williams "Happy" listing a series of socially inappropriate behaviors. This relatability makes him popular with fans of all ages, but these

Figure 1.2 Weird Al showcases the absurdity of covert operations by setting the actions of the C.I.A. to a bubblegum pop song and amplifies the satire through a fun animated video. "You need a quickie confession? We'll start a waterboarding session!" Still from "Party in the C.I.A." Weird Al Yankovic (2011).

examples are not satirical. However, when he deploys his lighthearted approach and wit to address institutions of power, he becomes a satirist.

Consider Yankovic's 2011 song, "Party in the C.I.A.," a parody of Miley Cyrus' pop song, "Party in the U.S.A." Yankovic describes the abhorrent everyday actions of the "men in black" who work for the Central Intelligence Agency (CIA), a foreign intelligence service of the United States federal government tasked with gathering and analyzing national security information overseas through interpersonal contact. The CIA has been tied to covert paramilitary operations, but this is rarely discussed publicly. Yankovic connects the upbeat, bubblegum pop melody of Cyrus' song to the some of the worst actions associated with the CIA, including, "I moved out to Langley recently with a plain and simple dream; wanna infiltrate some third-world place and topple their regime" and "...staging a coup like yeah, brainwashing moles like yeah," as well as unethical and inhuman practices: "You need a quickie confession? We'll start a waterboarding session!" This friction between musical form and lyrics draws attention to the questionable policies associated with the American government through a shadow organization.

Strategy 3: Magnification

Magnification exaggerates or amplifies a singular or relatively small moment to critique a larger social phenomenon. Although individual events or comments can go unnoticed or be dismissed as inconsequential, exaggerating smaller incidents by making them ridiculous or "over the top" reveals patterns within individuals or institutions that are absurd or ridiculous.

In April of the 2016 presidential primaries, the *Boston Globe* Editorial staff collated the promises then-candidate Donald Trump made on the campaign trail including deportations, trade wars, border walls, stricter libel laws against the press, and expanding the Immigration and Customs Enforcement (ICE). The Boston Globe Editorial staff turned this campaign rhetoric into a satirical artifact that parodied a

Figure 1.3 *The Boston Globe* Op-Ed presents a hypothetical front page should Donald Trump be elected president (2016). *Source*: Boston Globe Media Partners, LLC.

front page and was featured in the opinion-editorial section. In the lower left-hand corner, the editor's note reads, "What you read on this page is what might happen if the GOP frontrunner can put his ideas into practice, his words into action."

"Editorial: The GOP must stop Donald Trump" (Boston Globe Editorial Staff, April 9, 2016)

By showing how Trump's statements would affect the future if he were to become president, *The Boston Globe* used satire to reveal the inconsistency of Trump's promises with pre-existing American tenets and values. This artifact exaggerated individual utterances to reveal how they were part of a larger political phenomenon. In addition, the associated articles elaborated the impact of each decision on domestic and international relations. *The Boston Globe* staff reinforced the idea that a promise made on the campaign trail had serious consequences in the real world.

Magnification also includes amplification, or "...saying the quiet part out loud." This strategy is prominent in **postmodernism**, which is an approach to prior cultural artifacts that involves skepticism and irony and deconstructs the theories, behaviors, and artifacts we have largely taken for granted or accepted as valuable. Postmodern satirical media artifacts are self-referential, aware of their source material, and do not hide the origins of their inspiration, while at the same time commenting on their origins.

"No Way to Prevent This," Says Only Nation Where This Regularly Happens (*The Onion* 2014-Current)

In 2014, *The Onion* posted a satirical headline to accompany an article summarizing a series of deadly attacks in Isla Vista, California, where a 22-year-old man attacked 20 people, killing six. The article satirized the rhetoric of gun policy in the United States by magnifying Americans' acceptance of mass death even though similar nations do not suffer from the same tragedy regularly.

> "This was a terrible tragedy, but sometimes these things just happen and there's nothing anyone can do to stop them," said North Carolina resident Samuel Wipper, echoing sentiments expressed by tens of millions of individuals who reside in a nation where over half of the world's deadliest mass shootings have occurred in the past 50 years and whose citizens are 20 times more likely to die of gun violence than those of other developed nations.

However, the power of this satirical artifact emerged over time as *The Onion* republished the article after every mass shooting, using the same headline and general content with only minor changes to the details (e.g., city, perpetrator, number of victims). In the span of seven years, the same title was published 18 times, actively connecting each of these supposedly disparate events to highlight the ridiculous rhetoric that implies that each is distinctive despite a clear pattern. The artifact itself also comments on formulas in reporting and journalism that inhibit larger institutional change.

Strategy 4: Flipping the Frame

To frame a message is to provide structure that focuses the audience's attention to certain components and away from others. This includes how information is conveyed, the source of the message, and even to whom the message is addressed. By changing any of these factors - as well as other aspects - the content is separated from the original frame to encourage an appreciation of the social phenomena being satirized.

Figure 1.4 Donaldo Trumpez, a fictional candidate for Mexico's president, says and does the same things as real-life Donald Trump, including emphasizing his model wife and flying a personal jet with his name emblazoned on the side. Still from "Mexican Donald Trump with George Lopez" (Funny or Die 2015).

George Lopez, Roy Wood Jr., and Sarah Cooper as Donald Trump

In each of these artifacts, the words and arguments of President Donald Trump were put into the mouths of comedians, thus inviting the audience to consider how they would respond if Trump's claims were made by different people.

"Mexican Donald Trump," features George Lopez in a large blonde wig sitting down for a fake interview with a Univision reporter. In Spanish, Lopez repeats Trump's famous lines adjusted for a Mexican perspective: When asked why he wants to be the president of Mexico, Lopez-as-Trump replies, "Because I want to make Mexico great again;" he talks about building a wall on the border with the United States, "...to keep out the Americans, who are coming here and ruining Mexico;" and claims Americans are sending "...their frat boy rapists to Cabo, to Cancun. They come for their spring break to get drunk and to rape each other." Although the lines are a direct reference to Trump, they take on new relevance when the United States is framed as a problematic northern neighbor (The Daily Show with Trevor Noah 2016).

"They Love Me," also known as "Black Trump," is a music video by Roy Wood Jr., with words written by Donald Trump. Leading up to this video, Wood, Jr., attempts to convince Trevor Noah that Trump's quotes are right out of a "...rapper's playbook... he brags about his money, he's disrespectful to women, and there's always fights at his concerts." To make his point, Wood, Jr., delivers Trump quotes over a hip hop beat in a blonde wig with a "Make American Great Again" red baseball cap. Each quote is captioned and dated at the bottom of the screen, ensuring the audience recognizes the original source. The entire music video also parodies rap videos with beautiful women in cocktail dresses and country club casual outfits, Wood Jr., counting money, and Jordan Klepper as the hype man.

In 2020, during the pandemic lockdown and concurrent election, author and comedian Sarah Cooper published 24 short videos on TikTok lip-synching Donald Trump's actual words at press conferences and other events, each earning over one million views. The first video, entitled "How to Medical," featured 49 seconds of the president's briefing on April 23, where he wondered out loud if ultraviolet light or disinfectant

Figure 1.5 Roy Wood, Jr. in a Donald Trump wig delivering direct quotes from Donald Trump with citations. Still from They Love Me (Black Trump) (*The Daily Show with Trevor Noah* 2016).

Figure 1.6 Sarah Cooper lip syncs Donald Trump's famous lines from a press conference early in the COVID 19 pandemic, "I see the disinfectant where it knocks it out in a minute one minute and is there a way we can do something like that by injection..." Still from "How to Medical" Sarah Cooper (2020).

could somehow be injected into the body to kill the virus. Cooper wore a blazer and delivered the lines as seriously as Trump himself, while cutting away to herself also playing a doctor who was visibly shocked and confused by the president's statements.

In each of these examples, the words of Donald Trump are echoed, repeated, and lip-synched by comedians, drawing attention to the messages by detaching them from the body of Trump and thus inviting the audience to question his claims. These segments resonated with viewers who were already skeptical of Donald Trump - unlike the front page artifact from The Boston Globe, which triggered conversations beyond anti-Trump constituents - but they nonetheless reveal how flipping the frame can underscore absurdities when seen through the lens of someone else.

It Happened There: Courts Sanction Killings by U.S. Security Forces (Keating 2014)
In 2013, Joshua Keating started writing a series of articles entitled "If It Happened There" for *Slate*. These articles retold American news stories in a style often reserved for how writers in the West talk about events in other countries. In 2014, he applied this lens to the growing national unrest surrounding the lack of accountability for the killing of Black men by police in the wake of Eric Garner. His story started by highlighting the militarization of local police forces against already marginalized Black communities:

> NEW YORK CITY, United States—The heavily armed security forces in this large and highly militarized country have long walked the streets with impunity, rarely if ever held accountable for violence committed against civilians. In recent weeks, however, several such incidents have ignited public anger and threatened to open new fault lines in a nation with a long and tragic history of sectarian violence.

This opening paragraph makes clear that the policing trends of the United States and its long history of racial tensions - topics that are often relegated to later paragraphs in non-satirical articles - are the focus of Keating's piece. Similarly, phrases like "highly militarized country" and "sectarian violence," are often deployed when discussing other countries and cultures that are perceived by Americans as less developed. The article then connects America's high violent crime rate to "...ruling regimes [that] have broadly expanded the policing and surveillance powers of the domestic security forces and instituted draconian sentences for even minor criminal offenses." By simply turning an Ameri-centric lens on the United States, the satirical artifact reveals the ridiculous and inconsistent ways journalists cover violence abroad as compared to at home.

Strategy 5: Juxtaposition
Finally, in its simplest form, satire juxtaposes the way we talk about and think about certain issues with the facts. Placing **rhetoric**, or the deliberate framing of speech and other compositional techniques to persuade, satire can reveal the myths that permeate our public discussions of issues, alongside reality makes the absurdity impossible to ignore.

The Trial of Robert Kelly (*The Boondocks*, S1E2, Cartoon Network 2005)
Developed by Aaron McGruder as a comic strip in 1997 and launched as a series on Adult Swim in 2005, *The Boondocks* satirizes Black American culture and American politics through the lens of Huey Freeman, a ten-year-old Black

What Is Satire? | 11

Figure 1.7 The fictional trial of R Kelly devolves into a performance by the defendant in the courtroom as the gallery, jury, and judge gush over his celebrity. Still from "The Trial of Robert Kelly" (*The Boondocks* 2005).

left-wing revolutionary who was moved from Chicago to the all-White suburb of Woodcrest, Maryland, by his grandfather. The comic and animated series feature the juxtaposition of all-American social and political narratives with the devastatingly logical and sometimes cynical perspective of Huey.

In 2005, Robert Kelly (R. Kelly), a popular musician accused of sexual misconduct and assault by multiple women and (underage) girls which resulted in multiple settlements and an indictment on child pornography charges that had yet to go to trial. The second episode of the series (Barnes 2005) postulated the circus that would result from R. Kelly's trial, including the media coverage, the public debate, and ultimately the trial itself. In addition to the throngs of fans outside the courthouse fawning over R. Kelly, the judge and jury refuse to believe the abundant evidence and victim testimonies, a point that baffles the prosecuting character, series regular, Thomas "Tom" Dubois. The closing argument by the defense features Kelly's lawyer playing a generic R&B song that causes the entire courtroom to dance. Huey stops the music and scolds the courtroom.

> What the hell is wrong with you people?! Every famous n*gga that gets arrested is *not* Nelson Mandela! Yes. The government conspires to put a lot of innocent Black men in jail on fallacious charges, but R. Kelly is *not* one of those men. We all know the n*gga can sing. But what happened to standards?! What happened to bare minimums?! You a fan of R. Kelly? You wanna help R. Kelly? Then get some counseling for R. Kelly. Introduce him to some older women. Hide his camcorder. But don't pretend like the man is a hero! [Huey begins to walk away, then returns] And stop the damn dancing! Act like you got some god-damn sense people! Damn! I'm through playing around here.

After this brilliant synthesis of the situation, Huey's brother, Riley, shouts, "Boooo. Hey! You with the Afro! Give it a rest. Beat it. Put the music back on!" The music restarts and the courtroom continues dancing. R. Kelly is ultimately acquitted, foreshadowing R. Kelly's real-world acquittal on child pornography charges in 2008.

> **Activity 1.1 Examples of Satire**
>
> Review the list of satirical outlets in Appendix A and consider how many of these outlets you are familiar with and which names are completely foreign to you. Then choose an artifact from your favorite satirical outlet from the list and consider it critically. What social phenomenon is the artifact satirizing? *Why* is this social phenomenon absurd, internally inconsistent, either by holding two or more conflicting expectations, statistically wrong, or in conflict with other societal expectations? *How* does the artifact draw attention to that absurdity using the five techniques described in this chapter?

Satire brings to light trends that have gone unnoticed, imploring the audience to change course. If these cautionary messages are not heeded, then the hypothetical may become reality. This episode was widely shared in the wake of the documentary *Surviving R. Kelly* (2019) because of its its prescient foretelling that synthesized the culture around celebrity criminal trials: The defendant's celebrity can cloud the judgment of everyone involved, making it impossible to hold someone with power and social influence accountable. Only Huey is willing to stand up and state the truth, offering dispassionate commentary that juxtaposes the intentional and inadvertent rhetoric of the prosecutor and fans with the reality. R. Kelly was allowed to continue his predatory behaviors that were eventually described in the documentary. Huey reminds us that when we seek to exonerate prominent cultural figures we adore despite evidence, we discard our collective humanity. R. Kelly would eventually be found guilty of racketeering and sex trafficking in September 2021.

Satire and Power: The Power of Marginalization Satire

Power, and those who hold it, establish, reinforce, and benefit from social hierarchies. Therefore, they are uniquely vulnerable to satire. At the same time, however, they are also uniquely immune from criticism and accountability because of their power. Satirists negotiate these difficulties by revealing the impact of structures instituted and maintained by those in power in ways that escape the ire of those in power.[1] Satirists are more than simply comedians or jesters; they have developed strategies to address the absurdities of power in a manner that obfuscates their critique. In so doing, they're often able to connect with like-minded individuals while avoiding the ire of those in power. Therefore, it is essential to define satire by what it *does* and not how it *looks*. According to famed satirist Garry Trudeau, creator of the comic *Doonesbury*:

> Traditionally, satire has comforted the afflicted while afflicting the comfortable. Satire punches up, against authority of all kinds, the little guy against the powerful. Great French satirists like Molière and Daumier always punched up, holding up the self-satisfied and hypocritical to ridicule.
>
> *(Trudeau 2015)*

---

[1] It is important to note that the historical information contained within the chapters are a small sample of the past and readers are encouraged to use this information as a launching point to learn more about social issues related to SES and class, gender, sexuality, and race, as well as other categories including but not limited to ability, age, and religion.

In each of the aforementioned examples, the satirist's goal is to speak truth to power by confronting authority and calling out injustices implicitly or explicitly. For example, Wilmore jokingly points out Obama's failed campaign promises (i.e., closing Guantanamo Bay) and human rights violations (i.e., drone strikes in international disputes) at the White House Correspondents Dinner. Orwell reveals the corruption of power that exist in political systems that advocate for individual equality in *Animal Farm*. Yankovic turns the serious and sometimes unethical practices of a government agency into a silly pop song in "Party in the CIA." McGruder begs the audience to see how adoration prevents society from holding powerful figures accountable by showcasing this absurdity through the lens of ten-year-old Huey. All these examples critique how power is wielded. Therefore, it is essential to identify and analyze the operationalization of power, especially long-standing historical power that advantages certain groups over others, to understand satire.

Hegemony, Ideology, and Discourse

"When satire is aimed at the powerless, it is not only cruel – it's vulgar."

– Molly Ivins

Hegemony is the power or dominance that one social group holds over others (Lull 1995). This "asymmetrical interdependence" describes the phenomenon wherein all groups within a social system adhere to an established dominance by engaging in practices that reinforce a "superstructure" of control (Gramsci 1971), thus maintaining power structures. In other words, those without power may exhibit beliefs and behaviors that maintain the dominance of those with historical power (e.g., women may believe that men are inherently less emotional or better leaders even though these beliefs may reinforce a gendered hierarchy). Originally used to describe socio-economic class structures, many scholars have since applied theories of hegemony to other categories, including race, gender, and ability.

Table 1.1 provides a visualization of the power spectrum in the United States regarding class, gender, sexuality, race, religion, and ability. At the top of the spectrum are groups that have historically been in power and continue to hold the majority of institutional power. For example, American academics, politicians, CEOs, and other important positions are disproportionately occupied by upper-class, cisgendered, White men (Lu et al. 2020). Conversely, the people at the bottom of the

Table 1.1 The spectrum of power in the United States for different social categories (adapted from Holtzman and Sharpe 2014, p. 25).

People with ↑ Greater ↑Power in the United States	People with Resources (land, money)	Cis Men	Heterosexual, Straight	White People (or Western European appearance)	Christianity, specifically Protestantism	People considered Able-bodied, Neurotypical
	Class	Gender	Sexuality	Race	Religion	Ability
People with ↓ Less Power ↓ in the United States	People without Resources	Cis Women, Trans People, Non-Binary People	Lesbian, Bisexual, Gay, Asexual, Queer	People of Color (or non-White)	Non-Protestant Religions or Spiritual Systems of Belief	People with Physical, Cognitive, Developmental Disabilities

spectrum, i.e., people with low-incomes, women, LGBTQ+ people, people of color, non-Christians, and disabled individuals, are considered **marginalized** because they are treated as less valuable than, or peripheral to, those in power. Furthermore, their treatment is evidenced by pervasive statistical disadvantages, e.g., lack of acccess to clean air and healthy food, lack of access to medical services, lower quality public education, and higher rates of incarceration.

The **processes of marginalization**, or the ways a group is forced to and kept at the periphery, are rooted in pre-existing power structures that have been established over millennia. Also known as **othering**, that is, to actively exclude, ostracize, alienate, and discriminate against, these processes include **social marginalization** or rhetorically devaluing groups through media (mis)representation and social interactions, **economic marginalization** or restricting certain groups from acquiring resources like limiting wages or prohibiting them from certain occupations and opportunities, and **political marginalization** or restricting certain groups from participating in civic life through voting restrictions or access to political representation. Over the past century, social justice (e.g., suffrage and civil rights) movements have increased a general awareness of hegemony and power structures, but major gaps between those in power and those who are marginalized still remain.

Marginalization satire is satire that critiques this social hierarchy and the processes that maintain it, including the treatment of people who have been historically marginalized. It dissects the social constructs that maintain the marginalization of certain groups by drawing attention to social norms, public memories, and identities (Terhune and Corsbie-Massay 2020; Rossing 2016). Marginalization satire is more than simply drawing attention to issues relevant to marginalized peoples; therefore it can be created by people from marginalized groups as well as those who are not marginalized. Most importantly, this sub-genre focuses on the history and processes of hegemony that affect everyone, including those at the top of the power spectrum.

Whereas hegemony refers to social hierarchy, **ideology** is a system of ideas and ideals, especially those that form the basis of policy. According to Stuart Hall (1981), ideology is the *articulation* of hegemony. The often unseen power structures (hegemony) manifest in the social beliefs on which institutions are built (ideology). Ideologies can be religious (e.g., monotheism, belief in reincarnation), economic (e.g., capitalism, deregulation), or political (e.g., democracy, communism, autocracy) (Hall 1981). However, other belief systems, including those that relate to categorical issues, are just as impactful. For example, the American Dream is the belief that if you work hard you can achieve a higher class in the United States regardless of the circumstances into which you were born (see Chapter 2). Heterosexism is the belief that the coupling of cisgender men and cisgender women is the only legitimate form of romantic relationship (see Chapter 4). White supremacy stems from the belief that White people are inherently superior to non-White people (see Chapter 5). All these ideologies reinforce the hierarchies outlined in Table 1.1 and impact how we think about, talk about, and interact with others. Ideologies are ripe for satire because individual adherence to these belief systems can defy logic or evidence. People will engage in irrational and unreasonable behavior, including behavior that harms themselves and others, to support and defend their ideologies, as will be described throughout this book.

Finally, **discourse** is the framing of an issue in media content using a particular angle or perspective to tell a story; that is, *how* do we talk about a given issue? Longstanding patterns in discourse have actively impeded Americans' awareness of social hierarchies by making certain frames appear "normal." When this occurs, it encourages audiences to ask the same questions and get the same answers (Chen 2012). In short, discourse draws on and supports stereotypes by causing people to look for specific answers to certain questions. Although discourse can be difficult to see, **content analyses**, or the systematic study of how an issue (or group) is framed across media artifacts, can reveal these trends. Here are some examples:

- Discussions of poverty in American news media shifted from focusing on structural causes of poverty in the 1960s, including low wages and lack of affordable housing, to the negative individual characteristics of people in poverty, including portraying them as lazy or cheats in the 1980s, a trend that remains in place today (Rose and Baumgartner 2013).
- An analysis of female gubernatorial candidates in the 2000 election cycle revealed that personal characteristics (e.g., appearance, personality) were more likely to be featured when the candidate was a woman whereas policy positions were more likely to be featured when the candidate was a man (Devitt 2002).
- Although the percent of Black Americans in poverty has remained at about 30%, an analysis of news magazine images revealed that the representation of Black Americans in news stories about poverty more than doubled from 30% to 70% between 1964 and 1967, a trend that continued throughout the rest of the twentieth century (Gilens 2003).

Framing and discourse (and **rhetoric**, or language primarily designed to persuade audiences, often in the absence of sincerity) reflect ideologies and can reinforce hegemony because these processes are most effective when they deploy preexisting associations to bypass audience awareness. However, framing and discourse (and rhetoric) can also *disrupt* hegemony, which is the goal of the marginalization satirist: To draw attention to these unspoken hegemonic processes, thus activating audience awareness and revealing the non-conscious responses to which we are no longer sensitized.

Predicting the Biggest On-Field Battles (*Key & Peele Super Bowl Special*, Comedy Central 2015)

The racialized treatment of professional athletes was brilliantly satirized by the comedy duo Keegan Michael Key and Jordan Peele in their 2015 Superbowl Special, which featured the two as sports talk show hosts "Bertram Skilling" and "Dante Pibb." In one segment (Key, et al.), the hosts brought on Harry Peters, the host of "No. YOU Shut Up," a title that parodies and satirizes the bombastic nature of television programming, to talk about the on-field battles in the upcoming Super Bowl. The interaction begins with Peters describing the impending clash between Tom Brady and Richard Sherman. He defines Brady as "...the hardest working, most intelligent players in the game," and Sherman as "...one of the most physically gifted creatures to ever grace the sport."

Skilling and Pibb push back, arguing "Sherman is a smart guy! He graduated Stanford." Peters then acknowledges this fact: "100 percent, he is very *articulate*," an adjective that is often used to describe intelligent people of color, but relies on a very low bar of intelligence (Sue et al. 2008). The camera then cuts back to the hosts as they exchange shocked looks. The segment continues with Peters comparing White and Black players while ratcheting up the "brains vs. brawn" dichotomy: White players are "cerebral" despite featuring individuals with their famously less-than-intelligent public personas, and Black players are described using words like "voodoo" and "magical skills he learned from his grandma," echoing stereotypes of Black people as primitive (Glenn and Cunningham 2009). By parodying the style of sports talk shows, Peters' seemingly offhand but racially-loaded comments become increasingly extreme as the clip progresses, revealing the racialized way that athletes are described and ultimately discussed.

The sketch follows a 2014 interactive content analysis published by *Deadspin* that allowed users to review the frequency of words used to describe White and Black NFL prospects in scouting reports (Fischer-Baum et al. 2014). Words like "speed" and "strength" were used evenly, but words like "smart" and "leader" were more than twice as likely to be used to describe White players than Black players. Conversely, words like "instincts" and "natural" were almost twice as likely to be used for Black players than White players. Interestingly, the word "however" was also more likely to be used for Black players than White players, indicating that scouts were more likely to qualify their earlier comments when referring to a Black prospect.

The interface was covered in many non-sports mainstream outlets because the opportunity to look closely at the disparate treatment of athletes by race was eye-opening for many while also providing an interesting and engaging visualization of racism to those sensitized to these issues. Ultimately, it provides a valuable tool through which to see the satirical artifact from Key and Peele that neatly connects the concepts of hegemony, ideology, and discourse. In reverse, it magnifies the racial trends in the discourse (i.e., how we *talk* about football players), thereby mocking the ideological supremacy of Whiteness (i.e., the belief that White people are intelligent regardless of their actions and behaviors, and Black people are relegated to physical "specimens") and disrupting the racial hegemony by encouraging the audience to laugh at its absurdity.

Stereotypes, Prejudice, and Discrimination

The clip also reveals how discourse is intimately connected to **stereotypes**: Widely held, fixed, and oversimplified images of a particular type of person (Gorham 2019) that can be catalyzed through media trends. By viewing mediated representations of specific groups, we associate certain groups with certain characteristics. In the above example, Black people are stereotypically associated with physicality and White people with intelligence. By amplifying these simplistic and faulty associations, Key and Peele implore the audience to acknowledge how the marginalization of Black people is perpetuated through often unquestioned discourse and stereotypes.

Stereotypes are also deployed and reinforced through the stories that we tell and the archetypes and "schemas" that we use to understand social events. **Archetypes** are recurring symbols or motifs in literature or art. Archetypal characters are often constructed through stereotypical associations (e.g., the dumb blonde, the damsel in distress, the White working-class buffoon, the Black or Latino "thug"). **Schemas** are basic narrative outlines or stories that serve as cognitive heuristics or mental shortcuts (e.g., "rags to riches" stories, Cinderella stories, the White savior). Stereotypes, archetypes, and schemas all promote simplified understandings of people and the world, thus limiting our ability to appreciate the value of the diversity of humanity and the range of individuals within any given group.

Stereotypes are different from **prejudices**, which are opinions or attitudes about an individual or a group and can be either positive or negative. Prejudices can be related to stereotypes because individuals can hold attitudes and opinions about groups based on associated stereotypes, especially if they have no interaction with said group. Similarly, ideologies inform our attitudes and prejudices. An ideology of White supremacy, that White people are intellectually superior to non-White people, projects a negative attitude on people who are not White. However, prejudices and stereotypes are not inherently correlated because one can have stereotypes of a group without prejudicial attitudes; people with low prejudice are aware of stereotypes but work to limit the impact of stereotypes on their conscious attitudes and behavior (Devine 1989). The *Key and Peele* sketch demonstrates this difference; hosts Skilling and Pibb do not accuse Peters of being prejudiced against Black people but rather focus on the stereotypical associations that Peters makes when he describes the different types of players.

Like ideologies, stereotypes and prejudices are rooted in what we think, believe, and feel, and they persist despite contrary evidence, making them ripe for satire. But satirizing these phenomena helps disrupt more troubling outcomes, including **discrimination**: Actions or behaviors that affect a target individual based on their group affiliation. Discrimination is connected to hegemony because longstanding biases in the decision making of people and institutions reinforce hierarchies (see Table 1.1). Furthermore, **individual discrimination** (i.e., the actions taken by single individuals that favor or harm a person based on their social category) and **institutional discrimination** (i.e., policies within institutions like education and politics that reinforce disparities of social categories) work together to systematically marginalize certain groups. Policies that prevent historically marginalized individuals from equitability participating in American institutions emerge from and reinforce individual prejudices, creating a discriminatory cycle that is difficult to disrupt.

Goobacks (*South Park*, S8E7, Comedy Central 2004)
In this episode, time travellers from 3045 come to present-day South Park, Colorado, through a time portal. We learn that the future is poverty-stricken and the only way to provide for one's family is to travel back in time to work for extremely low wages, put those earnings into a bank account, and then wait a millennia for it to increase in value for future generations. Excitement quickly becomes prejudice as present-day South Park changes in response to a wave of people from the future: Present-day residents are losing their jobs to the future people, teachers must learn how to teach crowded classrooms of students who speak different languages, and ethnic enclaves emerge all over the city.

The episode parallels many of the debates regarding immigration in the real world, but the audience's attention is focused on how Stan Marsh, one of the four main characters, changes in response to the time travellers. At the beginning of the episode,

Figure 1.8 The boys walk through South Park's ethnic enclave, "Little Future," with stereotypical sampling of ethnic neighborhoods including hanging livestock and tricked out cars. Still from "Goobacks" (*South Park* 2004).

Stan is fascinated with the first man from the future, but his snow shovelling business quickly fails because the time travellers work for menial wages. At a town hall meeting, Stan is swept into the social panic in response to the wave of time immigrants as the meeting devolves into a cacophony of "They took our jobs!", discourse that reinforces the stereotype that (time) immigrants are job-stealers, and the term "goobacks," a reference to the anti-Latino slur "w*tb*cks," becomes a common "time-bashing slur." This results in prejudice and discrimination against the time immigrants to protect the ideologies and hegemony of present-day South Park.

The episode replicates our current immigration discourse in an exaggerated allegory: The same current anti-immigrant language used regarding immigration (e.g., taking American jobs, changing culture, draining public resources through overcrowded schools) is replicated in this narrative but applied to an impossible community, that of time travellers. The creators of *South Park*, Trey Parker and Matt Stone, demand viewers acknowledge the process by which we come to stereotype, hate, and discriminate against immigrants. This is a heavy episode but one that has aged extremely well because it mirrors how we actively marginalize others, perhaps even our own descendants, and refuse to address the larger global (and temporal) problems that we ourselves may be causing.

Satire vs. Mocking: Issues of Directionality

The satirist must take care to not carelessly repeat stereotypical, prejudiced, and discriminatory statements without explicating the subsequent problems. When this happens, artifacts intended as satirical only repeat hateful content by "lampooning" or mocking already marginalized groups. To **mock** is to make fun of someone or something in a cruel way; similarly **"Punching down"** refers to any content that targets individuals who are of a lower status, thus further disenfranchising the disenfranchised. According to Trudeau (2015), "Ridiculing the non-privileged is almost never funny—it's just mean." Content that punches down while claiming to be satire demonstrates a lack of understanding (or denial) of the traditional purpose of satire to "comfort(ed) the afflicted while afflicting the comfortable."

The 2015 attacks on the *Charlie Hebdo* office in Paris ignited an international conversation on the differences between satire and mockery. *Charlie Hebdo* is a self-described left-wing satirical magazine whose original focus was to critique the absurdities of the French government. In the early 2000s, the magazine published several cartoons that featured multiple images of the prophet Muhammed making jokes at the expense of ideologies associated with fundamentalist interpretations of Islam. The visual representation of Muhammed, seen as sacrilegious to Muslims, was perceived as attacking Muslims, an offense compounded by placing him in disrespectful positions. On January 7, 2015, two men claiming affiliation with Al-Qaeda opened fire on the *Charlie Hebdo* offices, killing twelve people.

A few months after the attacks, Garry Trudeau (*Doonesbury*) delivered an indictment of *Charlie Hebdo* and how "satire" has been used as an excuse for mocking:

> By punching downward, by attacking a powerless, disenfranchised minority with crude, vulgar drawings closer to graffiti than cartoons, Charlie (Hebdo) wandered into the realm of hate speech, which in France is only illegal if it directly incites violence. Well, voila—the 7 million copies that were published following the killings did exactly that, triggering violent protests across the Muslim world, including one in Niger, in which ten people died.
>
> *(Trudeau 2015)*

The magazine argued that its representations were satirizing the lack of free speech within fundamentalist Islamic communities. However, many, including the current French president Nicholas Sarkozy, argued that targeting a minority ethnic group using images and symbols known to be inflammatory bordered on hate speech. Muslims, people who follow the faith of Islam, are a growing and systematically marginalized minority in France. They are often concentrated in ethnic enclaves outside the city and suffer disproportionately from unemployment, a lack of education, and discrimination (Francois 2020). By mocking this group, *Charlie Hebdo* encouraged audiences to laugh at the beliefs and lives of a marginalized group. Although the desire to satirize the *lack* of free speech in a democratic society may be admirable, the execution was lazy as well as arguably ineffective and counterproductive.

To ascertain if media is satire or mocking, one must determine if the content encourages critical thinking about power structures. The satirist must understand the systems of power against which they are pushing back, and how these systems have led to the (mis)treatment of certain groups over time. The satirist must be a historian first and a satirist second; jokes without historical awareness should not be considered satire because they are not intentionally speaking to historical processes. Conversely, jokes that merely reinforce historical disparities and continue to oppress already-disadvantaged are simply cruel.

The next section will address how marginalization satire is interpreted by different people, and how ethical satirists hone their messages to ensure that an audience correctly interprets their critique.

The Inconsistent Effects of Marginalization Satire

Satire that addresses processes of marginalization can reinforce preexisting social hierarchies and belief systems by repeating hidden cultural and psychological processes, as described in the preface. This is an issue for all satire given the historic need for satirists to obfuscate their intended meaning to avoid the ire of those in power. However, in the case of marginalization satire, messages that are misinterpreted by the audience can be actively counter productive by further marginalizing already marginalized groups.

Archie Bunker and the Lovable Bigot

All in the Family launched in 1971 on CBS. Produced by Norman Lear, the sitcom ran for eight years. It featured Archie Bunker (played by Carroll O'Connor), a working-class man of Irish descent frustrated with contemporary culture. His daughter Gloria (played by Sally Struthers) and her husband Michael (played by Rob Reiner) advocated for women's rights, civil rights, and queer rights, the major social movements of the time. Meanwhile, Archie's wife, Edith (played by Jean Stapleton), was a dutiful housewife who tried to avoid the overtly political strife in her home.

Figure 1.9 Michael, Gloria, Archie, and Edith debate in the living room from *All in the Family* (1971–1979). *Source*: Bettmann / Contributor / Getty Images.

All in the Family centered on the conflict between Archie and the younger generation. As the patriarch of an intergenerational family on either side of the political divide of the 1960s, he would regularly express "traditional," often stereotypical, prejudiced, and discriminatory, views about marginalized groups to which Gloria and Michael would object. He made no effort to conceal his own bigotry, which he often claimed was simply "fact." Lear intended to demonstrate that Archie's views of the world were antiquated and wrongheaded and expected viewers to laugh at Archie and empathize with Gloria and Michael because "Mike is always the one who is making sense. Archie at best will work out some kind of convoluted logic to make a point. But it's always foolish" (Lear 1971).

However, Vidmar and Rokeach found that American and Canadian respondents reported that the show appealed more to the "...racially and ethnically prejudiced members of society than to the less prejudiced members" (1974, p. 45). For example, there was an "Archie Bunker for President" movement during the 1970s composed of people who unironically shared the ideologies and attitudes of Archie. They misinterpreted the satire. Rather than laughing at the absurdity of Archie's stereotypes and prejudices, they *agreed* with Archie despite Lear manifesting a voice of reason through Gloria and Michael.

Similar characters have emerged in the wake of *All in the Family*, including Homer Simpson from *The Simpsons*, Eric Cartman from *South Park*, and Michael Scott from *The Office*. Despite efforts to present these characters as undesirable and the embodiment of what *not* to do, some viewers empathize and agree with them because these characters embody viewers' preconceived notions and attitudes about certain groups. At the Conservative Political Action Conference (CPAC) in 2018, Texas Senator (and self-proclaimed Simpsons superfan; Buzzfeed Video 2015) Ted Cruz said, "I think the Democrats are the party of Lisa Simpson and the Republicans are, happily, the party of Homer and Bart and Maggie and Marge." Unsurprisingly, this hot take was met with laughter and derision. Other *Simpsons* fans around the world ironically and dispassionately explained that Homer's character was constructed as an example of what *not* to do and who *not* to be. Simpsons showrunner Al Jean posted on Twitter: "Ted, they're not saying 'boo,' they're saying 'Cruz.' Oh, wait, they are saying 'boo'" (Jean 2018), a reference to the 1995 *Simpsons* episode, "A Star is Burns."

If undesirable characters, or characters that the viewer is not supposed to idolize or emulate, are deployed, their turpitude must be consistently portrayed and underscored, presenting a tricky puzzle for the satirist. The lovable bigot is an important trope but one that is regularly misunderstood and for whom the general appeal is fading. After teaching diversity and satire for almost a decade, the satire of Archie Bunker and Homer Simpson is more likely to offend than educate. These characters promote a history of discrimination by espousing prejudicial attitudes, but they are situated as examples of what *not* to do, a subtlety that can be easily lost, especially because these programs revolve around these main characters.

To understand marginalization satire, the audience must be aware of how long-standing social hierarchies (i.e., hegemony) connect to belief systems (i.e., ideology) and attitudes about groups (i.e., prejudice), impacting how we think about (i.e., stereotypes), talk about (i.e., discourse) and treat groups differently (i.e., discrimination), which in turn reinforces long-standing social hierarchies. If any of these components are missing, the satire may be rendered ineffective. *The next few sections describe the process by which satire may be misinterpreted and the difference between satire and discriminatory behavior.*

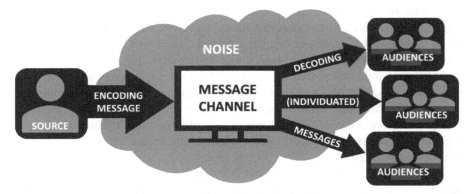

Figure 1.10 Communication Process Model (adapted from Shannon 1948).

Communication Process Model

Two important concepts that help us understand how satire is received are polysemy and reception theory. Derived from the English prefix for "many" and the Greek suffix for "sign," **polysemy** is the phenomenon in which a message can have multiple meanings, explaining why satire is difficult to consistently parse. Similarly, **reception theory** states that the interpretation of a message depends on what the user brings to the message (Hall 1973). In other words, viewers will interpret messages in line with their pre-existing belief systems.

These processes are captured in the **communication process model** (Shannon 1948), which represents how the source of messages, such as Norman Lear or Al Jean and *The Simpsons* writers, **encode** specific meanings into content. The message is then transmitted through a channel, in this case, video and television, to audience members who **decode** their own meaning from the message. Anything that obstructs or interferes with the encoding, transmission, or decoding of the message is considered **noise**. The encoding of satire may be clear to the message source as well as to the audience members that are prepared to decode the message as intended, but pre-existing hegemonic structures, ideologies, and discourse add disruptive noise, causing some audience members to misinterpret the intended meaning.

Stuart Hall (1980) describes three possible modes of message interpretation: **Dominant**, **oppositional**, and **negotiated**. Dominant audiences interpret or decode a message as intended by the sender, whereas oppositional audiences interpret or decode the message differently from its intended meaning. Often, oppositional audiences do not bring the same body of knowledge to the message as the sender. Negotiated audiences can decode the message as intended while also engaging in alternative interpretations, producing new meaning from a given text that may not have been intended by the sender.

Satire is often criticized for preaching to the choir and making jokes that only resonate with those already familiar with the topic (Flanagan 2017). However, oppositional audiences are problematic because their interpretation of the messages can undermine the satirists' goals. Marginalization satire demands that audiences critically consider hegemonic processes that have been framed as unquestioned and "normal" social phenomena. The process of pointing out the stereotypes or discriminatory language involves repeating the problematic phrases and concepts (e.g., Richard Sherman is "very articulate" from "Predicting the Biggest On-Field Battles"). Stereotypes are ripe for satirical critique, but understanding a satirical critique of stereotypes often relies on the audience's prior knowledge of the stereotype and its associated problems. For audiences who lack this knowledge, the satirist may perpetuate the stereotype, and continue to socially marginalize historically marginalized groups, rather than disrupt it because they may simply laugh at the stereotypes and not at the absurdity of stereotypes.

Stereotype Pixies (*The Chappelle Show*, S3E2, Comedy Central 2006)
The misinterpretation of marginalization satire is at the heart of Dave Chappelle's famous departure from Comedy Central in 2005. In an interview with *TIME Magazine* (Farley 2005), Chappelle described the moment that caused him to question the direction of the show and whether he should continue. The second episode of the third season featured a series of "stereotype pixie" sketches. In one sketch, Chappelle plays himself on an airline faced with the decision of chicken or fish. A stereotype pixie (also played by Chappelle) appears as a tap-dancing minstrel caricature in blackface, much like a devil on one's shoulder, and encourages Chappelle to eat the chicken. Desperate to not appear stereotypical, Chappelle requests the fish only to find out the airline is all out of fish and he will instead receive *fried* chicken, a food even more stereotypical. The blackface caricature becomes increasingly animated as the segment cuts between the dancing pixie and Chappelle appearing frustrated and tortured. Eventually, a White man sitting nearby offered to switch plates, reconciling his dilemma.

Figure 1.11 Dave Chappelle dressed as a early 20th century minstrel in blackface encourages real life Dave Chappelle to engage in stereotypical behavior. Still from Stereotype Pixies (*The Dave Chappelle Show* 2006).

> **Activity 1.2 What Are *You* Laughing At?**
>
> Laughter does not always indicate that the audience has understood the joke. Revisit the artifact you selected in Activity 1.1. First, consider the social phenomenon that the artifact is satirizing. *What does the audience need to know to "get" the satire as intended by the satirist? How might audiences interpret the artifact if they do not already have the knowledge?*
>
> Second, search online for reactions to this artifact. *What messages did the satirist encode (i.e., intend) and what messages did the audience decode (i.e., interpret)? How did they align or deviate?*

Other sketches in this episode include a Latino pixie and an East Asian pixie, each embodying stereotypes that the main character desperately attempts to resist. These sketches satirize the experience of marginalized people who are fearful of inadvertently reinforcing the stereotypes used against them. This experience emerges from what W.E.B. Du Bois (1897) referred to as **double consciousness**, in which marginalized people are aware of who they are and of how the rest of the world sees them and are constantly battling these two states. To be marginalized and be subjected to stereotypes is to experience perpetual internal conflict, a uniquely absurd experience that Chappelle reveals with humor and exaggeration.

However, upon showing this sketch to the live audience, Chappelle recalls one White man laughing profusely at the blackface caricature, not at the impact of blackface on Black people today and the process of stereotyping that causes Black people to be hyper vigilant about not appearing stereotypical. A lack of awareness regarding the phenomenon of double consciousness, regardless of whether the viewer is aware of Du Bois' formal name, means that the viewer will not interpret the message as Chappelle intended. Concepts that have not received much attention in the public sphere are difficult to satirize because of the audience's ignorance. People who are aware of these processes of marginalization laugh at the stereotypes; people who believe that the stereotypes as truths laugh at the historically marginalized group. In an analysis of Chappelle's work, Haggins (2007) argues that "…the way in which specific cultural stories are read can either contribute to or undermine hegemonic notions of race… [and] how it was being read by multiple audiences: in other words, what exactly are they laughing at?" (p. 228).

Strategies for Satirical Literacy OR How to Read This Book

Media literacy is the ability to understand the process by which content is produced and distributed and, therefore, parse deeper meanings associated with it. Put more concisely, it is "the ability to access, analyze, evaluate, and create media in a variety of forms" (Aspen Media Literacy Leadership Institute). Understanding, interpreting, and creating satire is a form of media literacy. By extension, **satirical literacy** is the ability to access, analyze, evaluate, and create satirical content that effectively demonstrates the absurdity of a social phenomenon and encourages the audience to think differently about their associated social interactions. The purpose of this book is to provide a robust description of major areas of marginalization, and apply these concepts to satirical examples to reveal the absurdity of marginalization processes.

This text is divided into four primary chapters: Socioeconomic status (SES) and class, gender, sexuality, and race. Each chapter begins with a definition of the key terms relevant to the subject matter and describes some of the historical phenomena and foundational statistics. As with the current chapter, major concepts are demonstrated through satirical examples; each analysis begins with a brief description of the satirical artifact and then explicitly connects the components of the artifact to the major concepts. Specific sub-areas and intersectional concerns are addressed, and each chapter closes with important things to consider (i.e., common errors) when creating content that satirizes the social category in the twenty-first century media environment. The four primary chapters also feature critical essays written by students as well as activities that encourage you, the reader, to engage more deeply with the concepts or reconsider some of your favorite artifacts.

The final chapter addresses social atrocities, some of the most egregious outcomes of marginalization. Although many believe that social atrocities like homelessness, rape, slavery, and genocide should not be satirized, we must point to the absurdities that result in some of the worst acts of humanity as a means of seeing and disrupting them when they inevitably occur again. The four main chapters will cultivate the skills to focus your satirical eye on the process, and aid in recognizing and analyzing the emotional reactions these atrocities elicit.

Within each chapter, readers should seek to answer the following key questions regarding the example artifacts provided within the text. These questions can then be applied to analyzing satire that they encounter in the real world.

Is It Satire?

Identifying satire can be difficult because the satirist focuses on issues that are often absent in the public sphere, or points at things that the audience has been trained not to see. Furthermore, in order to keep the audience guessing, the satirist will obfuscate the message both as a self-preservation strategy and as a means of commenting on the issue itself. These qualities of satire, coupled with the rapid expansion of media outlets and forums where satire may live, demand that the satirist intentionally construct their message and include appropriate indicators they are disseminating satire. Highet (1962) describes four indicators of satire:

1) **Explicit Definition:** The author states the content is satire (e.g., Orwell's *Animal Farm* was originally published with the subtitle *A Contemporary Satire*).
2) **Pedigree:** The content comes from a long line of satirical content or is branded as such (e.g., the White House Correspondents Dinner, which has been a traditional satirical venue for decades).
3) **Disguised Pedigree:** The content adopts the theme and methods of earlier satirical content (e.g., disguising satire as news as in the *Boston Globe's* "front page" satirizing of Trump dates back to political cartoons, broadsheets, and television programs like *That Was the Week That Was*, originally broadcast on the BBC in 1962).

4) **Acknowledged Pedigree:** The content quotes known satirists (e.g., the re-voicing of Donald Trump by comedians in the 2016 and 2020 election cycles calls back to "Black Bush," a 2004 sketch where Chappelle echos the lines of George W. Bush in the lead up to the Iraq War, and Richard Pryor's "The First Black President" from 1977).

The satirist does not stumble into satire. It is a specific writing genre and style, and therefore, satirists must effectively "wink" at the audience or feature some cue explicitly to indicate the content is satire. Earlier satirists like Aristophanes addressed audiences in the middle of the play to "...focus their attention on the central message" (Highet 1962, pp. 27–28). This wink may be subtler in current satire, but it is still necessary to ensure the audience reads the content as satirical and laugh *with* the satirist. Furthermore, these cues protect the satirist by allowing them to point to their intentionality if the satire is misinterpreted.

> Poe's Law: "Without a winking smiley or other blatant display of humor, it is utterly impossible to parody a Creationist in such a way that someone won't mistake for the genuine article."
>
> *(Poe 2005)*

In some cases, specifically traditional satirical outlets, this wink may be implied through the venue itself (e.g., *The Onion*). However, there are many instances in which content labeled as satire is not read as such, especially with websites that are unfamiliar to a general audience (e.g., Duffle Blog). In many of the interpreted examples described in the section The Inconsistent Effects of Marginalized Satire above, the winks were either missed or actively ignored. For this reason, critical readers are encouraged to actively search for the wink to confirm the content as satire and to be able to discuss satire with others, especially those who do not necessarily recognize satire at first glance.

What Is Being Satirized and How?

> "The type of subject preferred by satire is always concrete, usually topical, often personal. It deals with actual cases, mentions real people by name or describes them unmistakably (and often unflatteringly), and talks of this moment and this city and this special, very recent, very fresh deposit of corruption whose stench is still in the satirists curling nostrils."
>
> *(Highet 1962, p. 16).*

Satirical artifacts point out absurdities in the real world. Therefore, one must begin with the real life absurdity on which the artifact is commenting in order to understand and analyze satire. This is the most difficult component of the analysis, especially when the absurdity seems obvious, but one must be aware of past trends to appreciate the satire because an awareness of history, theories, and research will ensure greater insight into the meaning of the message. Ultimately, satire can address issues that we are hesitant to discuss in polite company because the issues are so troubling, which is absurd in itself because our hesitancy to discuss these issues perpetuates disparities and discrimination. Each chapter outlines some disparities and historic injustices[1] that are essential to understanding the featured artifacts and the exercises described throughout the chapter connect jokes to key terms, past events, and theories.

Bumper Sticker: If Jesus does return, I'm pretty sure he'll be stopped at the airport. (Ephemera)

In 13 words, this bumper sticker directly calls out the ironic overlap of religion and politics. To understand the satire, one must be aware that Jesus, contrary to popular imagery, was not an Anglo man with light hair and eyes. Rather, he was Middle Eastern, and specifically a Palestinian-Jewish man. This bumper sticker also references how people of Palestinian and Middle Eastern origin are frequently stopped at the airport and profiled as terrorists, a stereotype that has only grown since the attacks of September 11, 2001. The bumper sticker highlights the absurdity of people who consider themselves followers of Jesus while also supporting anti-immigration policies and racial profiling of Middle Eastern individuals in the United States. For these segments of the American population, their religious beliefs, which value a specific Middle-Eastern man, are at odds with their political beliefs that people from the Middle East pose a threat to the American way of life.

How Does the Content Make You Feel?

> "The final test for satire is the typical emotion which the author feels and wishes to evoke in his readers. It is a blend of amusement and contempt. "In some satirists, the argument far outweighs the contempt. In others it almost disappears; it changes into a sour sneer, a grim smile, or a wry awareness that life cannot all be called reasonable or noble."
>
> *(Highet 1962, p. 21)*

In some sense, all satire is entertaining because it is designed to elicit emotional responses in the viewer. As described by Highet, satire makes the reader simultaneously feel amusement and contempt. Although an emotional response is an

---

Activity 1.3   Starting with Disparities

Research a disparity, such as education, socioeconomic status, or incarceration, which is associated with a given demographic characteristic (e.g., weight) or group (e.g., women, Muslims). What is the history of this disparity and how is it currently perpetuated? How has this disparity evolved into stereotypes, prejudice, and discrimination, and how have these processes become normalized discourse? Why is this process absurd and how might one draw attention to it using allegory, parody, magnification, flipping the frame, or juxtaposition? How have satirists accomplished this previously?

Figure 1.12 "I'm offended by this potato" A meme demonstrating that offensiveness is subjective therefore the argument that content is "offensive" is an ineffective argument.

essential test for satire, it is often lost in the expectations of entertainment as amusement. Therefore, critical readers must be keenly aware of their own emotions to analyze satire. We are rarely asked to explain why we feel a certain way toward an entire group. In fact, asking "why" people hold a given prejudice can reveal the nonsensical, ludicrous, and often stereotypical rationalization behind their attitude. Facing the underlying processes behind our prejudices will inevitably elicit feelings of discomfort or "cringe." Again, because marginalization satire draws on the hegemonic process we have been trained *not* to see, simply acknowledging these phenomena, disparities, and absurdities can be painful.

This book is about more than why we laugh. Rather, it is an organized exploration into what makes us uncomfortable or offended. There are many examples of satirical artifacts being criticized because audiences blame the satirist for their negative emotional reaction (e.g., cringe) before (or without) considering the social phenomenon being satirized. In other cases, something may be labeled as "offensive" without elaboration, which is often an outcome of an emotional response. If something qualifies as satire, it is important to consider the satirist's goals with every line, shot, or interaction, as the feelings of discomfort are often intentional.

> "Satire is, by definition, offensive. It is meant to make us feel uncomfortable. It is mean to make us scratch our heads, think, do a double-take, and then think again."
>
> – *Maajid Nawaz*

Additional Activities

> **Activity 1.4   Implicit Association Task**
>
> Select and complete at least two iterations of the Implicit Association Task (IAT), available at implicit.harvard.edu/implicit. Consider the test and how it made you think about the processes of stereotyping as compared to prejudice and discrimination. Focus on your personal experiences across the tests and engage with your discomfort. Why are you uncomfortable? What does this reveal about the cognitive processes of stereotypes, prejudices, and discrimination?

> **Activity 1.5   Laughing While Learning**
>
> Since its launch in 2014, HBO's *Last Week Tonight with John Oliver* has been heralded for its balance of entertainment and education. The show stands out as a widely embraced and rarely misunderstood instance of satire for several reasons. Over half of the time is spent sharing information either directly or embedded within a joke, information is presented in brief bursts, and Oliver's jokes are preceded by an information and a clip. These techniques ensure the audience is prepared with consistent information to laugh at the given joke as intended (Terhune and Corsbie-Massay 2020). *Watch an episode of Last Week Tonight with John Oliver (HBO) available online. Consider how new information gleaned while watching the episode changed your reception of the jokes.*

References

https://www.amazon.com/Ephemera-Inc-stopped-airport-Sticker/dp/B07FSVWNPX.

@AlJean. (22 February 2018). @TheSimpsons Ted they're not saying "boo" they're saying "Cruz". Oh, wait, they are saying "boo". Twitter.

'No way to prevent this,' Says only nation where this regularly happens. (27 May 2014). The Onion.

Barnes, R. [Writer], McGruder, A. [Writer], Taylor, Y. [Writer], and Bell, A. [Director] (13 November 2005). The trial of Robert Kelly. In: *The Boondocks [TV Series]*. Adelaide Productions.

Bennett, K.E. (2022). The Refractive Comic: Nanette and Comedy From Inside Identity. Television & New Media.

Brennan, N. [Writer], Chappelle, D. [Writer], and Cundieff, R. [Director] (16 July 2006). Black Howard Dean & Stereotype Pixies. In: *Chappelle's Show [TV Series]*. Marobru Inc.

Buzzfeed Video (30 June 2015). Ted Cruz auditions for the Simpsons. YouTube. youtube.com/watch?v=_K0sRkvX4KE (accessed 3 May 2022).

Chen, C.H. (2012). "Outwhiting the whites": An examination of the persistence of Asian American model minority discourse. In: *Race/Gender/Class/Media: Considering Diversity Across Audiences, Content, and Producers* (2nd Edition) (ed. R. Lind), 146–153. Pearson.

The Daily Show with Trevor Noah. (28 April 2016). "They love me" music video - Black Trump (ft. Jordan Klepper): The Daily Show. YouTube. youtube.com/watch?v=JSBGDC0rKWU (accessed 3 May 2022).

Devine, P.G. (1989). Stereotypes and prejudice: Their automatic and controlled components. *Journal of Personality and Social Psychology* 56 (1): 5–18.

Devitt, J. (2002). Framing gender on the campaign trail: Female gubernatorial candidates and the press. *Journalism & Mass Communication Quarterly* 79 (2): 445–463.

Du Bois, W.E.B. (1897). Strivings of the negro people. *The Atlantic Monthly* 80 (August): 194.

Farley, C.J. (14 May 2005). Dave speaks. TIME Magazine.

Fischer-Baum, R., Gordon, A., and Haisley, B. (8 May 2014). Which words are used to describe white and black NFL prospects? Deadspin.

Flanagan, C. (May 2017). How late-night comedy fueled the rise of Trump. The Atlantic.

Francois, M. (8 December 2020). France's treatment of its Muslim Citizens is the true measure of its republican values. Time.

Funny or Die (11 September 2015). Mexican Donald Trump with George Lopez. YouTube. youtube.com/watch?v=T0noDEI2nLY (accessed 3 May 2022).

Gilens, M. (2003). How the poor became black. In: *Race and the Politics of Welfare Reform* (ed. S. Schram, J. Soss, and R. Fording), 101–130. The University of Michigan Press.

Glenn, C.L. and Cunningham, L.J. (2009). The power of black magic: The magical negro and white salvation in film. *Journal of Black Studies* 40 (2): 135–152.

Gorham, B. (2019). Media effects: 2.1: The social psycholofy of stereotypes and bias: Implications for media audiences. In: *Race/Gender/Class/Media: Considering Diversity Across Audiences, Content, and Producers* (ed. R.A. Lind). New York City: Routledge.

Gramsci, A. (1971). *Selections from the Prison Notebooks*. New York City: International.

Haggins, B. (2007). *Laughing Mad: The Black Comic Persona in Post-soul America*. New Brunswick, NJ: Rutgers University Press.

Hall, S. (1973). Encoding and decoding in the television discourse. Discussion Paper. University of Birmingham, Birmingham.

Hall, S. (1981). The whites of their eyes: Racist ideologies and the media. In: *Silver Linings : Some Strategies for the Eighties* (ed. G. Bridges and R. Brunt), 28–52. London: Lawrence and Wishart. https://archive.org/details/silverliningssom0000unse/page/n5/mode/2up.

Hall, S. (1980). Encoding/decoding. In: *Culture, Media, Language* (ed. S. Hall, D. Hobson, A. Love et al.), 128–138. London: Hutchinson.

Highet, G. (1962). *Anatomy of Satire*. Princeton, NJ: Princeton University Press.

Holzman, L. and Sharpe, L. (2014). *Media Messages: What Film, Television, and Popular Music Teach Us about Race, Class, Gender, and Sexual Orientation*. New York City: Routledge.

Keating, J. (3 December 2014). If it happened there: Courts sanction killings by U.S. security forces. Slate.

Key, K. [Writer], Peele, J. [Writer], Talarico, R. [Writer], and Benz, P. [Director] (30 January 2015). Super bowl special. In: *Key and Peele [TV Series]*. Den of Thieves.

Lear, N. As I read how Laura saw Archie. New York Times. (10 October 1971). https://www.nytimes.com/1971/10/10/archives/as-i-read-how-laura-saw-archie-as-i-read-laura-.html.

Lu, D., Huang, J., Seshagiri, A., Park, H., and Griggs, T. (9 September 2020). Faces of power: 80% are white, even as U.S. becomes more diverse. New York TImes.

Lull, J. (1995). Hegemony. In: *Gender, Race, and Class in Media: A Critical Reader* (ed. B. Yousman, W. Yousman, G. Dines et al.), 41–44. California: SAGE Publications.

McClennen, S. (2011). *America according to Colbert: Satire as Public Pedagogy*. New York City: Palgrave Macmillan US.

McClennen, S. and Maisel, R. (2014). *Is Satire Saving Our Nation?: Mockery and American Politics*. New York City: Palgrave Macmillan US.

Parker, T. [Writer, Director], Stone, M. [Writer], and Graden, B. [Writer] (18 April 2004). Goobacks. In: *South Park [TV Series]*. Braniff.

Poe, N. (11 August 2005). Big contradictions in the evolution theory, page 3. christianforums.com.

Rose, M. and Baumgartner, F.R. (2013). Framing the poor: Media coverage and US poverty policy, 1960–2008. *Policy Studies Journal* 41 (1): 22–53.

Rossing, J.P. (2016). Emancipatory racial humor as critical public pedagogy: Subverting hegemonic racism. *Communication, Culture & Critique* 9 (4): 614–632.

Sarah Cooper. (2020, 24 April). How to medical. YouTube. youtube.com/watch?v=RxDKW75ueIU (accessed 3 May 2022).

Shannon, C.E. (1948). A mathematical theory of communication. *The Bell System Technical Journal* 27 (3): 379–423.

Sue, D.W. et al. (2008). Racial microaggressions against Black Americans: Implications for counseling. *Journal of Counseling & Development* 86 (3): 330–338.

Swift, J. (1726). *Gulliver's Travels*. London: Benjamin Motte.

Terhune, P. and Corsbie-Massay, C. (2020). Satirical education or educational Satire?: Learning and laughing on last week tonight. In: *Laughter, Outrage and Resistance* (ed. L. Henson and M. Jankowski), 165–184. New York: Peter Lang Publishing.

Trudeau, G. (11 April 2015). *The Abuse of Satire*. The Atlantic. https://www.theatlantic.com/international/archive/2015/04/the-abuse-of-satire/390312/.

Vidmar, N. and Rokeach, M. (1974). Archie Bunker's bigotry: A study in selective perception and exposure. *Journal of Communication* 24 (1): 36–47.

Wilmore, L. (2016). White House Correspondents' Association dinner. C-SPAN (30 April 2016).

Yankovic, A.M. (2011). *Party in the CIA (Parody of Party in the U.S.A By Miley Cyrus) [Recorded by Weird Al Yankovic]*. On Alpocalypse [MP4 file]. United States: Way Moby.

2

Satirizing Socioeconomic Status (SES) and Class

> *"It's called the American Dream because you have to be asleep to believe it."*
> – George Carlin

Socioeconomic status (SES) and class are integral to the American experience and to the process of marginalization. Although we frequently talk about the marginalization of race, gender, and sexuality, the oppression of those groups is often operationalized through systematic economic disadvantage, making SES foundational to the rest of this book. Furthermore, SES and class are less discussed in the United States compared to these other categories because America is usually framed as a "classless society" where the socioeconomic class into which one is born is perceived to be less relevant than one's talent, merit, and hard work. We are led to believe that any person, with enough effort, can move out of the class into which they were born and the economic based caste systems of the "Old World" in Europe and of less developed nations in the Global South do not apply.

However, as will become clear throughout this chapter, that rhetoric of the American Dream is in contrast to reality, and instead, the institutionalized structure of money, resources, and opportunities have been weaponized to maintain the dominance of some groups while marginalizing others. This chapter will define SES and class as well as the stereotypes, prejudice, and discrimination that emerge from the resulting social categories.

Do Americans Dream of Class Mobility? Defining Socioeconomic Status (SES) and Class

Although socioeconomic status and class are often used synonymously, defining each of these terms is essential to understanding how the denial of resources is associated with marginalization. **Socioeconomic status (SES)** is one's position in a social hierarchy based on objective indicators of economic value (e.g., income, wealth), as well as the potential for acquiring monetary value (e.g., education, career). It is essential to distinguish between **income**, which is the amount of money that an individual earns by working, and **wealth**, which is the combined value of one's assets, including property and investments. Although these two concepts are

Diversity and Satire: Laughing at Processes of Marginalization, First Edition.
Charisse L'Pree Corsbie-Massay.
© 2023 John Wiley & Sons, Inc. Published 2023 by John Wiley & Sons, Inc.

related, one can have income with no wealth (e.g., living paycheck to paycheck) and wealth with no income (e.g., $1 salary club, see later in this chapter).

Conversely, **class** is the cultural and social categorization of individuals based on SES, which can be indicative of social networks and behavioral expectations (e.g., political attitudes, membership in certain clubs, activities). It is the social expectations and opportunities that come with belonging to a certain socioeconomic group. As described by Scott and Leonhardt, classes are "...groups of similar economic and social position; people who, for that reason, may share political attitudes, lifestyles, consumption patterns, cultural interests, and opportunities to get ahead" (2005). Therefore, class is not just income, assets, and education. Class is also the community and customs that people may participate in when they have a certain level of income, assets, and education. In this manner, class and expectations of class can be used to perpetuate socioeconomic inequality over time.

Consider the typical categories of class: Lower, middle, and upper. Each category comes with a cluster of stereotypes that manifest in prejudices and discrimination even though they are objectively associated with resources and access. We frequently stereotype people in the upper classes as inherently intelligent or hard-working without recognizing these are outcomes of access to resources that allow them to act upon their intelligence or take advantage of opportunities. A higher SES *affords* education, healthcare, a nice home, and nice clothes. It also provides access to healthy food, breathable air, clean water, and a network of people who also have access to these resources (Scott 2005). Conversely, we stereotype people in the lower classes, who may be on welfare or lack formal education, as lazy or unintelligent. Often, we do not recognize that people in lower classes lack access to education, healthcare, healthy food, breathable air, clean water, or a network of people who have access to these resources. This failure to recognize the disparities in resource availability encourages and reinforces stereotypes.

Scientists: Rich People, Poor People May Have Shared Common Ancestor. (*The Onion* 2014)

> *ITHACA, NY—According to a study released this week by geneticists at Cornell University, substantial evidence indicates that rich people and poor people—disparate populations long thought to be entirely unrelated—may have once shared a single common ancestor. "After conducting careful DNA analysis, our research team was taken aback to discover that the wealthy and the working class actually have a considerable number of genetic similarities," said study co-author Kenneth Chang, adding that despite the disparity between the modern-day affluent and low earners in terms of behavior, appearance, and lifestyle, numerous genetic markers revealed that their predecessors may have once lived beside one another without any noticeable differences. "Side by side, poor people and rich people look almost nothing alike, of course. It took months of chromosomal comparison to discover that links exist between, say, a top-level consultant at Bain Capital living in a gated community and a mother of three relying on multiple low-wage jobs to survive. And upon close inspection, it is possible to detect subtle, but striking, physical resemblances between these vastly different peoples." Scientists also determined that the ultra-rich were closely related to jellyfish and other soft-bodied invertebrates.*

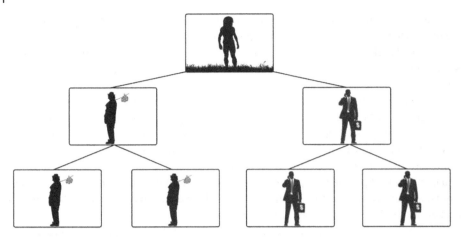

Figure 2.1 The evolution of class: "Rich People, Poor People May Have Shared Common Ancestor" (*The Onion* 2014).

In fewer than 200 words, this 2014 article from *The Onion* satirizes the phenomenon of SES as a social category. It presents a faux discovery: Reality is "discovered" because discourse has diverted collective attention and understanding away from reality. The first quote from the "expert researcher," who was surprised that "…the wealthy and the working class actually have a considerable number of genetic similarities," is amusing because we know that it is true. It also elicits feelings of contempt because the statement acknowledges that the social segregation and the subsequent perceived disparities between these groups are so expansive that they might as well be two separate species.

Furthermore, by parodying scientific articles and language, the artifact points to the need to acknowledge and recognize the depth of unquestioned differences that are often taken for granted. We know that we are all human, but we do not think about or treat each other as such because of these rhetorical differences. We are born into a certain SES and with that comes cultural socialization of a specific class. However, due to socioeconomic segregation, these nuances can result in a social distance that appears to be more than simply access to money, resources, and opportunity; they are interpreted as innate differences between individuals.

Despite these sociocultural differences, there is a pervasive belief that with enough hard work, anyone can move up from the class they were born into. This is the **American Dream**, the national ideology that people can work their way out of their life circumstances because the United States provides them unique opportunities for ascending the class hierarchy. In his 1931 book *The Epic of America*, James Truslow Adams states that in the United States, "…life should be better and richer and fuller for everyone, with opportunity for each according to ability or achievement" (2017, p. 410) regardless of social class or circumstances of birth. In short, the American Dream is the promise of a higher class for anyone who works for it. This sentiment is associated with **capitalism**, an economic system where trade and industry are controlled by private owners for profit rather than by the state. Individuals within a capitalist system can profit from their own labor, amass resources, achieve a higher class, and pass this wealth on, often to their own families. Because of these rhetorical opportunities to transcend the class in which one was born, America is often falsely described as a "classless society."

Despite this "promise," research regarding social mobility reveals that the chances of out-earning one's parents has become increasingly difficult with every generation

---

Activity 2.1   100+ Items of Privilege

In 2014, *Buzzfeed* published a quiz entitled, "How Privileged Are You" written by Rega Jha and Tommy Wesely. It featured 100 measures of **privilege** or life experiences related to one's social categories that provide *unearned statistical advantages* in life; in short, being privileged means *not* being disadvantaged. Although racial and gendered privileges and disadvantages are frequently discussed in the public sphere, more nuanced privileges and disadvantages related to class as well as how it intersects with sexuality and religion are harder to ascertain. An adaptation of the quiz is available in Appendix B, with each item rephrased to focus on what we do and do not know are privileges. Consider which items from the class/SES section you did not know were advantages, and how they affect one's chances of advancement.

---

starting with those born in 1940 (Hiliger 2015). Almost all Americans born in 1940 were able to out-earn their parents. Those born in 1960 and 1970 had about a 60% chance to do so, and those born in 1980 had a 40% chance (Chetty et al. 2017). In 2012, only about 8% of men born in the bottom fifth of the economic spectrum made it to the top fifth in the United States (DeParle 2012), a statistic that varies only slightly by race, gender, and geographic location.

Despite this declining opportunity for mobility, Americans are more likely than the British, French, Italians, and Swiss to overestimate social mobility (Alesina et al. 2018). More than half (53%) of American millennials expect to become millionaires during their lifetime (Adamczyk 2019) even though the top 10 nations with the highest mobility index are all in Europe according to the World Economic Forum. The United States comes in at 27, just behind Lithuania (World Economic Forum 2020). It is clear that the idea of America as the "land of opportunity" has sustained even though access to opportunity is shrinking.

Many researchers have attributed the decline in mobility to the changing policies of the twentieth century, specifically stagnating wages, tax cuts for the wealthy that remove essential funds from the national budget, and greater individual debt. The cruel irony of this phenomenon is that the opportunity to advance for younger generations has been stifled by the policies of past generations. Americans' dream of improving their individual status involves hoarding money and assets, thus advancing themselves at the expense of others (Reeves 2017). Furthermore, this individualism also fosters the assumption that others have not achieved similar accomplishments because of their individual failings rather than inequalities embedded in society. Commonly referred to as the **just world phenomenon**, our tendency to believe that the world is fair and that people get what they deserve leads us to believe that people who are in dire straits brought it upon themselves through their own inaction or inherent character flaws rather than institutional structures that make it practically impossible to succeed. A strong belief in a just world is associated with blaming the poor, and a weak belief is associated with identifying external causes of poverty, including world economic systems, war, and exploitation (Harper et al. 1990).

Old Economy Steve

The meme Old Economy Steve emerged on Reddit in 2012 to satirize how older Americans' ignorance of changing economic prospects manifested in their tendency to hold younger Americans to a standard that was no longer applicable. The meme featured a classic portrait of a young White man from the 1970s. The top line featured a quote that might be uttered by many from the Baby Boomer generation (born 1946–1964) speaking about their own accomplishments to a Millennial (born 1981–1996). The bottom line reinforced how the economy and the system had changed in the decades since, demonstrating the absurdity of the top line in the current economic environment. The meme quickly gained popularity online because of pervasive frustration among young adults with Baby Boomers naively repeating the rhetoric of the American Dream in the absence of reality.[1]

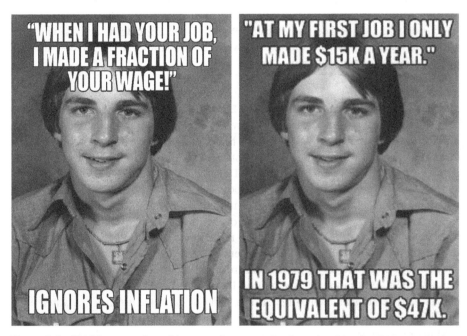

Figure 2.2 "Old Economy Steve" A meme demonstrating how the rhetoric of money among older generations no longer applies given economic shifts.

The Intersectionality of the Self-Made Man

Similarly, Americans champion the idea of the "self-made man" who acquires the "wealth they possess by patient and diligent labor" (Henry Clay, 1832). In capitalist societies like the United States, individual value is associated with resources, including land, money, and commodities. Attaining wealth and elevating one's class is effectively synonymous with attaining social value. However, this idea of the "self-made man," and it is nearly always a "man," is ironic because their success has historically relied on the unpaid labor of others. Since its inception, the United States has always been a land of opportunity for some at the expense of others because land-owning men of European descent were the only individuals allowed to profit from their own labor.

---

[1] This is also done well in the SNL sketch "Millennial Millions" (NBC 2019). https://mashable.com/video/snl-millennial-millions-rachel-brosnahan.

Women were restricted from owning property, pursuing higher education, and following the vast majority of career paths. Instead, they were expected to do the unpaid domestic labor that was required to maintain the home so that men could amass wealth outside the home (i.e., the "breadwinner"), effectively supporting the dreams of their husbands and children. As Nora Ephron explained during the 1996 commencement address at Wellesley University, "We weren't meant to have futures, we were meant to marry them. We weren't meant to have politics, or careers that mattered, or opinions or lives; we were meant to marry them" (Ephron 2012). Women who were expected to work (i.e., working- and lower-class women, women of color) were then employed to do domestic labor in other people's homes and paid less than men who could work outside the home. Ultimately, the American dream of elevating one's SES for women was only available through marriage and becoming a dutiful housewife.

Poverty is Sexist

In 2018, one year after the MeToo movement gained worldwide attention, Connie Britton wore a sweater to the Golden Globes with the statement, "Poverty is sexist." Many sought to dismiss her claims by applying the common adage that "poverty doesn't discriminate." However, as will be discussed in the next chapter on gender, a phenomena is considered "sexist" if it reinforces disparities based on sex and gender. Her sweater was satirical because it drew attention to the absurdity of the socioeconomic situation of women around the world. The impact of this satirical artifact was

Figure 2.3 Connie Britton wore a sweater to the 2018 Golden Globes embroidered with the phrase: "poverty is sexist" to draw attention to intersectionality of gender and poverty. *Source*: David Fisher / Shutterstock.com.

especially pronounced because it was worn at such a prominent and elegant event where most women don designer gowns. In response, Britton wrote this in *Entertainment Weekly* (2018):

> *Here's what I mean: 130 million girls around the world are denied an education. Women in developing countries account for less than half of all students enrolled in lower secondary school. In 18 countries, a man is legally empowered to prevent his wife from doing a job of which he doesn't approve. And women in low-income countries have less access to financial institutions and the internet than men. In Africa, nearly three out of four new HIV infections are in adolescent girls. So women around the world are more deeply entrenched in the effects of poverty, and they have fewer opportunities to escape. In other words: Poverty is sexist....*

Similarly, racial discrimination was fueled by limiting opportunities and resources for certain groups. European settlers in the sixteenth century occupied land originally inhabited by Indigenous peoples and killed approximately 56 million people across North, South, and Central America. As colonists began to establish communities and take advantage of this land through the seventeenth and eighteenth centuries, hundreds of thousands of enslaved Africans were brought to the United States to labor as chattel property and forced to work without pay because they did not own their own bodies or their own labor. Similarly, as colonists began to "go West" in the nineteenth century to take advantage of the frontier, Indigenous Americans and Americans of Mexican descent were forced off their land, their primary means of capital, to make room for Americans of European descent to homestead and create wealth. Asian migrants were responsible for building much of the infrastructure in the westward migration even as they were refused access to citizenship and property. The opportunity to amass resources while systematically removing the opportunities of others to do the same undermines the American narrative of the "self-made man."

Homeland Security: Fighting Terrorism Since 1492 (Matthew Tafoya 2001)
This image was created by Matthew Tafoya, a member of the Navajo Nation, in the wake of the September 11, 2001, attacks on the World Trade Center and the Pentagon, which sparked "homeland security" initiatives. It points to the paradoxical nature of the American Dream and who has access to opportunity by considering for whom the land has been promised and from whom it needs to be protected. The photograph from 1886 features Geronimo and fellow members of the Bedonkohe band of the Apache people. Still a household name, Geronimo, along with other members of the Apache Nation, fought against Mexican and United States military campaigns attempting to occupy Native lands. The Bedonkohe band served to secure their homeland against invading terrorists, a story that took on greater significance for Tafoya after 9/11, who recalled thinking "Now *they* know how it feels" (Corman 2004).

It is clear that the rhetoric of the American Dream conflicts with the reality of social advancement, undermining the narrative of SES and class in the United States. *The next two sections will address stereotypes of lower and upper classes and how they work to limit opportunity and mobility even in American "classless" society.*

Figure 2.4 "Homeland Security: Fighting Terrorism Since 1492" An image created by Matthew Tafoya that has since been turned into a meme with multiple iterations available online (2001). *Source*: Bill Strain / Flickr / CC BY 2.0.

Pulling Yourself up by Your Bootstraps: Satirizing Stereotypes of Scarcity

The ideology of the American Dream, that anyone can succeed with hard work, inhibits awareness of stereotypes regarding who advances and why. Although class-based stereotypes may be harder to see than those pertaining to gender, sexuality, and race, they are interwoven into our understanding of others. For example, there is a pervasive ideology in the United States that hard work equals success. Inversely, those who do not work hard will not be successful. The converse (i.e., those that are successful have worked hard) and the contrapositive (i.e., those who are not successful have not worked hard) are often also interpreted to be true. These statements represent the core of class-based stereotypes in the United States, which assumes those who do not advance are lazy or inherently unintelligent.

These stereotypes are present in news and entertainment media. In the 1960s, more than 90% of news stories about poverty featured a structural frame (i.e., poverty results from institutional barriers to advancement like a lack of affordable housing), but during the 1970s, 1980s, and 1990s, this was present in about 60% of articles. Instead, the coverage shifted to individual frames (i.e., poverty results from individual issues like laziness and dysfunction), which captured the idea that, "…the poor avoid work and are content to stay at home and have children" (Rose and Baumgartner 2013, p. 29). By the 2000s, structural frames had fallen to less than half of stories, and the "lazy" frame was used in more than half of stories (Rose and Baumgartner 2013). At the same time, the "white working-class buffoon" became a standard trope in sitcoms (Butsch 2003). From Ralph Kramden on *The Honeymooners* (1955–1956) and Archie Bunker on *All in the Family* (1971–1979) to Al Bundy on *Married with Children* (1987–1997) and Jay Pritchett on *Modern Family* (2009–2020), this archetype has been constructed by writers and producers who rarely come from the working class and who encourage audiences to laugh at the delightful incompetence of working-class White men.

For Labor Day We Asked: 'Why is the Working Class So Lazy (Funny or Die 2015)

By Natalie Falk

The *Funny or Die* clip "For Labor Day We Asked: 'Why is the Working Class So Lazy?'" portrays a fake "man on the street" news interview in which a man asks people why the working class is so lazy. The answers are mostly ironic, silly, or random. They include responses like, "I think if they've taken the initiative to work harder to be born to rich parents, like I did, they wouldn't be in the situation they're in now," "Well I'm very rich so I never really think about them," and "It's got to be all that beer, it makes them stupid… educated men drink scotch." At the end, a working-class man is interviewed, and he describes how he goes into work every day without fail, even when he is injured. Finally, he asks the looming question, "So who's the lazy ones?", to which he responds, "Rich people and the politicians."

This video satirizes the common, stereotypical idea that members of the working class are lazy. The false assumption is they remain in the working class merely because of their individual traits and not due to the structural barriers they face. Holtzman and Sharpe describe the influence of media in corroborating this idea. Shows like *The Simpsons* portray members of the working class as foolish or lazy, thus deserving of their place in a lower class. These shows (and most of mainstream media) ignore the external reasons for the lack of class mobility, such as a limited access to opportunities. One must understand this trend to understand that the ironic responses in the video are meant to be satirical.

The 2003 book chapter "Ralph, Fred, Archie and Homer: Why television keeps re-creating the white male working class buffoon" by Richard Butsch explains how mass media's portrayal of class "justif[ies] class relations of modern capitalism" by underrepresenting the working class and overrepresenting the upper class. Butsch found that only a few large companies (mainly the broadcast networks) decide the content of the programs that a large percentage of audiences watch. Due to the risky and costly nature of major programming decisions, many network executives are inclined to avoid new ideas and continue programming shows with middle-class characters that have been proven to attract audiences and advertisers. This information provides context for why the working class is so underrepresented in television, which ultimately increases the misconception about the "laziness" of the working class that is satirized in the video.

This artifact from *Funny or Die* satirizes some of the absurdities of class, including the common misconception that members of the working class are in that class because of their own laziness rather than external or societal reasons. The responses may seem silly, but they criticize and reflect on the absurdities of the misconceptions of the working class, thereby commenting on a societal problem that deserves attention.

These trends ensured that people of lower SES were thought of as lazy and incompetent at best and conniving cheats at worst. As media promoted the idea the poor are inherently bad and undeserving, the public was less likely to support safety net policies and programs that help them out of poverty. Unsurprisingly, government policy shifted accordingly with a marked decrease in social welfare programs provided by the government in the 1980s (Rose and Baumgartner 2013) and an increase in the rhetoric of individual self-reliance, often referred to as neoliberalism.

The phrase "pulling yourself up by your bootstraps" is commonly deployed to refer to the expectation that people can work their way out of any bad situation. Interestingly, the term was popularized in the early nineteenth century as a ludicrously far-fetched task. In the early twentieth century, its definition evolved to refer to seemingly possible tasks that simply required effort and ingenuity, including moving up from the class into which you were born. Today, the phrase is often used to cajole individuals into trying harder despite a lack of resources or critique claims that institutional barriers make advancing uniquely difficult. However, embedded in this collective misuse of the term is a lack of awareness around the experiences of those in the lower class. It is physically impossible to pull oneself up by one's bootstraps, yet it is used unironically to critique those who have not been able to advance. As Martin Luther King, Jr. stated in a 1967 interview with NBC News (2018), "It's all right to tell a man to lift himself by his own bootstraps, but it is cruel jest to say to a *bootless man* that he ought to lift himself by his own bootstraps" (emphasis added).

The Pervasiveness of Poverty

Approximately 34 million (12%) Americans, lived in poverty in 2019 (US Census Bureau, 2020). However, almost two-thirds (61.8%) of Americans will spend at least one year in poverty (2015), which is an income of about $1,000 a month for a single individual ($2,000 a month for a family of four). Furthermore, 20% of Americans are considered "lower class," because they earn less than twice the poverty line. In addition, one-fifth of American children live in poverty and almost one-half (43%) are considered low income (Koball et al. 2018). These are sizable segments of the population and yet their suffering is largely dismissed due to the belief that poverty is a character flaw and poor people are simply lazy. Interestingly, this too is counter to the numbers: The hours worked by those in the bottom fifth of the economic strata

Activity 2.2   A Living Wage Word Problem
A **living wage** is the minimum income necessary for someone to meet their basic needs including food, housing, and clothing. The living wage is rarely considered when calculating poverty thresholds (living wage.mit.edu) or the **minimum wage**, or the lowest wage that employers can legally pay employees. Visit livingwage.mit.edu. What is the living wage in your neighborhood? What is the minimum wage? How many full-time (35 hours per week) minimum wage jobs must one person hold in your neighborhood in order to live? How many part-time (20 hours per week) minimum wage jobs would it take? At approximately 100 waking hours a week, how much time does that leave every day for time for yourselves, family, and friends? What does that mean for people's quality of life and the pursuit of their dreams? How could you highlight this absurdity satirically?

Figure 2.5 "Walmart Checkout Lady" meme is captioned to demonstrate that being employed, even in multiple jobs, does not guarantee a living wage.

increased by 22% from 1979 to 2007, whereas hours worked by those in the top fifth increased by just over 5% (Mishel 2013). People at the bottom end of the income spectrum must work harder to survive given that wages have not increased over the past 45 years when accounting for inflation (DeSilver 2018).

Class disparities also manifest through lack of access to non-financial resources. About 23 million Americans live in **food deserts**, which are urban areas where it is difficult to buy affordable or good quality fresh food (Haines 2020), 10% of Americans will experience food insecurity at some point, and 4.1% have very low or chronic food security (Coleman-Jensen 2021). Some two million Americans do not have access to clean drinking water and basic plumbing (Jagannathan 2019), almost half do not have access to clean air (Hahn 2020), and more than 30 million American children attend underfunded schools (The Century Foundation 2020). Each of these resources are required for individuals and communities to thrive, but they are disproportionately allocated to communities already rich in resources.

The conflation of SES with individual characteristics reduces public support for social welfare policies and programs by reframing poverty as an individual flaw instead of an institutional failing. Because of these complexities, the stereotypes of people considered lower class as lazy cheats, who are undeserving of help, continue unabated, despite the pervasiveness of poverty. These class-based stereotypes are laid bare in a 2014 clip from *The Daily Show with Jon Stewart*, in which Stewart parallels the conservative rhetoric of welfare programs and tax breaks.

Slumdogs vs. Millionaires, Part 1 (*The Daily Show with Jon Stewart*, Comedy Central 2014)

> As you know, there is a bit of a divide in this country: income inequality. The left thinks it's unfair because of systemic disadvantages built in for the less affluent. The right thinks it's unfair because apparently those disadvantages aren't systemic enough.

With this joke, Stewart sets the stage for by highlighting how systemic inequality benefits those at the top of the hierarchy. The clip then features a montage of Fox News figures talking about those without resources as "a nation of takers," "welfare cheats," "freeloaders," "the moocher class," and "…subsided freeloaders that would rather watch Jerry Springer on the couch or occupy a park than go out and earn a living." Collating these stereotypes encourages the viewer to think about how people at the lower end of the socioeconomic spectrum are talked about in conservative media. Exasperatedly, Stewart says, "I wish there was some shorthand way to represent their feelings toward the recipients of these benefits graphically," then cuts to a brief animation that features an outstretched hand breaking through the center of a map of the United States, threatening the viewer while begging for a handout.

After pausing for the audience's incredulous laughter, Stewart offers a brilliant and humorous read of the visual rhetoric:

> What note do you give the graphic designer? "Give me the dirt-stained hand of the moochy poor bursting, *Alien*-like, through this once-mighty nation. And then give me a little ragtime underneath it. It's a morning show."

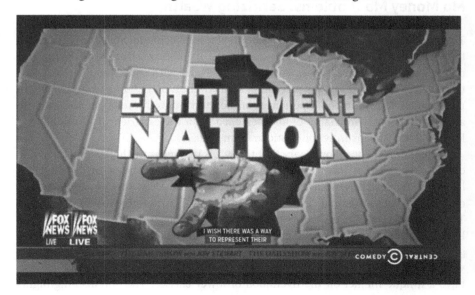

Figure 2.6 Stewart dissects the visual rhetoric of an animated image used in Fox News coverage of Occupy Wall Street and social welfare programs. Still from "Slumdogs vs. Millionaires, Part 1" (*The Daily Show with Jon Stewart* 2014).

Embracing the adage that a picture is worth a thousand words, Stewart explicates the sentiment that is conveyed in this brief graphic. He flips the seemingly inadvertent speech into a more purposeful representation of stereotypes to reinforce the audience's attitudes toward struggling Americans. This strategy of explicating metaphors and exaggeration underscores the stereotyping embedded within the messages themselves.

Stewart then focuses the audience's attention on how the aforementioned stereotypical rhetoric affects policy by showcasing how prominent Republican politicians deploy these assumptions, such as John Boehner, the Speaker of the House at the time, and Mitch McConnell, who would soon become the Senate Majority Leader in 2015. They rationalize ending temporary unemployment benefits and eliminating other social welfare programs, like healthcare subsidies for low-income Americans, to offset their associated cost. Stewart parodies this tradeoff magnifying the inevitable outcomes of such a trade-off:

> (Mockingly) I would happily extend your unemployment benefits for the mere cost of your healthcare. It's like a wonderful "Oh Henry" story with an ironic twist. (Mockingly) "You know, honey, I sold on our food to get you that doctor's appointment." "What? I stopped treating my cancer to get you a banana! We should have talked."

By describing the hard, zero-sum thinking that is deployed to prevent social welfare spending, the clip reveals the absurd treatment of those at the bottom of the socioeconomic hierarchy and how stereotypes of these individuals drive policy. The clip then shifts to reveal the the other side of the spectrum: How positive stereotypes of those at the *top* of the social hierarchy are used to rationalize maintaining costly policies that benefit *the wealthy*.

Mo Money Mo Problems: Satirizing Wealth

The public discourse regarding people in lower socioeconomic classes is rooted in the experiences of those at the top end of the income spectrum who have more power, opportunity, and access (Butsch 2003). Those with such resources also own the means of production, thus propelling many of the aforementioned stereotypes in mass media. However, the experiences of the individuals in the upper classes, who are simultaneously in charge of and detached from the experiences of middle and lower classes, are absurdly solipsistic in themselves.

Solipsism is the view or theory that the self is the only one that can be known to exist. In the case of intergroup interactions, it is the psychological tendency to believe that our experiences are the only experiences, an easy thing to believe when one is not exposed to other experiences. Solipsism is also impacted by hegemony. That is, individuals in the upper classes may not be aware of how the "other half lives," regardless of their social power and the fact that their actions impact these groups. The aforementioned clip reveals how the classist attitudes of those in power, who are clearly of a higher SES than those on whom they are passing judgement, have a unique impact on the livelihood of lower classes. The clip also highlights how the rationalization of costly government policies, such as tax cuts, are also driven by stereotypes. By contrast, those at the bottom end of the socioeconomic spectrum are intimately aware of how the middle and upper class live because their lifestyles are featured in media content and serve as aspirational models. The decisions of those at the bottom of the socioeconomic spectrum also rarely impact those at the top.

Slumdogs vs. Millionaires, Part 2 (*The Daily Show with Jon Stewart*, Comedy Central 2014)
Returning to *The Daily Show with Jon Stewart* example, the second half of the clip makes the disparate impacts of these solipsistic processes evident by cutting to the same politicians contradicting themselves when arguing *against* offsetting temporary tax cuts for wealthy Americans because the costs no longer need to be offset.

- "We should never have to offset the cost of a deliberate decision to reduce tax rates" (Sen. Jon Kyl, R-AZ).
- "What you're trying to do is get into the Washington game, and their funny accounting over there" (Rep. John Boehner, R-OH).
- "This is the existing tax policy that has been in place for ten years. Why did it all of a sudden become something that needs to be (quote) 'paid for'?" (Sen. Mitch McConnell, R-KY).

By juxtaposing the politicians' own rhetoric of which government policies must be paid for (i.e., those that help those in the lower classes) and which do not need to be paid for (i.e., those that help those in the upper classes), the inconsistency of their arguments becomes evident. Stewart then returns to the original critique by exaggerating the stereotypes and the processes behind these contradictory reactions through an impression of Mitch McConnell: "Why do we have to pay for it? It's been in existence for over 10 years. Giving money to rich people doesn't cost anything. All the payment we need is their beautiful smiles."

The majority of class-based satire has focused on the absurdity of life in the upper classes and their ability to exercise power without accountability. Although this may not initially appear to be a process of marginalization, it is essential to understanding how the lower classes continue to suffer. *The Daily Show with Jon Stewart* clip points at how those in power who make decisions that benefit those at the top of the hierarchy, to the detriment of those at the bottom of the hierarchy. It reveals the solipsism among the upper classes, coupled with the impacts of their actions.

It is not surprising that people with resources have no need for cross-class awareness, but this lack of awareness also manifests in actual psychological differences between classes. In Antony Manstead's 2018 review of the psychological research on socioeconomic status and class, they explain the disparities between those in the middle and upper classes compared to those in the lower and working classes regarding their perceptions of the world, individual autonomy, and expectations of opportunity. Lower-class individuals are more likely to see their lives as *interdependent* (i.e., impacted by the experiences and decisions of others). By contrast, middle-class and upper-class individuals are more like report an *independent* cultural ideal, meaning individuals are autonomous and able to determine the outcome of their lives (Manstead 2018). This difference then manifests in one's expectations of others; middle-class and upper-class individuals are more likely to believe that people *can* pull themselves up by their bootstraps, regardless of the circumstances in which they find themselves.

Similar to the etymological evolution of "pulling oneself up by one's bootstraps," the term "meritocracy" emerged as a satirical term in Michael Young's book *The Rise of the*

Meritocracy (1958) as an indictment of the emphasis on merit. In Young's dystopian novel, socioeconomic class divides have been replaced with merit-based class divides. Those who have merit constitute the ruling elite and those who are determined to be without merit constitute the disenfranchised masses leading to a segregation wherein those in the upper classes experience autonomy while all the talent and "merit" have been siphoned from the lower classes. In the decades since its publication, the term **meritocracy** has been embraced unironically to describe governments or societies where ability determines one's power and status. In these systems, people are supposedly judged by their potential and not by their social categories. But this emphasis only changes the language while maintaining the associated processes of marginalization given the role of resources like a quality education in the actualization of merit.

The Hunger Games (Suzanne Collins 2008)
Although *The Hunger Games* franchise is commonly understood as a commentary on the rampant consumerism and bloodlust of television audiences in an era of reality television, the dystopian world that Collins created also satirizes the American class structure. Districts 1 and 2 are at the top of the hierarchy, incredibly wealthy and awash with resources, whereas residents of District 12 live in poverty and are forced into unsafe working conditions to provide resources to the higher districts. The social ladder is made obvious in the numerical district ranking and reinforced by the living conditions and available opportunities especially as the districts (i.e., classes) compete during The Hunger Games, where two "tributes" (players) from each district are pitted against each other in a battle to the death.

Tributes from Districts 1 and 2 are referred to as "career" players who have spent their entire lives training for the games. The resources available to them from their social position of birth allow them to excel in this competition. The deployment of seemingly objective metrics like "skill" and "talent" benefit those with resources like training facilities and a network of prior winners while rhetorically detaching their success from their systemic advantages. When success is rationalized as the outcome of individual efforts, it is easy to ignore how resources associated with merit can be amassed among those who have access to them, and withheld from those who do not. The audience then sees this world of excess and privilege through the lens of, and ultimately comes to empathize with, the residents of the lower districts who are doomed to failure based on the literal circumstances of their birth. They are stratified and defined by seemingly arbitrary characteristics of which they have no control, and concepts like fairness, individuality, and even free will are nonexistent.

Advantages for Some by Disadvantaging Others

In the book *Dream Hoarders*, Richard Reeves (2017) describes how those in the top 20% of the income spectrum actively restrict access and opportunity for those in the bottom 80% under the auspices of providing for their own. An insular focus on protecting oneself and one's immediate family contributes to the **wealth gap**, the disparity in overall financial worth (including income and assets) between classes, which widens the gulf between those who control the allocation of resources and those who lack resources. The wealth gap is different from **income inequality**, or the uneven distribution of income throughout a population, which perpetuates disparities in a fundamental resource: money.

Many of the items of privilege featured in Activity 2.1 revolve around the cost of being poor or the cost-saving capacity of *not* being poor; a lack of resources inhibits one from attaining resources, and having resources allows one to amass more resources. Items like "I don't have any student loans," "I work in a salaried job," and "I have never done my taxes myself" may just seem like nice things at first but they are advantages associated with having resources that allow one to accumulate more resources: Not having student loans means not having to pay a percentage of your income to Sallie Mae (now the SLM Corporation); salaried jobs also mean consistent income, regardless of changes to hours worked or sick days, thus allowing one to make future plans on a stable foundation; hiring an expert to do your taxes allows one to take advantage of loopholes in expanding tax laws and ultimately save money in the long run (e.g., Donald Trump famously paid $750 per year in federal taxes in 2016 and 2017). This is the absurdity highlighted in the Tom Toles cartoon in Figure 2.7: The wealthy have more opportunities to spend less and save more, such that it is confusing for them to pay any taxes at all.

Similarly, amassing *wealth*, made easier through access to financial consultants, reduces the need for a steady *income*. In 2013, Mark Zuckerberg famously joined the $1 salary club by insisting on collecting one dollar annually while still retaining a worth of about $75 billion due to his investments in Facebook (now META) and other companies. Although he reports almost no income, he is still one of the

Figure 2.7 "The rich are above us all, and below," a political cartoon by Tom Toles (2019). *Source*: Phil Venditty / Flickr / CC BY 2.0.

wealthiest people in the world. Similarly, when asked if his wealth made it impossible for him to understand the plight of ordinary Americans while on the campaign trail in 2011, Mitt Romney (unironically) said, "I'm also unemployed."(Zeleny 2011).

Furthermore, many of the items listed as class privileges combine to create a cushion: Health insurance limits the impact of an unexpected illness on one's finances and investments can be liquidated to access cash. This is what makes Romney's "joke" about being unemployed so problematic; being without income or unemployed, is hardly a danger for a man worth $250 million and who made approximately $13.7 million in capital gains investments, taxable interests, and dividends the year that he ran for president (Cohan 2012). Those at the upper end of the socioeconomic spectrum do not need to think about the details of making ends meet, which is a unique privilege. Money brings its own advantages including *not* being in perpetual fear of being without money.

Solemn Jeff Bezos Realizes He Could End Up Like Homeless Man If Just Few Hundred Thousand Things Go Wrong (*The Onion* 2019)
Consider a 2019 post from *The Onion* entitled, "Solemn Jeff Bezos Realizes He Could End Up Like Homeless Man If Just Few Hundred Thousand Things Go Wrong." It features a fictional Jeff Bezos, founder of Amazon and the wealthiest person in the world with a net worth of almost $200 billion, contemplating what it would take for him to fall through the cracks into poverty.

> "I could suddenly lose my job, my health insurance, my mansions, my planes, become addicted to every drug, break every bone in my body, be arrested for arson, and deal with the fallout of a mass amnesia where nobody knows me, and then I'm left completely penniless with nowhere to go. It really is only by the grace of God that none of those things plus a few million others have not yet happened to me."

Bezos has a vast cushion of wealth and enjoys an important benefit of class that is rarely discussed: The ability to survive unexpected expenses. In January 2020, just before the pandemic, fewer than half (41%) of Americans had enough savings to cover a $1,000 emergency (Leonhardt 2020). In a 2022 survey, it was revealed that almost two-thirds (64%) of American workers live paycheck to paycheck (Dickler 2022). Strikingly, almost 40% of Americans making over $100,000 annually also suffer from this lack of financial security (Hoffower 2021), even though a household income of $100,000 is widely considered the benchmark of middle class. Economists attribute this lack of financial security to business management strategies that focus on benefiting shareholders over employees, and maintaining outdated pay practices (Bersin 2018). The wildly different experiences of the CEO and the average employee are highlighted in the final line: "At press time, just to be safe, Bezos was meeting with Amazon's board of directors to discuss further cuts to employee benefits."

The adage that "satire punches up" takes on a multifaceted meaning when targeting those in power at the top of the socioeconomic ladder. A plutocracy is a society in which the government is ruled by the wealthy. The United States is commonly referred to as a democracy, a system of representative government wherein the whole population or all eligible members can participate. However, the democratic quality of the United States is undermined by capitalism, which enables those who accumulate resources to influence government (Reich 2007). Mocking the upper classes for their inability to realize "how the other half lives" while simultaneously controlling access to resources for the "other half" is a tried-and-true approach to class-based satire. The absurdity of this power relationship is also easy to highlight, thereby holding the powerful accountable for their deficiencies and the subsequent impacts on societal institutions.

What Is the Answer? Make Everyone Middle Class!

By definition, the "middle class" is just that: Between upper class and lower class. Pew Research Center defines the middle class as those earning between two-thirds and double of the median household income (Bennet et al. 2020): People making between $45,000 and $135,000 yearly in 2020. However, middle class is also defined by education and occupation. People with bachelor's degrees or professional occupations that require post-graduate degrees (e.g., teacher, nurse, accountant) are considered to be middle class by virtue of their career. Ultimately, both definitions are true even though they can be conflicting, e.g., an adjunct college professor teaching at three universities without health insurance who is living below the poverty line (Flaherty 2020) may still be considered middle class by some. Alternatively, nuclear power reactor operators (the occupation of Homer Simpson) are one of the highest paid "working class" jobs, earning a median income of over $100,000 (Kiersz and Hoff 2021).

Activity 2.3   Class Commentary in Political Cartoons

Political cartoons have historically been a favorite venue for class-based satire that targets the upper classes, especially as the penny press newspapers of the nineteenth century made newspapers accessible. Search online for political cartoons over the past 150 years in national and local newspapers that satirize solipsism (insular self-protectionism). Find one from each of the following periods and make note of trends across time.

- 1875–1900
- 1900–1929
- 1930–1945
- 1946–1970
- 1970–2000
- 2001–Current

Nation's Rich and Powerful Wondering When Rest of Americans Will Just Give Up (*The Onion* 2018)

By Gianna Carideo

In this satirical article posted by *The Onion*, the writers use a picture of a busy Iranian city to illustrate American society in Washington. This article details the top 20% of the American economic system's views on the middle, working, and unemployed classes. The folks being surveyed do not understand why these other classes even try to get ahead in the current economy. They admit to controlling the media, financial, and political institutions to further their wealth. They also admit to lying about trickle-down economics to the lower classes for them to accept their fate. Finally, the top-tier classes expressed their renewed hope and optimism given the lack of lower-class voter representation.

(Continued)

> (Continued)
>
> This article uses satire to provide a commentary on social class, a division of a society based on social and economic status. Writing from the point of view of the upper class, *The Onion* illustrates the power imbalances that exist in the American economic and social classes. In this case, the American Dream is restricted to those who are already established in the upper class. As stated in the article, "What exactly is wrong with them? I mean, there's no possible way they'll ever stop us from getting everything we want, so the poor—and I suppose what's left of the middle class—are only delaying the inevitable." This illustrates that the American Dream is only possible for the upper class, at the expense of lower classes. The Scott and Leonhardt (2005) article confirms this opinion, as they state, "Americans are arguably more likely than they were 30 years ago to end up in the class into which they were born" (p. 3). In this article, it is acknowledged that, though many self-starters are now multi-millionaires and billionaires, American citizens are more likely to be confined to the same class they are born into. This supports *The Onion*'s article because if there is a higher chance of being held to your same class no matter how hard you work, why would Americans even try in today's society?
>
> Haugerud's 2012 article entited "Satire and dissent in the age of Billionaires" supports the views of *The Onion*. One quote stood out: "How extreme wealth intermingles with politics is one of the most provocative issues of our era." This quote supports the statement in *The Onion*'s article that describes the upper class' influence on media, politics, and financial institutions. It should also be noted that this article was posted in May of 2018. This month, the United States economy surged, which left the upper class with more money in its pockets.
>
> I thought that this article did a good job of describing the imbalances that exist within the American socioeconomic class system. I believe that by writing in the point of view of the most privileged, *The Onion* is able to provide a unique point of view that is not normally illustrated when describing issues that exist in this institution.

Given these discrepancies, middle class means something different from its seemingly objective classification. According to Dennis Gilbert (1998), Americans in the middle class are comfortable with the means to purchase occassional luxuries and experience "a combination of self-direction and freedom from routinization at work" (p. 285).[2] Ultimately, we define middle income as similar to us (Kamp 2009). The phrase "growing the middle class," is a mantra for American politicians attempting to connect with their constituency, not because the majority of Americans are middle class but because the majority of Americans believe they are middle class. Most Americans (70%) think they are middle class, when in reality only 50% are (Martin 2017).

Media perpetuate the idea that most Americans are "middle class" by presenting the interests of the upper classes as general concerns and not emphasizing the structural economic concerns of the lower classes (Mantsios 2001). "By downplaying economic insecurity and representing 'the middle' as a 'state of mind,' the media encourage

---

2 This subjective sense of satisfaction and stability is ironic in a society that promotes materialism and consumerism.

working-class individuals to identify with a politically neutralized 'universal middle class' (Bullock et al. 2001, p. 231). When running for president in 2012, Mitt Romney defined middle income as "$200,000–$250,000 and less" (Frank 2012) even though the median household income at the time was about $50,000, and claimed that his tax policy was, "for the great middle class, the 80 to 90 percent of us in this country" (Falcone 2011), indicating that Romney considered himself "middle class" despite being worth $250 million at the time. When all people consider themselves middle class, including people who objectively qualify as wealthy, the resulting struggle is ripe for satire.

The political cartoon by Nick Anderson in figure 2.8 connects Romney's lack of understanding of class-based experiences with the glad-handing and folksy approach required of American politicians. In the cartoon, Romney eagerly reaches out his hand to a member of the middle class and makes what he interprets as a lighthearted bet that amplifies his ignorance. As described, many Americans do not have $1,000 for emergencies, so the idea that they would have $10,000 for a friendly bet is ridiculous despite it being pocket change to someone worth $250 million. But more importantly, the bet itself, that Romney is in a lower tax bracket is insulting because money earned on investments is taxed at a lower rate than income. Because Mitt Romney is unemployed coupled with his ability to hire the best financial consultants and tax lawyers to take advantage of all possible tax loopholes, it is likely that he pays a lower percentage of his income in taxes. The voter's frustration with this situation is evident; he stares at Romney with a doubtful look and refuses to offer his hand in return.

Although the middle class is defined by objective qualifiers, mass media has emphasized visual representations of the American Dream and the good life for those who identify as middle class. In this mediated environment, the American Dream became salient, concrete, and constructed around what one's life looked like, not just one's accomplishments. Middle-class families are understood to be living in a standalone house in the suburbs with a two-car garage and a white picket fence; a television in the family room, a dinner table with nice china, top-end appliances, and a family vacation to Disneyland. In this case, the material goods that one could purchase indicated one's accomplishments, and the *material* middle class American Dream became the goal and stories of the American Dream often featured the "horror" of falling off one's position in the social ladder (McGrath 2005). Interestingly, this is not what most Americans believe will bring them happiness; they believe friends, family, and health will (Manstead 2018), but nonetheless, this illusion of the house, car, etc., remains concrete in the collective imagination despite major social changes in the decades since.

Furthermore, the mediated presentation of lower and working classes that entails a lack of education and stable occupations, as well as a brash sense of humor and "classless" or crass behavior, often does not address a difference in their possessions. Working-class television families also have standalone houses with multiple bedrooms, attached two-car garages, and spacious backyards (see Roseanne, 1988-1997; Married… with Children, 1987-1997; Mom, 2013-2021). Although the sets might imply that these families are middle class, class distinctions emerge in the scripts. Money is a regular plot point in working-class sitcoms, and families are constantly concerned about money resulting in possessions that are not as nice compared to wealthier television families. The humor in this genre comes from their perpetual desire for a nicer life and the lengths to which the family will go to achieve it. This phenomenon is satirized in the opening credits of *The Simpsons*,

Figure 2.8 "Mitt Romney meets the middle class" a political cartoon by Nick Anderson (2012). *Source*: Nick Anderson / THE CARTOONIST GROUP.

where the "couch gag," the last moment in the opening sequence that differs from episode to episode, draws attention to the ubiquitous and cliché couch component of any family sitcom.

If the definition of "middle class" means nothing, then what does it take to become part of the middle class? As described by Thorstein Veblen in his 1899 book *The Theory of the Leisure Class*, the leisure class is the class between the lower and upper classes. Members of the leisure class can be identified by their desire to emulate the appearance of earning as much as the upper classes (pecuniary emulation), engaging in the activities of upper classes (conspicuous leisure), and having similar possessions to those of the upper classes (conspicuous consumption). Ultimately, being middle class is to have nice things but not be opulent. A culture of buying on credit allows individuals to maintain socioeconomic illusions, resulting in a steadily increasing culture of consumerism and materialism over the past 150 years.

Babbitt (Sinclair Lewis 1922)
Twenty-three years after the publication of Veblen's book, Sinclair Lewis published *Babbitt*. It's a story of George F. Babbitt, whose name entered public discourse as "...a person and especially a business or professional man who conforms unthinkingly to prevailing middle-class standards" (Merriam Webster). Babbitt is introduced as a man who "...made nothing in particular, neither butter nor shoes nor poetry, but he was nimble in the calling of selling houses for more than people could afford to pay." Further mocking his (lack of) contribution to society, Lewis goes on to provide an

Figure 2.9 The couch gag from The Simpsons has become a memorable pop culture artifact in its own right, but the frame itself parodies the wholesomeness of the all-American family as presented on television.

extremely detailed explanation of Babbitt's identity as an amalgamation of simultaneously meaningful and meaningless objects.

> On his watch-chain were a gold penknife, silver cigar-cutter, seven keys (the use of two of which he had forgotten), and incidentally a good watch. Depending from the chain was a large, yellowish elk's-tooth-proclamation of his membership in the Brotherly and Protective Order of Elks....

The novel is a long-form lampooning of the cliché emerging middle class, satirized by a man so woefully mediocre that he believes to be of value because of the appearance of his home, his family, his occupation, and his supposedly innate intelligence, which comes from a blind adherence to the things that he has been told are valuable. *Babbitt* underscores the flaws in the desire to become part of the middle class for the sake of being middle class while simultaneously acknowledging that the middle class is incredibly alluring.

Laughing at SES and Class in the Twenty-First Century

Class and socioeconomic status continue to be difficult topics to discuss and subsequently satirize in the United States, which impedes our ability to disrupt these patterns. This chapter has focused on marginalization processes with respect to wealth and resources. An inability to advance is attributed to individual failings, and this lack of awareness regarding how class impacts society as well as one's own attitudes allows classist stereotypes and prejudices to be maintained and unquestioned. Furthermore, the isolation and insular experiences of those in the top 20% of the socioeconomic spectrum, which is exacerbated by other categories of historic advantage including gender and race, are a major factor in the marginalization processes that discriminate against lower-status groups. The stereotypes that are used to diminish, dehumanize, and ignore the experiences of those at the bottom are problematic and absurd, and the belief that some people are better than others simply because they have access to more resources can pervade one's sense of self and exacerbate prejudicial attitudes and discriminatory behavior.

The complexity of satirizing class, especially in traditional broadcast media, is compounded by socioeconomic barriers to the media industry. Excelling within this industry often requires a college degree from a prominent school, a prolific social network, and a willingness to take underpaid or unpaid internships to build one's résumé, all of which require resources. The stratification of media professionals affects the content they create. As Richard Butsch describes, media producers overwhelmingly grow up in middle-class to upper-class homes, and "…the tight schedule and deadlines of series production leave no time for becoming familiar enough with working-class lifestyle to be able to capture it realistically" (2003, p. 581). Given the role of media in constructing the collective knowledge about certain groups (see Chapter 1), especially for those who have no interaction with members of the group, the solipsism of media producers makes criticizing the class system in the United States rare.

However, the rise of social media in the twenty-first century coupled with other low-cost communication technologies has allowed for a wider range of voices to be represented in the public sphere, resulting in more diverse satire. In the case of class and SES, social media platforms like Twitter and Facebook have emerged as powerful spaces for user-generated satire, alongside cable and streaming outlets, that targets socioeconomic status and class.

On September 26, 2019, a story began circulating in the news cycle that donors associated with Wall Street would not contribute to the Democratic party if Elizabeth Warren, a prominent proponent for increasing taxes on the wealthy to address income inequality, was selected as the Democratic nominee in the 2020 primaries (Schwartz 2019). In response, Law Boy, Esq. (@The_Law_Boy) posted, "…once a month some hedge fund manager or another goes on TV and says like 'if you vote for anyone who says the rich have too much power I swear to god I will dictate the course of this election'" (2019), drawing attention to America's implicit plutocracy by saying the quiet part out loud.

However, simply expanding opportunities does not mean that every joke in these platforms qualifies as satire especially given the longstanding approach of mocking low-income Americans for simply being low-income, instead of asking *why* they cannot access resources. When satirizing SES and class, it is important to remember:

Being in poverty or struggling financially is not a personal shortcoming. There is a trend in mainstream media to mock those at the bottom of the socioeconomic ladder for stereotypical assumptions of their personalities, demeanor, and intelligence. The trope of the "country bumpkin" or "yokel" are rooted in the stereotype that those in rural, low-income communities are incompetent. These cruel jokes continue to marginalize rural Americans and ensure their community is not seen as robust, dynamic, and complex.

There are unintelligent and lazy people, as well as intelligent and resourceful people at every income stratum; satire focuses on actual disparities of power, not assumed disparities in intelligence. Intelligence is not correlated with wealth or resources, but recognition of intelligence is. This institutionalized approach to merit and value is rooted in a flawed system that is ripe for satire. As a community, Americans are largely unaware of how wealth and merit is distributed. In this environment, simply stating facts can satirize the institution and disrupt discourse.

It is crucial to hold institutions and individuals that control and ultimately benefit from socioeconomic systems accountable. Although mocking the rich for their solipsism may feel good, merely making fun of individuals allows classist systems to continue unabated. It is easy to ignore the larger issues when individuals are blamed for institutional problems because simply removing the targeted individual still allows the larger problems in the institution to remain unchecked. Satirizing SES and class means showing audiences what they have been encouraged not to see and dispute the flawed ideologies regarding wealth and value that they have been encouraged to believe.

Additional Activities

Activity 2.4   Play SPENT
Satire can exist in any media format. As described in the introduction, it does not necessarily have to be entertaining but does require audiences to recognize the absurdities of society, causing them to feel amusement and contempt at the same time. The online game SPENT invites players to take on the role of someone who is living at the poverty line and must get through the month on $1,000. It's a powerful tool to consider the process of decision making when living paycheck to paycheck. Many students begin the game with the idea that they will be able to survive the month on the limited income, but as the game continues and life happens, things like deciding to leave a note or drive away from a small fender bender, losing hours at work to attend their child's school play, or treating the family pet when it needs a trip to the vet will test the player's personal morals and ethics. Ultimately, this game reveals how class privilege operates by taking these things for granted. This game demands that players take the perspective of an often-maligned group, which is often blamed for their own status because they supposedly make poor decisions. After playing it, they can appreciate the absurdity of living at the poverty line and the absurdity of the stereotypes and rhetoric that is deployed in the public sphere about people placed in this situation.

Figure 2.10 SPENT, a free online interactive game where the user attempts to make it through one month on minimum wage, informs users how their short-term decisions can have long-term consequences. (2011).

Activity 2.5   Spotting American Dream Rhetoric

For many, the American Dream is a term students learned in high school while discussing the mass migration from Europe in the early twentieth century or possibly while reading F. Scott Fitzgerald's *The Great Gatsby*, but the idea of the American Dream is everywhere and is used to universally connect with audiences because of its simultaneously concrete imagery (e.g., a suburban house with a white picket fence and a two-car garage) and its nebulous promise that one's future will be better by simply being on American soil. In short, it means nothing and everything at the same time and is rhetorically deployed by politicians, advertisers, entertainers, journalists, and everyday people, often without definition or discussion, as a placeholder for an idealized America.

Consider how the American Dream is discussed in your favorite media content (e.g., television programming, movies, books, music, news outlets, influencers), either implicitly or explicitly. Using the communication process model (Chapter 1), consider the encoded (i.e., how is the sender is defining the American Dream) and decoded meanings (i.e., how are the receivers/audiences interpreting the American Dream) of the message and how this idea is used to connect with audiences. In addition, consider how the sender and receiver's class status work as noise that results in different interpretations of the message.

References

Adamczyk, A. (3 May 2019). More than half of millennials think they'll be millionaires—here's what the data suggests.CNBC.

Adams, J.T. (2017). *The Epic of America*. New York: Routledge.

Alesina, A., Stantcheva, S., and Teso, E. (2018). Intergenerational mobility and preferences for redistribution. *American Economic Review* 108 (2): 521–554.

Bersin, J. (2018). Why aren't wages keeping up? It's not the economy, it's management. Forbes. https://www.forbes.com/sites/joshbersin/2018/10/31/

why-arent-wages-keeping-up-its-not-the-economy-its-management/?sh=29fad4c3397e (accessed 3 May 2022).

Britton, C. (13 January 2018). Connie Britton: Yes, poverty is sexist. Here's why. Entertainment Weekly. www.nativesovereigntees.com.

Bullock, H. E., Fraser Wyche, K., and Williams, W. R. (2001). Media images of the poor. *Journal of Social Issues*, 57 (2): 229–246.

Butsch, R. (2003). Ralph, Fred, Archie and Homer: Why television keeps re-creating the white male working class buffoon. In: *Gender, Race and Class in Media: A Text-Reader* (ed. G. Dines and J. Humez), 575–585. Sage Publications.

Chetty, R., Grusky, D., Hell, M., Hendren, N., Manduca, R., and Narang, J. (2017). *The fading American dream: Trends in absolute income mobility since 1940. Science*, 356 (6336): 398-406.

Cohan, W. (5 October 2012). Mitt Romney is worth $250 million. Why so little? Washington Post.

Coleman-Jensen, A., Rabbitt, M.P., Gregory, C.A., and Singh, A. (September 2021). Household Food Security in the United States in 2020, ERR-298, U.S. Department of Agriculture, Economic Research service. https://www.ers.usda.gov/webdocs/publications/102076/err-298.pdf?v=4757.2

Collins, S. (2008). *The Hunger Games*. New York City: Scholastic Press.

Comedy Central. (9 January 2014). Slumdogs vs. Millionaires: The daily show with Jon Stewart [Video].Comedy Central. www.cc.com/video/rlp7xz/the-daily-show-with-jon-stewart-slumdogs-vs-millionaires

Corman, C.A. (October 2004). 9/11 and Acoma Pueblo: Homeland security in Indian country [Newsletter]. *Common Place* 5 (1). http://commonplace.online/article/911-and-acoma-pueblo/ (accessed 3 May 2022)

DeParle, J. (4 January 2012). Harder for Americans to rise from lower rungs.New York Times.

DeSilver, D. (7 August 2018). For most U.S. workers, real wages have barely budged in decades. Pew Research Center.

Dickler, J. (11 May 2022). Two-thirds of Americans live paycheck to paycheck as inflation continues to climb. https://www.cnbc.com/2022/05/11/two-thirds-of-americans-live-paycheck-to-paycheck-as-inflation-climbs.html (accessed 11 May 2022)

Ephron, N. [WellesleyCollege]. (27 June 2012). Nora Ephron speaking at Wellesley college commencement 1996 [Video].YouTube. youtube.com/watch?v=DVCfFBlKpN8

Falcone, M. (23 September 2011). Mitt Romney's middle class moment. ABC News. https://abcnews.go.com/blogs/politics/2011/09/mitt-romneys-middle-class-moment (accessed 3 May 2022).

Flaherty, C. (20 April 2020). Barely Getting By. Inside Higher Ed. https://www.insidehighered.com/news/2020/04/20/new-report-says-many-adjuncts-make-less-3500-course-and-25000-year accessed (3 May 2022).

Frank, S. (14 September 2012). Romney thinks $250K is 'middle-income'. NBC News. https://www.nbcnews.com/news/world/romney-thinks-250k-middle-income-flna999527 (accessed 3 May 2022).

Funny or Die (2015). For Labor Day we asked "Why is the working class so lazy?" [Video].YouTube. youtube.com/watch?v=5gAYE8xv3dY

Gilbert, D.L. (1998) *The American class structure in an age of growing inequality*. Belmont, CA: Wadsworth Publishing Company.

Hahn, J. (21 April 2020). Nearly half of the US population is breathing dirty air. Sierra Club.

Haines, M. (19 May 2020). Pandemic Worsens 'Food Deserts' for 23.5 Million Americans. VOA News.

Harper, D.J., Wagstaff, G.F., Newton, J.T., and Harrison, K.R. (1990). Lay causal perceptions of third world poverty and the just world theory'. *Social Behavior and Personality: An International Journal* 18 (2): 235–238.

Haugerud, A. (2012). Satire and dissent in the age of Billionaires. *Social Research: An International Quarterly* 79 (1): 145–168.

Hoffower, H. (16 September 2021) 60% of millennials earning over $100,000 say they're living paycheck to paycheck. Business Insider. https://www.businessinsider.com/high-earning-henry-millennials-six-figure-salaries-feel-broke-2021-6 (accessed 3 May 2022)

Jagannathan, M. (23 November 2019). 2 million Americans don't have access to running water and basic plumbing. Marketwatch.

Kiersz, A. and Hoff, M. (28 May 2021). 30 blue-collar jobs with the highest salaries. Business Insider. https://www.businessinsider.com/highest-paying-blue-collar-jobs-in-america (accessed 3 May 2022)

Koball, H. (2018). Basic facts about low-income children. National Center for Children in Poverty.

Law Boy, Esq. [@The_Law_Boy]. (26 September 2019). once a month some hedge fund manager or another goes on TV and says like "if you vote for anyone&[Tweet]. Twitter. https://twitter.com/The_Law_Boy/status/1177281875552940033

Leonhardt, M. (22 January 2020). 41% of Americans would be able to cover a $1,000 emergency with savings. CNBC. https://www.cnbc.com/2020/01/21/41-percent-of-americans-would-be-able-to-cover-1000-dollar-emergency-with-savings.html (accessed 3 May 2022)

Manstead, A.S. (2018). The psychology of social class: How socioeconomic status impacts thought, feelings, and behaviour. *British Journal of Social Psychology* 57 (2): 267–291.

Mantsios, G. (2001). Class in America. In: *Race, Class, and Gender in the United States* (ed. P.S. Rothenberg and S. Munshi). New York: Worth Publishers. https://4.files.edl.io/a774/05/10/19/053156-125d68d9-cdf2-4efb-94a8-412482541061.pdf

Martin, E. (30 June 2017). 70% of Americans consider themselves middle class—but only 50% are. CNBC. https://www.cnbc.com/2017/06/30/70-percent-of-americans-consider-themselves-middle-class-but-only-50-percent-are.html (accessed 3 May 2022).

McGrath, C. (8 June 2005). *In Fiction, A Long History of Fixation on the Social Gap*. New York Times.

Mishel, L. (30 January 2013). Vast majority of wage earners are working harder, and for not much more [Issue brief]. *Economic Policy Institute* 348 (1).

NBC News (4 April 2018). MLK talks 'New Phase' of civil rights struggle, 11 months before his assassination | NBC News. https://www.youtube.com/watch?v=2xsbt3a7K-8a (accessed 11 May 2022).

NBC. (19 January 2019). Millenial millions: Saturday night live [Video]. NBC. nbc.com/saturday-night-live/video/millennial-millions/3867395.

Reeves, R.V. (2017). *Dream Hoarders: How the American Upper Middle Class is Leaving Everyone Else in the Dust, Why that is a Problem, and What to Do about it.* Brookings Institution Press.

Reich, R. B. (2007). How capitalism is killing democracy. *Foreign Policy* (162): 38.

Rose, M. and Baumgartner, F.R. (2013). Framing the poor: Media coverage and US poverty policy, 1960–2008. *Policy Studies Journal* 41 (1): 22–53.

Schwartz, B. (26 September 2019). Wall street democratic donors warn the party: We'll sit out, or back Trump, if you nominate Elizabeth Warren.CNB.

Scientists: Rich people, poor people may have shared common Ancestor. (25 July 2014). The Onion.

Scott, J. (16 May 2005). Life at the top in America isn't just better, its longer. New York Times.

Scott, J. and Leonhardt, D. (15 May 2005). Shadowy lines that still divide. New York Times.

The Onion. (23 May 2018). Nation's rich and powerful wondering when rest of Americans will just give up.

The Onion. (17 October 2019). Solemn Jeff Bezos realizes he could end up like homeless man if just few hundred thousand things go wrong.

TCF study finds U.S. Schools underfunded by nearly $150 billion annually. (22 July 2020). The Century Foundation.

Toles, T. (13 October 2019). Opinion: The rich are above us all, and below [Comic]. Washington Post.

World Economic Forum. (2020). The social mobility report 2020. http://reports.weforum.org/social-mobility-report-2020/social-mobility-rankings

Young, M. (1958). *Rise of Meritocracy*. Thames and Hudson.

Zeleny, J. (16 June 2011). Romney: 'I'm also unemployed'. New York Times.

3

Satirizing Gender

"You're born naked, and the rest is drag."

– RuPaul

Assumptions about gender have been built into our social, political, and economic institutions. The common understanding of gender in the United States is that we are born male or female and move through the world with this identity as if these categories result in a wide variety of psychological, personal, interpersonal, and lifelong decisions, such personality, occupation, or presentation. This understanding of gender has been normalized in social interactions and media. From a very young age, we learn that there is a "right" and "wrong" way to behave as a man or a woman. We watch as individuals who do not conform to these socially agreed-upon behaviors are mercilessly mocked and persecuted. We may even participate in this socialization, sometimes inadvertently, despite our own experiences. This chapter describes the absurdities of narrowly defining masculinity and femininity and how these gendered norms impact individuals and society.

The Unbearable Binaries of Gender: Defining Sex and Gender

Sex and gender are not the same even though we have used them synonymously in the United States. They often cluster together, but denote two different phenomena that are essential to understanding the absurdity of gender. **Sex** is a biological category socially constructed through individual judgement, often at birth. Prior to the advent of genetic testing, being identified as a male or female at birth meant the presence or absence of external genitalia that resembled a penis. If newborns possessed an identifiable penis, they were labeled "male." If they did not, the newborns were labeled "female." There was no nuance for external reproductive organs mislabeled as penises (e.g., enlarged clitorises) or the variety of biological reasons as to why a newborn would not have a visible penis (e.g., a buried or hidden penis).

By contrast, **gender** is the individual identity (often but not always) associated with one's sex-based category or how we understand ourselves and how we present ourselves to others. What we wear, how we carry ourselves, and the names and

Diversity and Satire: Laughing at Processes of Marginalization, First Edition.
Charisse L'Pree Corsbie-Massay.
© 2023 John Wiley & Sons, Inc. Published 2023 by John Wiley & Sons, Inc.

pronouns we use for ourselves develop over time as we come to present as a **man** (the gender expression generally associated with being male), a **woman** (the gender expression generally associated with being female), or **non-binary** (i.e., identifying as both man and woman or neither man nor woman and sometimes moving between these genders; includes gender-fluid). For most people, their gender conforms to the sex assigned to them at birth. These people are commonly referred to as **cisgender**. Those whose gender does not conform to their sex assigned at birth are commonly referred to as **transgender**.[1] These categories are neither robust nor immutable, but they have been treated as simple and distinct, resulting in a limited understanding of humanity that becomes absurd as one digs deeper.

Figure 3.1 "It's kind of weird when you think about it" WTFrame Comics (2020). *Source*: WTFrame Comics.

---

1 The prefix "trans-" in Greek literally means "across, over, or beyond." In some cases, people who identify as transgender may undergo surgery to affirm their gender identity, but this is not always the case. To be *trans* means simply to identify *beyond* the sex category assigned to one at birth.

Thanks to advances in genetics, we now recognize that XY sex chromosomes are largely associated with male development, and XX sex chromosomes are largely associated with female development, but this distinction is also complicated. Although the majority of humans, and sexed animals in general, exhibit one of these two sets of sex chromosomes, several other combinations of sex chromosomes exist (e.g., XXY [Klinefelter Syndrome], XXX [Triple X Syndrome], and XYY) thereby complicating the simplistic understanding of biological sex.

In recent years, the term **intersex** has been widely adopted to refer to individuals whose anatomy or genetics does not neatly adhere to the categories of male and female. Intersex people constitute approximately 1.7% of the population, comparable to the frequency of people with red hair. Although intersex people have existed since the dawn of humanity, they have been forced to adhere to the gender binary and categorize as either a man or a woman regardless of their genitals, genetics, or identity. Some have even gone so far as to perform surgery on children with ambiguous genitalia (Greenfield 2014). Stories abound of individuals being categorized one way at birth, only to discover later in life that their biology was more complex. Only recently have American institutions allowed individuals to feature a third, non-binary gender marker on their documentation after a 2015 lawsuit filed on behalf of Dana Zzyym who was denied a passport because they identified as neither male nor female (Hernandez 2022).[2]

In short, whereas sex is a socially constructed biological category, gender is the presentation of oneself that is often, but not always, associated with a sex-based category. We learn how to present and perform our gender through **socialization**, i.e., learning how to behave in a way that is acceptable to society, where we are explicitly and dispassionately told what boys should do and what girls should do, similar to how one learns table manners. From the moment children are labeled a boy or a girl respectively, they are awash in blue or pink clothes, gifted trucks or dolls, and encouraged to behave (or not punished when they behave) aggressively or emotionally (See Activity 3.1).

Childhood Gender Roles In Adult Life (Buzzfeed 2014)

By: Ryan Drum

The video "*Childhood Gender Roles in Adult Life*" from Buzzfeed stars a man and a woman in their twenties. They work in an office and are continually subjected to gendered products and biased treatment. For example, the man is given a blue laptop to work on, "manly" tea to drink, and coffee cups labeled with "stud." The woman, on the other hand, is given a pink laptop, soothing "women's tea," and a coffee cup labelled "princess." Both people show clear discomfort when being presented with these items. When the man gives orders in a meeting, he is commended for his "leadership skills" while the woman is being shushed for being "bossy." The video ends with the man and woman happily switching items.

The video confronts the prevalence of gender expectations in society that are taught throughout childhood and persist into adulthood. The blue laptop

(Continued)

---

2 Born intersex, Zzyym's gender-identity is medically supported.

> (Continued)
>
> covered in stickers of dinosaurs and tools are used as examples of gendered toys and products being sold to boys. Similarly, the pink laptop covered in jewelry and princess crowns are examples of gender-normative symbols that girls are encouraged to accept. Gender norms are forced on the characters in the video numerous times with everything from coffee cup designs to clothing colors. It is not as if it's illegal to violate these rules, but the characters who follow them receive praise; if they break them, they are scolded. As a result, this video shows the subtle yet powerful ways gender roles shape society. Gender has become a self-regulating force in which people police one another as to not be considered different.
>
> This clip tackles the idea that society has deemed certain actions, colors, and ways of life to be associated with a certain sex when in fact they have no inherent association. This video also makes its arguments by offering examples that most Americans have experienced during childhood. Gendered toys still cover aisles in toy stores to this day, and pink and blue clothing are still used to perform gender. Using universal examples and placing them in an absurd context is a powerful weapon in satire, and it is used effectively here.

The phrase **nature vs. nurture** often accompanies debates regarding issues of gender. In this argument, "nature" refers to the gendered behaviors and expectations that are supposedly innate to one's sex category assigned at birth. Conversely, "nurture" refers to the gendered behaviors and expectations instilled over time by one's environment. For most social scientists, the argument is not nature *vs.* nurture, but rather nature *and* nurture; that is, we are simultaneously affected by biological phenomena outside of our control (e.g., hormones), but much of what we learn regarding how to engage based on the gendered body in which we live comes from nurture, or *socialization*. We are socialized from birth to regard these behavioral expectations as normal, even within supposedly objective educational spaces, a phenomenon referred to as the **hidden curriculum** (Basow 2004; Margolis 2001). This pervasive overt and implicit information about social categories often makes it difficult to see how these expectations are constructed.

> **Activity 3.1 Doing Your Gender "Wrong"**
>
> Consider a moment when you learned that you were doing your gender "wrong." How have gendered expectations been reinforced by others including your friends, family, and even strangers? How did this experience affect your understanding of gender as an identity and as a performance?

The next two sections will focus on the absurdities of masculinity and femininity before addressing issues of gender as it pertains to transgender and non-binary individuals in the United States and those working to disrupt the gendered norms.

Real Men Wear Pink: Satirizing Masculinity

Although many of the conversations regarding gender and issues of marginalization tend to focus on the expectations of femininity and the experiences of women, it is important to contextualize the absurdity of the gender binary from both ends.

In its simplest form, **masculinity** is the culturally agreed-upon expectations that come with being categorized as male. Although everyone's individual masculinity is different and expectations of masculinity differs between cultures and over time, adhering to masculine attitudes and behaviors is an important part of maintaining a **patriarchy**, or a system of society or government in which men hold power and women are largely marginalized. Connell and Messerschmitt (2005) refer to this as **hegemonic masculinity**, which is "The pattern of practice (i.e., things done, not just... role expectations or identity) that allowed men's dominance over women to continue... only a minority of men might enact it" (p. 832). In American society, concrete aspects of manhood include tangible features like physical strength, facial hair, and a low voice. Alternatively, abstract forms of masculinity, including resilience to pain, assertiveness, and socioeconomic stability (i.e., "being a provider"), are not immediately evident at first glance, but include the behavioral or psychological expectations associated with being a man.

Through these definitions of masculinity, it becomes clear that masculinity is constructed as the opposite to (or the complement of) **femininity**, or the culturally agreed-upon expectations that come with being categorized as female. Being masculine is effectively framed as *not being feminine*; men are expected to be physically strong, resilient, assertive, and economically self-sufficient, whereas women are expected to be physically weak, overly emotional or vulnerable, coy and apprehensive, and economically dependent. These complementary constructions contribute to the gender hegemony or hierarchy. More importantly, as one learns how to become a man by embodying masculinity, they also learn that being perceived as feminine is less manly and subsequently abhorrent.

American Male (Michael Rohrbaugh 2016)

The 2016 short film *American Male* was created by Michael Rohrbaugh and produced by MTV's "Look Different Creator Campaign," a pitch competition for media artifacts that comment on privilege. It is a dark reflection on how gendered norms, specifically the juxtaposition of masculinity and femininity, can negatively affect American men. The protagonist, a muscular young White man, moves through a house party where he performs masculinity: Watching sports, drinking beer, and objectifying women. This footage is intercut with shots of him at home alone, revealing the work required to achieve this presentation of masculinity: Lifting weights, taking steroids, and physically and emotional abusing himself (e.g., slapping himself, screaming at his reflection). The voiceover describes the behavioral expectations of masculinity in contrast to the behavioral expectations of femininity.

Order beer, not wine, and beef, not chicken. Never light beer though and no tofu. Can't get more gay than tofu...
Women cross their legs when they sit. Men keep their legs open.
Women hold books across their chest. Men hold them at their sides...
Women wear bright colors like pink, yellow, and purple. Men wear dark shades of blue, brown, green, grey and black.
Women play woodwind or string instruments, like the violin, or the flute. Men play brass or percussion...
Women sing, dance, and perform on stage. Men play sports, watch sports, and talk about sports.
Women write in diaries. Men journal.
Women cook. Men grill.

The film closes with a flashback to the protagonist as a child, describing the years of choices that brought him to his current understanding of masculinity. "At a young age, I began to observe the people around me. The way they talk, the way they walked, what they said, where it got them." By the end of the film, the protagonist's struggles lead the audience to feel sympathy and even empathy for him: "Now I am no longer a person but a set of social cues." Although satirical, the film's direct criticism of gendered norms borders on dispassionate commentary.

American Male underscores that the social construction of masculinity is aggressively not feminine and shows the excessive measures that men may take to ensure their performance of masculinity is precise and socially acceptable. Gendered differences include major life decisions like school majors (e.g., "men are better at math") and appropriate occupations ("avoid the arts unless you live on the coasts") as well as seemingly non-conscious behaviors, such as how people walk ("women move their hips when they walk, men move their shoulders"), talk ("Women use exclamation points. Men use periods."), and eat ("order beer, not wine"). The audience is encouraged to be amused at the explication of details, such as the gendering of colors or the way people hold their books, and contempt toward a society that subjugates a child's individuality in adherence of these simple binaries.

As is demonstrated throughout the film, being seen as feminine, or being *accused* of anything associated with femininity, can threaten masculinity. Many studies demonstrate the real effect of femininity-as-threat: Men are less likely to take "pink-collar jobs" or jobs that have been historically dominated by women (e.g., schoolteacher, healthcare worker) (Miller 2017), women out-earning their husbands increases the risk of divorce (Killewald 2016; Parker and Stepler 2017), and simply the thought of a man earning less than his wife resulted in a 24-point shift in support for Trump over Clinton leading up to the 2016 election[3] (Cassino 2018).

Furthermore, being seen as feminine can provoke harmful behaviors. Men will avoid activities framed as feminine or weak to appear more manly, often to their own detriment, including purchasing eco-friendly products (Brough et al. 2016) or wearing a mask during the COVID pandemic (Glick 2020). The term **toxic**

---

3 Men who were asked this question after the head-to-head comparison of Clinton and Trump reported a 16% preference for Clinton; men who were asked this question before the head-to-head comparison reported an 8% preference for Trump. The order of questions had no impact on Sanders-Trump comparisons.

> **GE Big Boys (*Saturday Night Live*, S44E8, NBC 2018)**
>
> *By James Carver*
>
> The *Saturday Night Live* skit "GE Big Boys" opens with an old-fashioned black-and-white advertisement. The husband comes home from work wearing a suit and carrying a briefcase. He asks his wife, "Honey, how do you keep the house so clean?" She responds by saying "A lady never tells." After she makes this statement, a line appears on the screen: "A woman's work is done better with GE household appliances." The color of the screen changes as a deep voice fades in and says, "These days, women are the breadwinners in 50% of American homes, and that means housework is a man's job." The clip then goes on to list "Tools to get the job done right, with GE big boy home appliances, such as a dishwasher with a 70-pound door, the big boy washing machine, which measures six feet high, the big boy ride on vacuum cleaner, [and] a spot remover modeled after a jackhammer." All the tools also run on gasoline, giving them an "F-" energy rating. The husband character in the skit is played by Jason Mamoa, a current icon of masculinity. Each time he uses one of the appliances, he lets out a "masculine" grunt and shows off his strength. After he closes the 70-pound dishwasher door, he exclaims, "I would like to see a woman do that."
>
> For the viewer to understand the jokes advanced in this clip, they must understand the difference between how products are marketed to men vs. women. In the past, marketers would code household appliances, such as a vacuum, as female. Humor can be found in Jason Mamoa "manning up" to complete house chores, and that the appliances used to complete the chores are appliances that are usually coded as masculine, including lawn mowers and jack-hammers.
>
> This skit comments on a few larger societal structures and phenomena. For one, the satire is commenting on the reality that the American home is changing. However, the skit takes this idea a step further by satirizing how companies now must target their audiences. In the past, as evidenced by the clip, they could target women in the home. But now since the home is changing, they must target *men* at home. How do they do this? By creating products that fall into stereotypical masculine desires. In addition, the skit comments on masculinity because masculinity is constructed around being a "man's man." A good-looking, extremely masculine man is cleaning the floors and house in a way that women can do. The crux of the joke is that masculinity is the opposite of femininity.
>
> The products in this skit are designed in a way that ensures men don't have their masculinity threatened when they do household chores, which is over-the-top and unnecessary. But the joke is that to sell these products to men, the product must be designed and marketed as "big boy" appliances, especially because they've been marketed so heavily for women in the past. All of this being said, I think *SNL* hit the nail on the head with this video.

masculinity describes a slew of negative behaviors in adherence of masculinity (Harrington, 2020), an absurd phenomenon that impacts the individual and society at large. In a patriarchy, where men and masculinity are socially desirable traits, then anything deemed feminine can be read as undesirable, resulting in a need to hyper-masculinize products traditionally framed as feminine, including yogurt (Smerdloff 2016), low-calorie soda (Zmuda 2011), and even tissues (Sherman 2018).

Intersectionality of Masculinity

The metrics of masculinity are constructed around intersectional assumptions and stereotypes, including those related to sexuality and class. As will be addressed in the next chapter on sexuality, heterosexual sexual prowess, that is being attractive and desirable to women and engaging in sexual activity with them, is also an indicator of American masculinity that combines concrete and abstract factors. It combines the concrete characteristic of physical ruggedness expected of "manly" men along with the abstract factor of desirability. This multiplicative effect is evident when considering these two components separately: Men who are considered rugged but not sexually attractive to women may be labeled gay and men who are sexually active with women without ruggedness are met with confusion (See Activity 3.2).

Masculinity is also constructed through class and socioeconomic status (SES). Men who are of a lower SES or who cannot provide for their families are considered to be less manly. Economic crises, or instances where financial ruin affects large segments of the population, are correlated with more suicides among men due to increased unemployment, with suicides among those aged 45-64 accounting for the increase in the United States (Chang et al. 2013), revealing the toxic association between earning money and one's identity as a man. Furthermore, the belief that America is a "classless society" in which any man can advance beyond the class into which he was born (i.e., the American Dream as described in Chapter 2) inhibits collective awareness of the intersection between SES and masculinity.

The Oblongs (WB, Cartoon Network 2001–2002)

The Oblongs, a 2001 animated sitcom, directly tackled the intersection of masculinity and class. The show featured a working-class family that lived in a valley that was polluted by the sewage runoff from the upper-class people that lived on the hill. Because of their ecological disadvantage, many of the valley residents were disfigured. The father, Bob Oblong (voiced by Will Ferrell), had no arms and legs. He perseveres with a smile on his face and does his best to keep his family in good spirits, a goal made easier by the fact that he and his wife, Pickles (voiced by Jean Smart), have an *amazing* sex life.

This satire of masculinity and class, in that Bob is physically "less of a man" while very much the head of his household, is highlighted in the juxtaposition with his boss, George Kilmer (voiced by Billy West). George is drawn with all of the trappings of masculinity; he is tall, wealthy, and handsome, with broad shoulders. However, George is neither smart nor admirable as he mocks Bob's manhood by making light of his dire financial situation. In the first episode, George confronts Bob for submitting multiple medical claims for his family and suggests, "Maybe you valley people wouldn't have so many health problems if you didn't live where the air is contaminated and the land befoul." When Bob reminds him that his family cannot afford to live in the hills, George mocks him by crying like a baby. Although the show is primarily class and social satire, the satire of masculinity through the relationship between these two characters cannot be ignored. Compared to Kilmer, the stereotypically perfect man, Oblong is clearly "more of a man" because he exhibits love of and for his family, has personal self-esteem, and is secure despite his lot in life.

Figure 3.2 The difference in masculinity between Bob Oblong and his boss George Kilmer are striking, including body type and voice quality, as well as income and wealth. Still from "Misfit Love" (*The Oblongs* 2001).

Historically, men have been respected and elevated by society. Therefore, masculine behavior has become the metric by which all individuals are judged. The valorization of masculinity has led to the collective devaluing, or marginalization, of those who do not (or are not allowed to) perform and occupy this valued position, a form of **misogyny**, or the dislike of, contempt for, and ingrained prejudice against women. Furthermore, because masculine traits like physical dominance and interpersonal

Activity 3.2   Cultural Differences Regarding Masculinity
The performativity of gender is particularly evident when considering how gendered expectations change over time and between cultures, which can be defined by race, ethnicity, religion, region, and SES. Although the current text focuses on the mainstream expectations of masculinity and femininity in the United States, it is important to recognize that understanding cultural differences is essential to seeing the variations of gender performance despite the rhetorical belief that the behaviors of men and women are biological. We like to claim that gendered differences are "natural" despite disparities between these and other large groups. Compare and contrast the expectations of masculinity in your culture and a culture different from your own; this can be based on ethnicity, nationality, religion, or even across time. What is expected of men and why? How do the differences between these two cultures reveal a disconnect between the rhetoric and reality of gender?

assertiveness are associated with masculine leadership, women are expected to demonstrate these characteristics and be punished for them with insults (e.g., bossy, b*tch). The following section will address the expectations of femininity and analyze artifacts that satirize the impossible expectations associated with this half of the binary.

Beauty is Pain: Satirizing Femininity

Femininity encompasses the culturally agreed-upon expectations that are associated with being categorized as female. In the United States, concrete physical expectations of femininity include being slim, delicate, and attractive. Abstract expectations of femininity include being nurturing, emotionally supportive, and vulnerable. Taken together, these expectations reveal that to be feminine is to be submissive as well as to be aware of and promote one's status as an object of desire. Domestic expectations of women are also built on gendered supportive and nurturing roles. The kinds of dreams that women are encouraged to have are intimately tied to the role of wife and mother, i.e., to be the perfect domestic housewife. With the women's movements of the twentieth century, women began to question those expectations and consider non-domestic dreams (see the gendered American Dream in Chapter 2).

Movies, television shows, popular music, magazines, and other mass media have consistently objectified the female body. **Objectification** is to treat an individual as an object or a thing, in this case, an object for the pleasure of men. This is reinforced through a media phenomenon called the **male gaze** (Mulvey 1973),[4] which describes the tendency to present women's bodies in a way that is assumed to be desirable to heterosexual men often by describing or showcasing their body first in a sexualized manner before describing them as a whole person with an individual identity (See Activity 3.3). Over time, women learn this sense of "to-be-looked-at-ness," and the work associated with being slim, delicate, attractive, nurturing and vulnerable allows this objectification to continue unabated.

At the same time, women who take agency over their status as an object of desire are criticized with insults like "slut" and "whore," or are labeled manipulative and dishonest in order to ensnare men. Femininity and marginalized experiences in general are often defined by a **double bind**, a situation in which people are confronted with two irreconcilable demands or a choice between two undesirable courses of action; it describes the phenomenon where someone is criticized for their choices regardless of what they are. This is demonstrated in the cartoon from Katarzyna Babis, which features three pairings of women representing a spectrum of appearance and life choices, and the comments and insults that are hurled at them for their choices. In short, women are "...damned if you do and damned if you don't."

Through socialization and the hidden curriculum, girls learn from a young age they should aspire to be feminine. "A girl learns that stories happen to 'beautiful' women, whether they are interesting or not. And, interesting or not, stories do not happen to women who are not 'beautiful'" (Wolf 1990). Women are expected to adhere to the "thin ideal," a physically fit exemplar that all women should meet, i.e.,

---

4 This phenomenon emerges because viewers identify with the protagonist of the film (usually male) who objectifies and looks at women.

> **Activity 3.3 Introducing Women**
>
> In 2016, Hollywood producer Ross Putman began a Twitter profile to share the intros for female leads in projects that came across his desk.[5] They all began with a physical and often sexualized description of the character. The profile, entitled @femscriptintros, featured the bio, "These are intros for female leads in actual scripts I read. Names changed to JANE, otherwise verbatim." Tweets include:
>
> - JANE, 28, athletic but sexy. A natural beauty. Most days she wears jeans, and she makes them look good.
> - JANE stands next to it (30s) dressed in a paramedic's uniform: blonde, fit, smokin' hot.
> - JANE is attractive, but there is a weariness in her. Life taking its toll.
> - JANE, 30s, a natural brunette beauty, adjusts the straps of an elegant black gown which hugs her perfect curves.
> - JANE, late 30s, attractive strong Latina, puts handcuffs on him.
>
> Revisit one of your favorite movies or television shows and consider how the primary female characters are introduced. Compare this to how the primary male character is introduced. Do we see their face first or their body? Is the audience asked to look at them directly, or are they shown through the eyes of another character? Do we hear them speak? How do these disparities reinforce our understanding of gender differences?

a "small waist and little body fat" (Low et al. 2003). The thin ideal, along with other physical expectations including no body hair and a soft voice can be juxtaposed with the expectations of masculinity, which requires being big and strong, with copious body hair and a deeply resonant voice. Women who do not exhibit feminine characteristics are quickly marked as masculine and insulted with terms like "mannish."

Girls also learn that these traits can be acquired with time and effort. In other words, femininity is not only *appearing* attractive but *doing the work to appear attractive*. On average, women spend 45 minutes longer getting ready each morning, more than 25% more on health and beauty products, and 40% more on clothes compared to men (Haynes 2017; Palmer 2012). Furthermore, the impacts of these disparities translate into differential treatment in the workplace. Research shows that women who spend more time and money on their hair and makeup often earn more money than women who go without makeup (Wong and Penner 2016). Coupled with the "**pink tax**," the extra costs associated with products targeted toward women, women face more barriers to elevate their status.

Girl You Don't Need Makeup (*Inside Amy Schumer*, S3E2, Comedy Central 2015)

Comedian Amy Schumer's show *Inside Amy Schumer* (2013–2016) on Comedy Central featured sketches, monologues, and other artifacts designed to satirize issues of gender, class, and race. In this 2015 music video that parodies the popular "boy band" pop music genre, Amy is initially encouraged to embrace her natural beauty

---

5 Before Putman, two tumblr blogs collated sexist casting calls: castingcallwoe and terriblecasting.

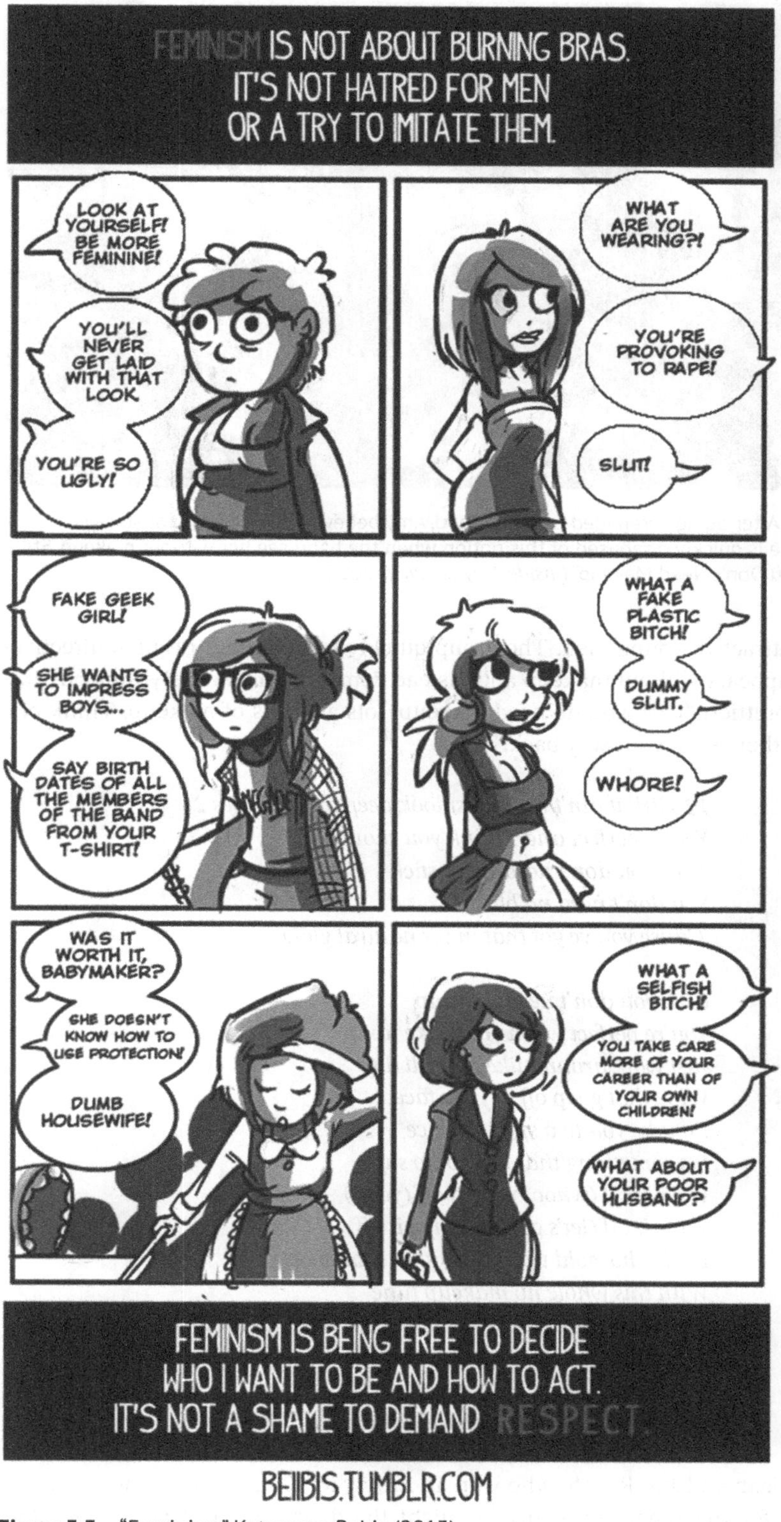

Figure 3.3 "Feminism" Katarzyna Babis (2013).

Figure 3.4 After being serenaded by a boy band, Amy believes that her natural state is beautiful; she is quickly disabused of this notion when the band see her without makeup. Still from "Girl You Don't Need Makeup" (*Inside Amy Schumer* 2015).

by a four attractive young men. The group quickly recants their original directives when she appears without makeup and instead demands she do everything possible to appear prettier: "Girl, you do need makeup; lots and lots of makeup. Think of a clown and then work your way back."

♪♪ *Girl, it ain't no lie just look deep into my eyes* ♪♪
You're perfect and I think you should know
That you don't need no lipstick
You don't need no blush
'Cause you've got that inner natural glow

...

Girl, you don't need makeup
You're perfect when you wake up
Just walk around like that all day
Wipe that goop off of your face
I'll take you to a special place
It's something that I've got to say
Wipe it off (whoo) wipe it off (yeah)
Wipe it off (let's go, girl) wipe it off
Ho-ho-ho-hold up, girl we spoke too soon
With this whole no makeup tune
We kinda changed our mind on the makeup thing
You'll be the hottest girl in the nation
With just a touch of foundation
Girl, I can't be seen with the ghost from "The Ring"

Kyle Dunnigan and Jim Roach, who won an Emmy for Outstanding Original Music and Lyrics for the song, repeatedly highlight the double bind of being feminine.

9 Non-Threatening Leadership Strategies for Women (The Cooper Review 2018)

By Josh Ives

Sarah Cooper's satirical blog, The Cooper Review, addresses patriarchal authority, hegemonic masculinity, and the male and female hierarchical relationship in the workplace in a post entitled "9 Non-Threatening Leadership Strategies for Women" featuring nine cartoon diptychs. Cooper's (2018) blog post begins with the disclaimer "In this fast-paced business world, female leaders need to make sure they're not perceived as pushy, aggressive, or competent. One way to do that is to alter your leadership style to account for the (sometimes) fragile male ego."

Cartoon #1 deals with setting a deadline, and under the heading of "THREATENING," shows a woman addressing a man with an annoyed look stating "This has to be done by Monday." Opposite that is the heading "NON-THREATENING" and shows the same woman and man (now with a happy face), but this time the woman states "What do you think about getting this done by Monday?" Under the cartoon is the text "When setting a deadline, ask your co-worker what he thinks of doing something, instead of just asking him to get it done. This makes him feel less like you're telling them what to do and more like you care about his opinions" (Cooper 2018).

Another cartoon deals with emailing a request. Under the heading of "THREATENING," it shows a woman sending the following email; "Send me the presentation when it's ready." Opposite that is the heading "NON-THREATENING" and displays an alternate email "Hey Jake!:-) Can I take a peek at your presentation when it's ready?:-) Thanks!!:-):-) !" Below the cartoon is the advice to "Pepper your emails with exclamation marks and emojis so you don't come across as too clear or direct. Your lack of efficient communication will make you seem more approachable" (Cooper 2018).

Cartoon #5 is about hearing a sexist comment. Under the heading of "THREATENING," it shows a man and woman sitting across from each other and the woman saying "That's not appropriate, and I don't appreciate it. Next to it is the heading "NON-THREATENING" with a thought cloud over the woman's head that reads "awkward laugh." The caption below states "When you hear a sexist comment, the awkward laugh is key. Practice your awkward laugh at home, with your friends and family, and in the mirror. Make sure you sound truly delighted even as your soul is dying inside" (Cooper 2018).

There are six more panels that address, in one way or another, the issue of gender hierarchy and hegemonic masculinity in the workplace. This blog post is good satire in that it uses humor to make people aware of the ridiculous notion that a woman who is in a position of authority must assume a subordinate role in the workplace to accomplish anything without bruising a man's ego or portraying herself as a "bitch." It forces one to see the absurdity in even questioning that a woman can hold a dominant position in the workplace.

Throughout the sketch, the group touts natural beauty but demands Amy work to achieve it. The melody and chord progression directly references One Direction's "What Makes You Beautiful" (2011), which features the chorus, "You don't know you're beautiful, that's what makes you beautiful," highlighting the social expectations of women to simply *be* beautiful without acknowledging the work that goes into it. The satire in this skit is most effective when it connects being attractive (and the related effort to maintain attractiveness) as synonymous with being a woman: "I didn't know that your lashes were so stubby and pale; Just a little mascara and you'll look female.... Please listen, girl what we're trying to say; Just get up an hour earlier; And you can make yourself much girlier." Women need to put effort into their appearance while maintaining the illusion of effortlessness.

Ultimately, femininity is a holistic expectation of moving through the world as an object of desire. The detrimental effects of attempting to achieve an impossible standard of physical beauty, which includes depression and eating disorders, has received a lot of attention (Grabe et al. 2008; Hausenblas et al. 2013; Karsay et al. 2018). Mass media images are often touched up at best or completely artificially constructed at worst. Whereas men are permitted to be dominant and agentic, women are expected to be submissive and demure by catering to the needs of men in interpersonal interactions and professional spaces. Women who seek leadership roles are often criticized for being bossy and "mannish," similar to women who do not adhere to the physical conventions of femininity. If an agentic woman attempts to occupy positions that have traditionally been held by men, she is expected to also be aware of her status as an object of desire and look good while doing it. At the same time, she should also not appear as overly threatening to the men in her orbit.

Intersectionality of Femininity

The expectations of femininity are also intersectional and are especially pronounced with respect to SES, and race. Although not all women are naturally conventionally attractive, it is expected that women will put time and effort into achieving conventional attractiveness. The ability to fulfill this societal expectation is disproportionately available to women of higher classes who have the resources to spend money on their appearance, devote time to the gym, purchase high-quality food, and access healthy outdoor spaces. With respect to race, expectations of attractiveness for women have long been dominated by Western, White European beauty standards. Women of different racial backgrounds who are less likely to be slim, have narrow facial features, or naturally straight or light hair, are socially punished for not adhering to these conventional beauty standards and are expected to work to achieve them.

Because American femininity has historically be constructed as pale, lithe, and ultimately White and upper class (Hall 1996; Kang 1997, Moon 1998), the physical and behavioral expectations of submissiveness becomes further complicated for women who are not White. Thicker body types prevalent among women of African or Indigenous descent can elicit insults. For example, Serena Williams and other muscular women athletes of color are regularly criticized for being "mannish" (Lichfield et al. 2018; Schultz 2005; Wilks 2020). Similarly, women of color who are subjected to stereotypes of being domineering or overly sexual will rarely be seen as sufficiently demure. Black and Latina women have long been associated with being interpersonally dominant (e.g., sassy) and hypersexual (e.g., Jezebel, vamp), thereby conflicting with feminine expectations.[6]

Typecast (A Royals Parody, Tess Paras 2014)

Originally performed at the CBS Diversity Sketch Comedy Showcase, actor and director Tess Paras shared a satirical video on YouTube underscoring the experiences common among women of color in Hollywood. In the 2014 clip, two Black American women and one Asian American woman meet at an audition. The three women lament the experience of seeing each other at the same casting calls, a wink to limited opportunities for women of color. The White male casting director enters and addresses each woman by name. When he comes to the Asian American woman, he says, "Tess Per- Puh- Paris, I don't know what that is. Is that Chinese? Is that Korean? Is that Thai? Is that American Samoan?" To which she responds with a smile, "It's whatever you want it to be!" He seems relieved as he puts down his clipboard and says, "All right, Chinese!" He then leaves the room and the women begin to sing.

> *I'm gonna play the white girl's nerdy friend. Of course! Obviously!*
> *I'm gonna play the white girl's other friend who is sassy.*
> *(Oh my god, you nailed that.)*
> *But she can't have two black friends. Two black friends?*
> *It gets confusing. So, I'm left out. I play the co-star nanny.*
> *Yeah, leading ladies are—quirky hipsters wearing vintage dresses. Tiny pouty pixies, blue-eyed and precious. We don't care—we're Zooey Deschanel in our dreams.*
> *But every breakdown's like: "sassy sidekick," "bitchy nerd," or "neighbor," oversexed Asian, "urban girl with flavor."*

Figure 3.5 Tess Paras and Haneefah Wood play the stereotypical friends of the White lead in the center, played by Stevie Nelson. Still from "Typecast (A Royals Parody)" Tess Paras (2014).

---

6 There is also a long history of labeling women of color who adhere to Euro-centric aesthetics as "attractive".

We don't care. We'll take any job right now, we swear.
And we're gonna be typecast. TYPECAST. Everyone starts somewhere!
I'll be a nurse! A thug who's tough. Any maid could look like us.
You know what would be cooler? (Cooler)
If I got my own series! And your own white friend, beige friend, brown friend, yellow friend.
"Submit all ethnicities."

This song's lyrics describe the limited roles available to women of color, the prevalence of these stereotypical trends in casting calls, and their resignation to these roles if they want to work as actresses. They are unable to access the same roles as White women because those roles do not exist. Furthermore, the roles that do exist for women of color are also class-coded (e.g., thug, maid, sex worker). Writers and producers have a "type" in mind and often seek to cast an actor that matches that type; as described in the lyrics, that White-coded type is "quirky hipsters wearing vintage dresses; tiny pouty pixies, blue-eyed and precious." This **typecasting** practice draws on and reinforces stereotypes (consider how the examples provided in Activity 3.3 that introduce female characters with their physique may limit considering a wider range of actors). The song and the accompanying video brilliantly demonstrate how this practice operates in the media industry and reveals the absurdity of this treatment through the eyes of the women whose representation and livelihoods are affected by it.

Much of the discourse focuses on the negative effects of femininity on women, but the complementary sexist puzzle of masculinity and femininity damages men and women by constructing narrow expectations of how people born with and without penises are supposed to behave. The next section will address how this rigid binary of sex to gender (and to sexuality, which will be discussed in Chapter 4) serves to advantage cisgendered and binary people and marginalize people who are trans or non-binary.

Satirizing Genderism: Beyond the Binary

Genderism is the belief that gender is rigid and binary; Erving Goffman (1977) used the term to describe the individual and social impact of lining up children along gendered lines. It is different from **sexism,** a term that encapsulates beliefs and historical trends that have afforded greater opportunities and resources for men than women, but both rely on rigid gendered expectations. That is, their power comes from the agreed upon unspoken and normalized difference in gender.

Like intersexed people, trans and non-binary people have existed since the dawn of humanity but the binary understanding of masculinity and femininity are deeply seeded. Abrahamic religions rooted in the origin story of Adam and Eve in the Garden of Eden may adhere to strict gender binaries because they believe these categories were bestowed by a monotheistic, all-knowing, infallible god. Alternatively, many cultures around the world have embraced third genders or gender fluidity, including the Bakla in the Philippines, the Muxe in Mexico, and the Hijras in India. Among Navajo communities in North America, the phrase **"two-spirit"** has emerged to describe individuals who embody both a masculine and a feminine spirit that predates European colonialism (Morales 2019).

The twentieth century featured many trans and non-binary figures but mainstream (read: heterosexual) conversation largely framed them as bizarre spectacles, focusing on sex change operations (e.g., Lili Elbe, Christine Jorgensen) or laughing at their existence (e.g., the recurring trans reveal episodes on *The Jerry Springer Show*, including "Surprise! I'm A Transexual," "I'm Marrying A Transexual," "My Boyfriend Is A Woman"). Furthermore, both heterosexual and queer communities have historically marginalized and dehumanized trans individuals; at the 1973 Christopher Street Liberation Day Rally marking the fourth anniversary of the Stonewall Uprising, prominent trans activist Syliva Rivera was booed by the crowd during her speech. Although the visibility of drag queens surged toward the end of the twentieth century with cultural figures like Divine and RuPaul as well as prominent films including *Paris is Burning* (1990), *The Adventures of Pricilla, Queen of the Desert* (1994) and *To Wong Foo, Thanks for Everything! Julie Newmar* (1995), there was little movement on the nuanced understanding of trans and non-binary people.

Despite this discriminatory environment, several important twentieth-century satirical examples addressed the experiences of trans and non-binary folks. Typically, the main character played with concepts of gender to show the audience that their construction of gender is just that, a construct. In Virginia Woolf's *Orlando: A Biography* (1928), a nobleman born in Elizabethan England mysteriously wakes up in a female body after spending several decades as a man, exploring a variety of social, sexual, interpersonal, and intrapersonal experiences. Woolf shows that constructs of sex and the impact of one's sex on their ability to move through the world more deeply. The book was adapted into a film in 1992 starring Tilda Swinton. In *The Rocky Horror Picture Show* (1975), Tim Curry plays Dr. Frank-N-Furter, a self-proclaimed "sweet transvestite."[7] In a parody of Frankenstein's monster, he experiments with creating life in the lab, animating Rocky, an attractive scantily clad muscle-bound man as a sexual plaything. Throughout the film, Frank-N-Furter dons women's clothes, acknowledges his manhood and masculinity, and invites his houseguests (and by extension, the audience) to embrace their own sexual diversity and "shiver with anticipation."

"It's Pat" (*Saturday Night Live*, NBC 1990–1993)

In a complex example that is worth exploring for its controversy, Julia Sweeney played Pat on *Saturday Night Live* in a dozen sketches in the early 1990s. In each, Pat was a socially awkward individual with an ambiguous gender expression that highlighted the collective inability to engage within individuals who do not adhere to gendered norms. Many jokes were rooted in Pat's cagey responses regarding their gender. In one episode, Pat is asked, "Would you say that you are more like your mother or your father?" To which they reply, "I'm a perfect combination of both!" (October 12, 1991; Season 17, Episode 3). These seemingly oblivious responses to the confusion and coded inquiries of others affirms Pat as a strong, independent individual who lives a largely boring and everyday life.[8] Pat's androgyny was

---

7 The term "transvestite" has a long and discriminatory history, usually referring to men who dress up in women's clothing for sexual pleasure. However, in the hands of Dr. Frank-N-Furter, the term is claimed as an identity, stripped of shame and instead worn as a badge of honor.

8 Sketches take place in the workplace, at the drugstore, at a hair salon, and at the gym as well as a few parodies of prominent contemporary movies (e.g., Basic Instinct, Single White Female, The Crying Game).

Figure 3.6 "Woman or sir, accept him or her, for whatever it might be. It's time for androgyny. Here comes Pat!" Still from theme song for "It's Pat" (*Saturday Night Live* 1991).

perplexing to others, and many punchlines revolved around people's distress in categorizing Pat. In one episode, the guest host Christopher Walken became so frustrated by Pat's ambiguity that he jumped out the window at the end of the sketch (October 24, 1992; Season 18, Episode 4).

The satirical intention to laugh at people's reactions to androgyny and gender ambiguity was further underscored in the *It's Pat* movie (1994). The villain character becomes so obsessed with discovering and outing Pat's gender that they send video of Pat doing karaoke to *America's Creepiest People* (a parody of *America's Funniest Home Videos*) in order to shame them and steal Pat's laptop to read their diary to discover their true gender. Both efforts backfire, as the pop band Ween invite Pat to be featured on a song and the diary reveals nothing, leading the villain to a mental breakdown.

However, the character Pat became the target of laughter from many audience members, revealing a lack of understanding of the satire. Instead of laughing at the responses of those around Pat, many people were laughing at Pat's gender ambiguity. In a 2019 interview with Dave Itzkoff of The *New York Times*,

> During her time at "S.N.L.", Sweeney said she was invited to be the grand marshal of several gay pride parades, which she interpreted as an endorsement of the character. But at other public appearances where she played Pat—say, the opening of a shopping mall in the Midwest—Sweeney said, "When I went there, I realized they were laughing at Pat."
>
> *(Itzkoff 2019)*

This is an important example of the inconsistent effects of satire described in Chapter 1. Pat was intended to reveal the stereotypes and prejudices of others by showcasing the social need for traditional gender markers and binary gender categorization. Instead, the character had the opposite effect because people could not see (and therefore could not laugh at) their own biases. Furthermore, "Pat" became an insult for gender non-conforming individuals, and several people have recounted experiences from that time where Pat was used to insult and attack them (Maglio 2017). This discriminatory deployment has tainted the character, despite Sweeney's original intentions.

Retroactive viewings of the character continue to spark heated conversations about who is the target of the joke. These ongoing discussions reveal that satirical messages will be interpreted differently by different individuals regardless of the satirist's intention. In addition, increasing collective awareness of the discriminatory treatment of gender-nonconforming people has rendered Pat ineffectual even if one can see the satire. According to Sweeney, the gag wouldn't stand the test of time: "You'd be able to say, 'What are your pronouns?'... And Pat would say, 'I'm so offended, they're obviously—' And then the joke would be over" (2019).

In the twenty-first century, robust conversations about trans individuals have focused on their experiences and a greater understanding of trans and non-binary people throughout history. However, the recency of this conversation means that artifacts effectively satirizing the structural institutions that reinforce the dehumanization and marginalization of trans and non-binary people are limited. Even prominent satirical outlets and satirists reinforce anti-trans and pro-binary rhetoric, often punching down and engaging in cruel mocking despite their status as purveyors social commentary and critique. *Saturday Night Live*, *South Park*, and *The Onion* all have artifacts that miss the mark when claiming to satirize the experience of trans, non-binary, and intersex people. In 2009, *The Onion* parodied a familiar trope in sports media listing the pros and cons of an athlete in an artifact entitled "Strong Side, Weak Side" targeting Caster Semenya, a South African track star and Olympian whose leaked gender testing records revealed an "intersex trait" despite being assigned female at birth and identifying as a woman. The infographic framed Semenya as a man: Her "strong" side featured words like "handsome," and "one of the guys," and her weak side read "definitely a guy," dismissing her identity as a woman and erasing her status as intersex for laughs. Interestingly, this artifact received little to no backlash in 2009, demonstrating how recently the public has become sensitized to the cruelty against those who do not adhere to binary gender norms.

User-Generated Satire

Web 2.0 and social media have provided more venues for marginalization satire by trans and non-binary individuals that addresses the absurdity of their experiences without gatekeepers who prioritize a genderist lens. This novel format also allows for threading, which collates artifacts that both comment on the experiences of marginalized people. One person can post a single joke and invite others to reply or quote-tweet, thus creating a supportive community through humor (Anderson 2019; Burns 2018).

Consider the common line, "How many [adjective] people does it take to change a lightbulb," which can be adapted to make fun of the experience of a wide range of people. Sometimes, these jokes are at the expense of the group being targeted, and sometimes they are at the expense of people who are discriminating against the group. For trans and non-binary people, this category of jokes is uniquely valuable in satirizing their own experiences.

> "How many trans people does it take to change a lightbulb? Just one, but it takes them 30 years to realize it needs changing"
>
> (@mspowahs, 2017)

> "How many trans people does it take to changea lightbulb? One to change it, literally everyone else to tell them to slow down and wait first"
>
> (@quinaryrose, 2017)

The format also allows for the lampooning of cis people who do not understand the experiences of trans and yet demand adherence to the gender binary.

> How many cis ppl does it take to change a lightbulb? idk the one that came w/the house still works, are u sure lightbulbs even need changing?
>
> (@mspowas, 2017)

> "why can't you just be happy with your bulb the way it is?" (credit @ AmyDentata)
>
> (@633nm, 2017)

In their simplicity, these jokes reveal the complexity of trans discourse and the frustration associated with social acceptance of one's whole self, especially when one has spent a lifetime deliberating over their identity. In doing so, these jokes push back on genderism and anti-trans prejudices in small but powerful ways. Social media means that these quips, which were once restricted to interpersonal and safe spaces, can be published online for all to see. Although these tweets may not be part of a formal movement, the systematic opportunities for trans visibility is an important step in the movement for trans acceptance and trans rights.

Feminism: Pushing Back on Genderism and Gendered Norms

In addition to discrimination against non-binary and transgender people, the entrenched nature of gendered norms is evident when considering the vitriol directed toward people promoting gender equality. By definition, **feminism** is the advocacy of women's rights for political, social, and economic equality. In recent years, feminism has focused on gendered norms in general, including critiquing the constructs of masculinity and femininity as well as the treatment of those who do not fit into this binary. Therefore, it is important to consider *feminism as the critical dismantling of gendered norms to disrupt their political, economic, and psychosocial effects.*

The history of feminism is long and arduous and inevitably goes back further than we think. However, the modern American history of feminism largely begins in the late nineteenth century with the push for women's **suffrage**, meaning the right to vote

> **The Women's Vote (*The Daily Show with Jon Stewart*, Comedy Central 2012)**
>
> *By Adam Brody*
>
> In 2012, as the Presidential election was heating up, *The Daily Show with Jon Stewart* ran a story about the "rise" of women voters. Jason Jones initially interviewed male political strategist Tad Devine before realizing the absurdness of talking about women voters without women present. So, he brought in five women who were leaders in important women's groups. As the interview begins, Jones still primarily directs his questions and his focus toward Tad. When the women get the chance to speak on what they feel about certain issues, Jones barely listens. Instead, he listens to Tad, who simply repeats the words of the women. At one point, Jones pulls out a laser pointer, and asks Tad, "What about this one down here. What's she feeling?" He does not bother to ask her himself. The video ends with a voice over that says, "The lesson is clear in 2012. Women finally matter."
>
> This video satirizes the inequality that women face in this country compared to men by showing an instance where their opinions are ignored in favor of a man's opinions. It also demonstrates the crude way in which women are typically treated with regards to politics. You would also never see a man being treated as rudely as these women were during this interview. This video is definitely taking a stance on gender equality and the way that women are taken advantage of in the professional setting.
>
> What makes this video good satire is the clear and overt joke it makes about the inequality between men and women. For example, there are a few times when Jones starts to make sincere comments toward the way women are treated in this country only to make a joke of it. One example is when he says "Change was going to begin with me" and then completely ignores the women he brought in to talk with.
>
> This is good satire because the way Jones behaves during the interview is a good representation of the way men treat women in America. The conversation was about what women voters want in the upcoming election, but the five women who were supposed to offer their input were not heard. Instead, the interview was dominated by men who claimed to know what women want. This is a cornerstone of sexism in this country: Women are constantly muted by men even when they are the subject of conversation.

in political elections. This **first wave** of feminism culminated in the nineteenth amendment in 1920 that codified women's right to vote in the United States. The **second wave** of feminism often refers to the social upheavals of the mid-twentieth century that focused on the social and economic limitations placed on women. Feminists during this time focused on increasing awareness of the plight of women, demanding equal pay, and changing attitudes toward women that kept them out of positions of power. The **third wave** of feminism refers to advances in the intersectionality of feminism in the late twentieth century, spurred by widespread adoption of the internet and greater global awareness of the plight of women worldwide. As Hillary Clinton declared in 1995 at the United Nations Fourth World Conference on Women in Beijing, "Human rights are women's rights and women's rights are human rights." Many scholars have described how waves of feminism are problematic and

82 | *3 Satirizing Gender*

foreground the experiences of White, often middle-class to upper-class White cisgendered women in the United States (Grady 2018). Although the Nineteenth Amendment determined that women could vote in the United States, this ability was not equitably distributed, as women of color were still largely prohibited from voting. Similarly, the second wave tended to focus on the forced domesticity of women, ignoring the experiences of working-class women and women of color who were working, often in jobs that were menial, underpaid, and disrespected. In addition, the patronizing lens of the third wave was evident as the focus of middle-class to upper-class women in the West was attempting to "save" women around the world. The feminism of the twenty-first century, commonly referred to as the **fourth wave**, has emerged as an intersectional and inclusive focus on the unique discrimination against of women of color, queer women, trans women, disabled women, sex workers, and more through digital grassroots campaigns like Black Lives Matter and the MeToo Movements.

Satirizing Anti-Feminists

Regardless of the focus, each of these movements has experienced a backlash. The push for suffrage during the early twentieth century was met with a slew of anti-suffrage and misogynistic political cartoons that mocked the intellectual capabilities of women. They blamed the impending demise of the American household on their desire for enfranchisement. A postcard from 1909 titled "Election Day" features a

Figure 3.7 Pro-suffrage postcard
Source: Artists' Suffrage League / Wikimedia Commons / Public domain.

Figure 3.8 Pro-suffrage postcard: *Source*: Puck Publishing Corporation / The Library of Congress / Public domain.

woman proudly going off to vote and a disgruntled man in a chair holding two children and a baby bottle; the caption reads, "What is a suffragette without a suffering household?" Women, a marginalized group that has been traditionally subjugated, are mocked and further marginalized for their attempt to attain equality (LaFrance 2016). These artifacts reinforce the pre-existing hegemonic dynamic that reinforces men as the decision makers and breadwinners, with the expectation that women are supposed to remain in the home.

However, other cartoons and postcards explicitly criticize and satirize those who are against equality movements. The labor of women is foregrounded in figure 3.7 in which the domestic expectations of women are used to justify unequal treatment even though a counter-stereotypical example stands directly in front of the man. In figure 3.8, women's suffrage is drawn as the foot of a giant woman moving forward. Those who would attepted to stop her are revealed to be trivial and ineffective, revealing the ridiculousness of efforts to hold back (technically more than) half the population. In both of these examples, the absurdity of unequal treatment as well as the ignorance of those in power seeking to maintain inequality are lampooned.

The same discriminatory and mocking images emerged during the "second wave" of feminism in the mid-twentieth century. During this period, feminists were characterized as bra-burning angry radicals, and feminism was contrasted with femininity (i.e., feminists were described as not feminine). Given the socialization that women should be feminine, seeking social, economic, and political equality was framed as masculine and could be interpreted as a threat to one's womanhood. The stereotype of feminists-as-manly could discourage women from identifying as feminists, thus allowing this problematic understanding of feminism to continue (Gundersen and Kunst 2019; Madison et al. 2014).

Ironically, mostly male media producers recognized that liberated women were a viable audience at the time, specifically non-domestic women and women who sought careers outside of the home. Their recognition led to content that satirized the marginalization processes of women. Shows like *The Mary Tyler Moore Show* (1970–1977, CBS) and *All in the Family* (1971–1979) emerged in the wake of the social justice movements of the 1960s.

In the first episode of *The Mary Tyler Moore Show*, which aired September 19, 1970, audiences are introduced to Mary Richards, a newly single 30-year-old woman with aspirations of working in television journalism. When she visits the station to inquire about a secretarial job, Mr. Grant, the director of the station, peppers her with questions regarding her age, religion, and marital status. Mary draws the ire of Mr. Grant when she attempts to push back on these problematic inquiries. In doing so, she reveals the complexity of simultaneously arguing for one's rights, maintaining one's femininity, and avoiding angering one's boss. The satire focuses on the experiences of women in the workplace and the double bind of the working woman.

Shows like *The Mary Tyler Moore Show* are credited with translating the women's movement of the mid-twentieth century into real-world interactions and delivering a palatable version of feminism into the American home. They showcased the unfair treatment of women in the United States and the marginalization processes to which they were subjected. In doing so, these programs satirized the experiences of women

Figure 3.9 Mary eagerly reaches out to Mr. Grant after he offers her the job of "Producer;" he is disinterested in her "spunk." Still from "Love is All Around" *The Mary Tyler Moore Show* (1970).

seeking equal treatment and foregrounded how older-minded individuals (often men) perpetuated inequalities even when they may not have considered themselves misogynistic or discriminatory (see *All in the Family* in Chapter 1).

Although the third wave of feminism is defined by an international and intersectional awareness, this moment in American popular culture was one of "girl power." Celebrities like Madonna, Oprah Winfrey, Roseanne Barr, Spice Girls, and Queen Latifah, along with prominent political figures like Hillary Clinton and Ruth Bader Ginsberg, ushered in a conversation about the potential of women. They were willing and eager to engage with and uplift young women while refusing to bend to gendered norms. At the same time, a surge in marginalized programming allowed women to participate in their own representation; sitcoms like *Roseanne* (1988–1997), *Blossom* (1990–1995), *Grace Under Fire* (1993–1998), *Living Single* (1993–1998), *Ellen* (1994–1998), and *Ally McBeal* (1997–2002) foregrounded powerful women and showed audiences the lived experiences of women. At the same time, traditional male-dominated outlets were still largely hostile to women. The term "feminazi" emerged as a pejorative term for radical feminists perpetuated by Rush Limbaugh and other right-wing pundits and women were largely excluded as writers and producers from many late-night talk shows and sketch comedy shows, thus limiting their ability to directly address gendered norms.

She TV (ABC 1994)
One important example of satire targeting gendered norms that stands out during this time is the short-lived sketch comedy show *She TV*, which ran on ABC in 1994. It was written by Bonny and Terry Turner, a husband-and-wife writing duo formerly

Feminism: Pushing Back on Genderism and Gendered Norms | 85

working with *Saturday Night Live*. The show was billed as exploring the female point of view and featured a cast of mostly women. Although the show ended after only six episodes, it remains a valuable example of how marginalization satire may not resonate with traditional mainstream audiences. In the opening sketch of the series, a parody of the cop drama *NYPD Blue*, the male lead detective in the precinct asks each woman if she is doing okay. After several agree quietly, one woman stands up and says:

> No Kelly, I'm not OK. I'm a single mother and I make one-third less the salary of my partner, but I have to be 10 times the cop he is because I'm a woman. Sipowicz wears the same suit every day. If I did that, I'd be laughed right out of the precinct. I have to work overtime so I can pay my babysitter. I have to get up an hour earlier to paint my face with makeup. So, don't even ask me if I'm OK. OK?

She then storms out. Another male cop turns to the lead detective and says, "So what's wrong with her," to which the lead detective replies, "That time of the month." This sketch addresses the experience of being a woman, enduring less pay, more time spent on one's appearance, and the ongoing disparagement. However, after clearly and succinctly laying out the disparities experienced as a women, her legitimate concerns are dismissed by her colleagues as menstrual related, a common misogynistic strategy to marginalize the voices of women. In this sketch, the quiet part is said out loud and the humor comes from satirizing those who would continue to marginalize women.

Figure 3.10   Cast of *She TV* (1994).

Laughing at Gender in the Twenty-First Century

Americans have begun to laugh at gendered norms on a national scale, but this conversation still seems like it is in its infancy. Legacy satirical outlets like late night talk shows, sketch comedy programming, and *The Onion* have begun to engage more critically with the effects of gendered norms and satirize the marginalization processes that maintain them. Other outlets that focus specifically on gender have also emerged targeting like-minded audiences like Reductress (launched 2013) and them. (launched in 2017). Furthermore, there has been a general disavowal of genderism among younger generations. Greater numbers of Millennial and "Gen-Z" Americans express the idea that gender is a spectrum (Wong 2015) and report a desire to explore their passions regardless of the norms in which they have been socialized. This shift has led them to embrace gender fluidity in real life, in dispassionate commentary, and in satire.

Despite these advances, the socioeconomic marginalization of women remains evident in the systematic devaluing of "pink-collar jobs" associated with feminized labor. These jobs are in childcare and domestic labor as well as other areas that are limited in advancement, such as secretarial work. This historic marginalization also manifests in the gender pay gap. Women make 82 cents for every dollar a man receives in the United States for the same work. This statistic is exacerbated when considering the intersection of race and gender; Black women make 62 cents, and women of Hispanic/Latin American descent make 45 cents for every dollar a White man makes. White women make 79 cents and Asian women make 90 cents, comparatively (Bleiweis 2020).

However, groups have emerged that openly embrace genderism and sexism in response to this increasing awareness, as has been the case with every wave of gender advocacy. The reframing efforts of conservative activists to synonymize multiple movements with a few radical extremists have successfully turned many women away from identifying as feminists (Elder et al. 2021; Rothermel 2020). Similarly, men's rights movements have organized in the early twenty-first century to argue that that the emasculation of men is the primary threat to society (Hodapp 2017; Rafail and Freitas 2019). They advocate for a wholesale return to gendered norms that has drawn support from both men and women worldwide, revealing the ideological strength of genderism and sexism.

Satirizing the processes of gender in this increasingly contentious environment can quickly go awry. Satire is especially difficult if it is unclear as to whether the satirist is pointing out the absurdity of gendered norms, the people who maintain gendered norms, or those who are on the side of hegemonic power. Some important things to remember when satirizing (or critiquing content that satirizes) gender:

Do not assume that critiquing people who adhere to gender constructs is the same as critiquing the construct itself. Critiquing masculinity is not the same as mocking men. Critiquing femininity is not the same as mocking women. Mocking an entire group is easy and often deployed for laughs without deeply engaging with social issues. These "jokes" make fun of people who are also subjected to gender norms while failing to elaborate the absurdity of these processes. As always, individuals in positions of power who hold and promote these ideas become a representation of institutionalized genderism and sexism, but effective marginalization satire disrupts the effects of their power, not just their personal ideology.

Do not mock people based solely on their gender. A common trope in male-dominated comedy is to dress men up as women and argue that is humor. However, these jokes continue to punch down by making fun of women simply *because* they are women. Although this has less of an impact when men are mocked for being men because of their historic positions of power, making fun of people for their gender is not satire. It is a lazy and cruel joke.

Gender roles are present and have impact, so do not dismiss them outright because you consciously choose to not adhere to them. With the recent generational shift in gender awareness, saying gender norms are "stupid" is easy if you personally choose to disavow them. but they are a part of society that must be addressed from their historical and long-standing roots. As with any ideology, satirizing a belief system requires a delicate touch to reveal their absurdity to someone who believes that they are "natural."

Additional Activities

Activity 3.4 Internalizing the Absurdity: When do you feel your most masculine? When do you feel your most feminine?

Regardless of your gender, consider when you feel your most masculine and when you feel your most feminine. What situations, activities, or emotions do you associate with masculinity and femininity? How does a heightened sense of masculinity make you feel? How does a heightened sense of femininity make you feel? Then ask a few friends or family members of different genders when they feel their most masculine and feminine and observe the trends. Even among individuals who consciously disavow gendered norms, how are these norms built into our sense of self and how do they affect our behaviors?

Activity 3.5 Drag as Satire

If femininity and masculinity are constructs that one can "perform," then performances that exaggerate the tropes of femininity and masculinity to comment on the absurdity of gender is a form of satire. As a performance genre, drag is an art that bends traditional understandings of gender. It features a person dressing in clothing and makeup often of the opposite sex to draw attention to the constructs of femininity and masculinity. Although drag queens, who are artists who exaggerate the expectations and trappings of femininity, are more present in popular culture, drag kings, who are artists who exaggerate the expectations and trappings of *masculinity*, make similar commentary on our gendered norms.

Whether you are a fan of drag or completely new to the art form, search for drag performances online and watch them through the lens of the material in this chapter. Early episodes of *RuPaul's Drag Race* (2009-), now-classic comedies like *To Wong Foo, Thanks for Everything! Julie Newmar* (1995) and *The Birdcage* (1996; an adaptation of the French film *La Cage aux Folles*, 1978), or the documentary *Paris Is Burning* (1990), which documents ball culture of the 1980s. How do these performances ask you to see the narrow expectations of femininity and masculinity, and the possibilities of playing within these spaces regardless of the body in which one was born?

References

Anderson, S. (3 September 2019). Trans Twitter turns bigoted tweet into a parody meme. Mashable. https://mashable.com/article/trans-twitter-bigoted-tweet-trans-rights-meme (accessed 13 May 2022).

Basow, S. (2004). The hidden curriculum: Gender in the classroom. In: *Praeger Guide to the Psychology of Gender* (ed. M. A. Paludi), 117–131. Praeger Publishers/Greenwood Publishing Group.

Bleiweis, R. (24 March 2020). Quick facts about the gender wage gap. Center for American Progress.

Brough, A.R., Wilkie, J.E.B., Ma, J. et al. (2016). Is eco-friendly unmanly? The green-feminine stereotype and its effect on sustainable consumption. *Journal of Consumer Research* 43 (4): 567–582.

Burns, K. (9 January 2018). Jokes About Being Trans — By Actual Trans People. Them. https://www.them.us/story/trans-jokes-by-trans-people (accessed 13 May 2022).

Cassino, D. (2018). Emasculation, conservatism, and the 2016 election. *Contexts* 17 (1): 48–53.

Caster Semenya (27 August 2009). The Onion. https://sports.theonion.com/caster-semenya-1819589541.

Chang, S.S., Stuckler, D., Yip, P., and Gunnell, D. (2013). Impact of 2008 global economic crisis on suicide: Time trend study in 54 countries. *The British Medical Journal* 347.

[Comedy Central]. (29 April 2015). Inside Amy Schumer - Girl, You Don't Need Makeup. YouTube.

Connell, R.W. and Messerschmidt, J.W. (2005). Hegemonic masculinity: Rethinking the concept. *Gender & Society* 19 (6): 829–859.

Cooper, S. (2018). *How to Be Successful without Hurting Men's Feelings: Non-threatening Leadership Strategies for Women*. Kansas City: Andrews McMeel Publishing.

Elder, L., Greene, S., and Lizotte, M. K. (2021). *Feminist and anti-feminist identification in the 21st century United States. Journal of Women, Politics & Policy* 42 (3): 243–259.

Glick, P. (30 April 2020). Masks and emasculation: Why some men refuse to take safety precautions. Scientific American.

Grabe, S., Ward, L.M., and Hyde, J.S. (2008). The role of the media in body image concerns among women: A meta-analysis of experimental and correlational studies. *Psychological bulletin* 134 (3): 460.

Grady, C. (20 July 2018). The waves of feminism, and why people keep fighting over them, explained. Vox. https://www.vox.com/2018/3/20/16955588/feminism-waves-explained-first-second-third-fourth (accessed 13 May 2022).

Greenfield, C. (8 July 2014). Should we 'Fix' intersex children? The Atlantic. https://www.theatlantic.com/health/archive/2014/07/should-we-fix-intersex-children/373536/ (accessed 12 May 2022).

Gundersen, A.B., and Kunst, J.R. (2019). Feminist≠ feminine? Feminist women are visually masculinized whereas feminist men are feminized. *Sex Roles* 80 (5): 291–309.

Hall, K.F. (1996). Beauty and the beast of whiteness: Teaching Race and Gender. *Shakespeare Quarterly* 47 (4): 461–475.

Hausenblas, H.A., Campbell, A., Menzel, J.E., Doughty, J., Levine, M., and Thompson, J.K. (2013). Media effects of experimental presentation of the ideal physique on eating disorder symptoms: A meta-analysis of laboratory studies. *Clinical Psychology Review* 33 (1): 168–181.

Haynes, C. (3 August 2017). True cost of beauty: Survey reveals where Americans spend most. https://www.groupon.com/merchant/trends-insights/market-research/true-cost-beauty-americans-spend-most-survey (accessed 4 May 2022).

Hernandez, J. (11 April 2022). U.S. citizens can now choose the gender 'X' on their passport applications. https://www.npr.org/2022/04/11/1092000203/gender-x-us-passport-applications (accessed 12 May 2022).

Hodapp, C. (2017). *Men's Rights, Gender, and Social Media*. United States: Lexington Books.

Itzkoff, D. (21 November 2019). Who is Julia Sweeney coming to terms with? It's Pat. The New York Times.

Kang, J.M. (1996). Deconstructing the ideology of white aesthetics. *Michigan Journal of Race & Law* 2: 283–359.

Karsay, K., Knoll, J., and Matthes, J. (2018). Sexualizing media use and self-objectification: A meta-analysis. *Psychology of women quarterly* 42 (1): 9–28.

Killewald, A. (2016). Money, work, and marital stability: Assessing change in the gendered determinants of divorce. *American Sociological Review* 81 (4): 696–719.

LaFrance, A. (26 October 2016). The weird familiarity of 100-year0old feminism memes. The Atlantic. https://www.theatlantic.com/technology/archive/2016/10/pepe-the-anti-suffrage-frog/505406/ (accessed 13 May 2022).

Litchfield, C., Kavanagh, E., Osborne, J., and Jones, I. (2018). Social media and the politics of gender, race and identity: The case of Serena Williams. *European Journal for Sport and Society* 15 (2): 154–170.

Low, K.G., Charanasomboon, S., Brown, C. et al. (2003). Internalization of the thin ideal, weight and body image concerns. *Social Behavior and Personality: An International Journal* 31 (1): 81–89.

Madison, G., Aasa, U., Wallert, J., and Woodley, M.A. (2014). Feminist activist women are masculinized in terms of digit-ratio and social dominance: A possible explanation for the feminist paradox. *Frontiers in Psychology* 5: 1011.

Maglio, T. (4 August 2017). Jill Soloway Cites 'SNL' Sketch 'It's Pat' as 'Awful Piece of Anti-Trans Propaganda'. *The Wrap*. https://www.thewrap.com/jill-soloway-its-pat-snl-hateful-awful-anti-trans-propaganda/ (accessed 13 May 2022).

Margolis, E. (2001). *The Hidden Curriculum in Higher Education*. United Kingdom: Routledge.

Moon, D. (1999). White enculturation and bourgeois ideology. In: *Whiteness: The Communication of Social Identity* (ed. T. Nakayama and J. Martin), 177–197.

Miller, C.C. (4 January 2017). Why men don't want the jobs done mostly by women. New York Times.

Morales, L. (26 January 2019). LGBT Navajos Discover Unexpected Champions: Their Grandparents. NPR https://www.npr.org/2019/01/26/687957536/lgbt-navajos-discover-unexpected-champions-their-grandparentsa (accessed 13 May 2022).

Mulvey, L. (1973). Visual pleasure and narrative cinema. In: *Visual and Other Pleasures* (ed. S. Heath, C. MacCabe, and D. Riley), 14–26. London: Palgrave Macmillan.

Palmer, K. (10 July 2012) The morning routine: 30% spend over a week in getting ready each year. https://today.yougov.com/topics/lifestyle/articles-reports/2012/07/10/morning-routine-30-spend-over-week-getting-ready-e (accessed 5 May 2022).

Paras, T. [TessTubeBaby]. (24 March 2014). Typecast (Lorde "Royals" Parody). YouTube.

Parker, K. and Stepler, R. (14 September 2017). As U.S. marriage rate hovers at 50%, education gap in marital status widens. Pew Research Center.

Rafail, P. and Freitas, I. (2019). Grievance articulation and community reactions in the men's rights movement online. *Social Media+ Society* 5 (2): 2056305119841387.

Rohrbaugh, M. (Director). (2016). American Male [Film].

Rose, M. and Cowie, C. [BuzzFeedVideo]. (31 March 2014). If childhood gender roles were forced on adults. YouTube. https://www.youtube.com/watch?v=381belOZreA.

Rothermel, A.K. (2020). "The other side": Assessing the polarization of gender knowledge through a feminist analysis of the affective-discursive in anti-feminist online communities. *Social Politics: International Studies in Gender, State & Society* 27(4): 718–741.

[Saturday Night Live]. (9 December 2018). GE Big Boys [Video]. YouTube.

Schultz, J. (2005). Reading the catsuit: Serena Williams and the production of blackness at the 2002 US Open. *Journal of Sport and Social Issues* 29 (3): 338–357.

Sharman, J. (Director). (1975). The Rocky Horror Picture Show. 20th Century Studios.

Sherman, E. (18 October 2018). Kleenex blows its branding with a gender bias problem. Inc.

Smerdloff, A. (22 January 2016). Yogurt is now being marketed as 'manly'. Vice.

Wilks, L.E. (2020). The Serena show: Mapping tensions between masculinized and feminized media portrayals of Serena Williams and the Black female sporting body. *Feminist Media Histories* 6 (3): 52–78.

Wolf, N. (1990). The beauty myth: How images of beauty are used against women. Random House.

Wong, J.S. and Penner, A.M. (2016). Gender and the returns to attractiveness. *Research in Social Stratification and Mobility* 44: 113–123.

Zmuda, N. (21 February 2011). Can Dr. Pepper's mid-cal soda score a 10 with men? Ad Age.

4

Satirizing Sexuality

> *"Everything in the world is about sex except sex. Sex is about power."*
> —Oscar Wilde

Sexuality is a complex concept that is often reduced to **sexual orientation**, or the type of person for whom one feels a sense of sexual attraction and the associated identity, or the specific sexual activities in which one engages. However, as the full scope of sexuality receives greater public attention, we become increasingly aware of the simplistic social norms and the inconsistencies between what we experience and what we are told we are supposed to experience. Furthermore, the marginalization processes of sexuality are not just interpersonal because sexuality is tied to marriage and the associated government opportunities including tax breaks, employee benefits, adoption, end-of-life care). This chapter describes the normative language and social expectations of heterosexuality before delving into the wider spectrum of sexuality and the institutional and individual discrimination against non-heterosexual sexualities and sexual identities.[1]

What's Love Got to Do with It? Defining Sexuality

As described in the last chapter, sex is not gender. By extension, gender does not indicate sexuality although there is a general assumption of to whom one is attracted *because* of their gender. The assumptions regarding sexuality may not be well understood due to the simplistic definition of sexuality that relies on physical interactions and disregards emotional or psychological desire, which is inadequate to convey the depth of sexuality and how a lack of understanding contributes to associated stereotypes, prejudice, and discrimination.

According to Oxford languages, sexuality is primarily defined as, "the *capacity* for sexual feelings" or the inner desire for "physical attraction or intimate physical contact between individuals." This definition relies on one's capacity to have physical or bodily

---

[1] Whereas the first two chapters focused on the marginalization of people who constitute a larger percentage of the population compared to the groups that are in power, i.e., poor and working classes, women and non-binary people, this chapter focuses on the treatment of a minority: people who do not identify as heterosexual.

Diversity and Satire: Laughing at Processes of Marginalization, First Edition.
Charisse L'Pree Corsbie-Massay.
© 2023 John Wiley & Sons, Inc. Published 2023 by John Wiley & Sons, Inc.

desires, a concept that is undermined by our recent discourse regarding asexuality. **Asexual** individuals are people who express low or no desire for intimate physical contact but may still engage in intimate emotional relationships, this includes individuals who may not experience physical desires due to psychological or physical conditions (e.g., depression, menopause). Although people may not experience desire for intimate physical contact, they may still express a desire for intimate *emotional* contact.

The second defintion offered by Oxford focuses on identity: "One's identity as derived from the gender or genders to which they are typically attracted." This definition is more in line with the traditional understanding of sexuality as sexual orientation and acknowledges that one's sexuality is separate from whether they are currently experiencing or have the capacity for sexual feelings. However, the issue of emotional intimacy is still absent from this definition. We may feel an emotional attraction before or even without a sense of physical attraction, in which case, we can have a sexuality or a sexual identity without ever actually engaging in sexual behaviors.

The way desire precedes sexual behavior reveals there is more to sexual identity than simply the gender or genders to which we are physically attracted. Consider the question: *When did you become aware of your sexuality?* People who are not heterosexual frequently express that they were aware of their sexuality before puberty. Technically, they were aware of their desires before the typical biological capacity for physical sexual attraction because of an existential disconnect between their (emotional and physical) experiences and a culture where heterosexuality is normalized and applied to pre-pubescent children from a young age. Martin & Kazyak (2009) describe trends in popular G-rated movies targeting children that promote hetero-romantic relationships as "exceptional, powerful, magical, and transformative" (p. 315).

Furthermore, these definitions ignore gender, which is fundamental to the understanding of sexuality. If gender was independent of sexuality, simply being attracted to one gender would have the same title regardless of the gendered body expressing it; for example, someone who was attracted to men would be categorized as andro-sexual, regardless of their gender.[2] Instead, if a person identifies as a woman and has historically been intimate with men, that person would be categorized as heterosexual. If a person identifies as a man and has historically been intimate with men, that person would be categorized as homosexual. Although these categories (heterosexual and homosexual) are clearly subject to change over time, the disparity in sexuality based on one's gender is essential in the definition of sexuality and sexual identity.

This book defines **sexuality** as a characteristic and identity associated with how one seeks and receives mature (i.e., adult) intimacy and interpersonal satisfaction, including meeting one's physical and/or emotional needs. It is both a distinctive feature of a person and affects their life, much like gender or race, and it is a personal identifier that can have positive or negative associations for each individual. Although sexual behavior can evolve into a sexual identity, one can also experience physical and emotional intimacy with certain gendered partners without identifying accordingly. The value of constructing sexuality in this purposefully broad manner will become clear when discussing physical and emotional attraction.

Sexual identity is the way one personally identifies as an extension of their sexuality. To use the language from Chapter 3 on gender, if you are attracted to someone

---

[2] Someone attracted to women would identify as gyno-sexual, regardless of gender.

Figure 4.1 Stop pushing a heteronormative agenda onto children (2017); *Source*: Sophie Labelle.

> **Activity 4.1   Understanding Sexuality**
>
> Recent research has found that the number of people who identify as "purely heterosexual" or "completely straight" is decreasing with each generation. Compared to 12% of Americans aged 45 and older, 27% of Americans aged 30–44 and 36% of Americans aged 18–29 identify as other than "completely straight" on the Kinsey scale (Moore 2015). However, we learn from a very young age what is expected of us in intimate adult relationships. Consider an artifact targeted to children, like a Disney movie, which features adult relationships. Consider how sexuality can be inferred from this artifact. Consider the following questions:
>
> 1. Does the artifact talk explicitly about non-heterosexual adult relationships? If it does, what does it say about sexual diversity? If it doesn't, what does the lack of conversation say about sexual diversity?
> 2. Is there a diversity of healthy adult relationships in this artifact or does it only feature male-female heterosexual relationships within the confines of marriage?
> 3. Does the artifact feature cross-gendered friendships? Do healthy cross-gendered friendships exist (i.e., without sexual tension)? Or do all cross-gendered relationships have an expectation of physical or emotional intimacy?
>
> If the answer to each of the first questions is "no," then the artifact is talking about sexuality only through the dominant lens of heterosexuality. When we talk about the representation of sexual diversity in child-targeted programming, the conversation often revolves around "exposing children to sexual content" where "sexual content" is a negative frame for non-heterosexual relationships. However, nearly all content targeting children expose them to mediated sexuality at a young age, and it just happens to be socially-sanctioned heterosexuality.

on the other side of the gender binary, you are categorized as **heterosexual**. If you are attracted to someone on the *same* side of the gender binary, then you are categorized as **homosexual**.[3] This model of sexuality is sometimes referred to as **monosexism** because it implies that one is either attracted to individuals of the opposite gender (i.e., heterosexual) or of the same gender (i.e., homosexual or gay). Monosexism reinforces many of the issues outlined in Chapter 3, specifically the socially sanctioned binary of gender. Other sexualities such as **bisexual** and **pansexual** refer to experiencing intimacy with more than one gender.[4] For example, the term **demisexual** refers to the need for emotional intimacy before physical or sexual intimacy.

Gay vs. Black by Wanda Sykes (I'ma Be Me, HBO 2009)

In 2008, after two decades of success in the entertainment industry, comedian Wanda Sykes revealed to the world that she was gay at a rally for marriage equality. In her

---

[3] For trans individuals whose gender does not align with the category assigned to them at birth, their sexuality is often framed in line with their self-identified gender.

[4] Some who are attracted to multiple genders prefer the term pansexual to remove the binary language. In this sense, one could be a non-binary bisexual. https://www.ygender.org.au/article/bisexuality-is-not-transphobic.

2009 HBO special *I'ma Be Me*, Sykes highlighted the absurdity of how others understand and treat sexuality.

> AS WANDA: There's some things that I had to do as gay that I didn't have to do as Black. I didn't have to come out Black. I didn't have to sit my parents down and tell them about my Blackness. I didn't have to sit them down. "Mom, Dad, I got to tell y'all something. I hope you still love me. I'm just gonna say it. Mom, Dad—. I'm Black."
>
> AS WANDA'S MOM: "What? What did she just say? Oh, Lord Jesus, she didn't say 'Black, 'Lord. Did she say 'Black?'"
>
> AS WANDA: "Mom, I'm Black."
>
> AS WANDA'S MOM: "Oh, Lord, Lord Jesus. Lord, Lord, Father God. Oh, bless, bless, Lord. Anything but Black, Jesus. Give her cancer, Lord. Give her cancer. Anything but Black, Lord."
>
> AS WANDA: It's like, "Mom, yeah, I'm Black. I'm—. That's just how it is."
>
> AS WANDA'S MOM: "No. No, you know what? You been hanging around Black people. You been hanging around Black people, and they got you thinking you Black. They twisted your mind."
>
> AS WANDA: It's like, "No, Mom, I'm Black. That's just how it is."
>
> AS WANDA'S MOM: "Oh, what—. What did I do? What did I do? I knew I shouldn't have let you watch Soul Train. Was it Soul Train?"
>
> AS WANDA: "No, Ma, it wasn't Soul Train, Ma. It's just who I am. I was just born Black."
>
> AS WANDA'S MOM: "Oh, you weren't born Black. I don't want to hear that. Uh-uh, you weren't born Black. The Bible says, "Adam and Eve," not "Adam and Mary J. Blige!"

In retelling her story of coming out to her parents, Sykes draws on an all-too-common narrative about parental fears of queerness. By replacing the word "gay" with "Black," Sykes reveals how the oppression and discrimination associated with sexuality is unique. There is little doubt as to whether or not one belongs to a given race, but the existence of non-heterosexual sexualities can be questioned and ultimately dismissed even by loved ones. Applying this argumentation to other identity categories reveals how these homophobic and anti-gay attitudes are nonsensical. Sykes flips classic homophobic rhetoric like the belief that being gay is contagious and the biblical story of Adam and Eve to showcase the absurdity of these lines when they are applied to sexuality, especially given that one's racial identity is rarely questioned or dismissed.

Sexuality-based communities also embrace different labels and identifiers, which can change over time for many different reasons, as with any identity-based group. The terms gay and lesbian have been deployed as gender-specific labels, associated with men who find intimacy with men and women who find intimacy with women, respectively. These terms are largely preferred to "homosexual," whose scientific-sounding deployment has been used to other (i.e., actively ostracize, alienate, and discriminate against a given group that is already marginalized) those who are not heterosexual by pathologizing non-heterosexual sexualities. Whereas "gay" and "lesbian" are more likely to describe friends, relatives, or neighbors, "homosexual" indicates an out-group identity that can negatively impact support for policies curbing anti-gay discrimination (Smith et al. 2018).

In the second half of the twentieth century, the term gay community gained traction during the sexuality-based civil rights movements as an umbrella term to indicate the community of people who identify with sexualities other than heterosexual. Occasionally, the term **sexual minorities** is deployed to indicate that people who do not identify as heterosexual are in the numerical minority. However, much like "homosexual," this term is rarely used by these communities and prioritizes the size of the community over the community itself. The word "queer" is more expansive than sexuality and includes anyone whose gender identity lies outside of the binary, meaning non-binary, intersex, and transgender people, regardless of their sexuality. *Therefore, throughout this chapter, gay will be used to refer to non-heterosexual sexualities and queer will refer to both non-heterosexual sexualities and non-cis genders.*

The rest of this chapter will explore trends in the popular American framing of sexuality, specifically the emphasis on heteronormativity, individual and institutional manifestations of homophobia and anti-gay attitudes, and the systematic erasure of nuanced sexual identities.

Satirizing Heteronormativity

People worldwide who identify as other than heterosexual account for approximately 5-10% of the population (Spiegelhalter 2015); this number changes depending on age, culture, time and even how the question is asked, but this is a working average for discussion purposes. Gay people have been forced to hide their sexual identities for centuries due to individual and institutional discrimination. In order to avoid persecution, gay people may lie about their personal lives or adopt heteronormative attitudes, behaviors, and ideologies as a survival strategy. **Heteronormativity** is the belief that a long-term monogamous relationship between a man and a woman is the ideal. It is the manifestation of statistics (i.e., the majority of people are heterosexual), hegemony (i.e., who holds power in society), and solipsism (i.e., the attitude that the self is the only thing that can be known to exist). It leads to the perspective of the heterosexual majority becoming normalized and consequently, naturalized. Simultaneously, all other sexualities are framed as deviant. We can observe heteronormativity in the discourse questioning whether homosexuality is a choice, the internalization of anti-gay attitudes by people who are not heterosexual, and the negative stereotypes of gay people and relationships.

When Did You Choose to be Straight? (Travis Nuckolls 2008)

On Valentine's Day in 2008, a three-minute video was posted to YouTube featuring on-the-street interviews of people in Colorado Springs. To begin, the interviewer asks, "Do you think gay people are born gay or they choose to be gay?" Many of the interview subjects said that believed gay people *choose* to be gay. The off-camera interviewer then asks a follow up: "When did you choose to be straight?" Respondents who had just indicated they thought being gay was a choice paused in response to this flipped question. Several appear to be caught in the absurdity of their own logic, admitting "That's a good point" or "You got me there." Several respondents answered that being straight was not a choice, to which the interviewer asks, "Do you think it is the same for gay people?"

The question of whether or not being gay is a choice is one of the most common discriminatory consequences of heteronormativity. When sexuality is framed as an **achieved identity**, or an identity that one *chooses* to pursue like an occupation, then

What's Love Got to Do with It? Defining Sexuality | 97

Figure 4.2 A early example of user-generated margainlization satire, "When Did You Choose to be Straight?" successfully parodied the person-on-the-street approach of late night shows, and showcased the absurdity of choice rhetoric in perpetuating anti-gay attitudes and policies (2008).

anti-discrimination statutes do not apply and sexually marginalized people are not eligible for the same legal protections against discrimination as **ascribed identities**,

---

Gay Wedding Advice (*Key & Peele*; Comedy Central 2014)

By Daniel Loftus

This 2014 skit starts with the Johnson family gathered together to discuss the wedding of Cousin Delroy. Delroy, who is not seen in the skit, is getting married to another man. So, the main family member who is standing in front of the family welcomes co-worker Gary, who is gay, to tell the family what to expect at a gay wedding. Gary proceeds to tell them that a gay wedding is just the same as a wedding between a straight couple. One man from the family speaks up and questions what people wear to the weddings and if he will sit in the "straight section." The man up front clarifies the question to Gary, telling him that the straight section would be different than the "gay section." Gary tells them there are no sections like that, and that it is just like a normal wedding. The family doesn't seem to understand because they think they will have to guess who is gay at the wedding. They continue to ask questions to Gary, such as when they will have to sing certain songs or "gay hymns." As the questions continue, Gary gets increasingly frustrated with the family for what he starts to see as "homophobia," like when one person asks if it is okay to gasp when the couple kisses. Eventually, Gary storms out, and it cuts back to the family, which thinks it now understands the workings of a gay wedding.

(Continued)

> (Continued)
>
> This clip is trying to show the ridiculous beliefs people hold, such as the "them and us" mentality so many straight individuals hold toward the gay community. The family, who is said to be entirely straight, assumes that a gay wedding has to be fundamentally different than straight wedding experiences. They express stereotypical ideas of what it means to be gay. In expressing absurd ideas of what a gay wedding would entail, such as pony shows and gay hymns, the characters anger an actual gay man in the skit.
>
> There are several greater societal structures at play in this clip. First, there is an idea of being opposed to gay sex and romantic involvement between men. The one character oversteps her boundaries by bringing up "anal sex," which made the others gasp, and that same character also said she would look away when the couple would kiss. Studies show that people are more accepting of gay couples receiving things like insurance benefits than they are of them showing affection in public (Ghaziani 2018). In this case, the family is willing to attend the wedding and allow the wedding to occur, but they are made uncomfortable by sex and affection that they would otherwise be fine with if the couple was a man and a woman. Overall, this clip makes many of the characters seem irrational by showing how their obsession with heteronormativity has gone so far that the notion a gay wedding can look the same as a normal wedding is unthinkable to them.

categories over which one has no control and that have been imposed by external forms (e.g., race and gender). By simply flipping the question, the video reveals the absurdity of considering (non-heterosexual) sexualities as an achieved identity that people choose to pursue.

The video is simple and effective in its execution. The interviewees do not hesitate to answer the original question because it is commonplace, albeit loaded and polemic. The underlying prejudicial implications are revealed when the interviewer flips the question by replacing "gay" with "heterosexual." The interview subjects are then forced to apply the discourse of nature vs. nurture to themselves. Similar to the monologue by Wanda Sykes, this strategy underscores the ridiculous one-sidedness of assumptions regarding sexuality. Furthermore, the audience watches in real time as these individuals reassess their beliefs about sexuality when faced with a question they have never faced but is regularly asked of people who are not heterosexual. This artifact does more than point out the conflict between the rhetoric and the reality by saying the quiet part out loud; it also models ways to engage with others who espouse these beliefs, inspiring many spinoffs in the years since on college campuses, within religious organizations, and internationally.

Heteronormative behaviors also include behaviors associated with heterosexuality. The concept of being "straight" is much more than a sexuality; it is a lifelong set of socialized expectations, and the pervasive belief is that one must act straight to gain respect, or adhere to the associated cisgendered, heterosexual, and behavioral gendered norms (Clarkson 2008). Heteronormativity is the expectation that all will align with their gender assigned at birth, marry an opposite-gendered person, and reproduce; and those who do not completely adhere to this life path will desire or attempt to pursue this life to the best of their ability. Heteronormativity accepts no deviance, and when one does not adhere to heteronormativity, the world must clearly be flipped on its head.

As described in the last chapter, our genitals are inspected at birth to determine sex. This is then documented, and this information determines our name, how we are treated, the clothes we are expected to wear, the toys we are expected to play with, and the way we are expected to behave. As we get older, this information translates into the subjects and interests that we are permitted to participate in. It also shapes the people with whom we can develop friendships and the spaces in which we are allowed to develop them. We also learn behaviors that are associated with finding intimacy in the opposite sex: How we should dress, carry ourselves, and speak to attract an opposite sexed/gendered mate. Although lifelong partnership depends on many other factors than one's ability to perform gender, we are socialized to believe that we can find someone with whom to marry, mate, and grow old *if we perform these gendered behaviors well.*

These behavioral expectations are internalized by everyone, including those who do not identify as cisgendered or heterosexual. This **internalized homophobia**, or the adoption of anti-gay attitudes by gay people, is correlated with many negative behavioral and health outcomes (Russell and Bohan 2006) because one believes that their life is not valuable if it is not "normal." It can be difficult to see how heterosexism pervades American society if one has never experienced this internal turmoil, but the experience is widespread among the gay community causing a parallel understanding of oneself and one's place in the world.

The Puppy Episode; Part 2 (*Ellen*, S4E23, ABC 1997)

On April 30, 1997, Ellen DeGeneres' character, Ellen Morgan, came out in a two-part episode of her eponymously named primetime sitcom, *Ellen*. The episode accompanied Ellen DeGeneres' formal coming out in *TIME Magazine* two weeks earlier after months of hinting and double entendres at public appearances. In the first part of the episode, Ellen Morgan deals with her feelings of attraction to Susan (played by Laura Dern) and discomfort with the intimate advances of Richard (played by Steven Eckholdt). At the end of Part 1, Ellen comes out to Susan and the entire airport terminal when she accidentally announces "I'm gay" over the loudspeaker.

The second part begins with Ellen Morgan describing a dream sequence to her therapist, played by Oprah Winfrey. Ellen expresses a lifetime of concern and fear over being gay, and Winfrey-as-therapist asks why she has kept it to herself all these years, to which Ellen replies:

> I don't know. I guess I thought if I just ignored it, just go away and I could just live a normal life… A house. The picket fence, you know, a dog or cat. Sunday barbecues. Someone to love, someone who loves me, someone I can build a life with. Just, I just want to be happy.

Ellen's aspirations, which she says kept her in the closet, reflect heteronormativity. Ellen outlines the absurd expectations of gender and sexuality embedded in the American Dream, the idea that the perfect life everyone wants includes materialistic expectations of a house, a spouse, and a family. The episode goes on to lampoon these expectations and the feeling of liberation when one recognizes that these desires have been externally constructed, allowing them to consider their own desires independent of heteronormative socialization.

To be queer is to *not* be straight and veer off the line from sex assigned at birth to gender to sexuality. This deviation can include non-binary and trans people who do not adhere to the sex that was assigned to them at birth, as well as people who do not find intimacy in opposite sex individuals, and individuals who find intimacy with multiple partners. This broad array of categories contained in the overarching term 'queer' includes those featured in the lesbian, gay, bisexual, transgender, and queer acronym (LGBTQ) as well as **pansexual**, which is defined as feeling a physical or emotional attraction to people independent of their gender. Individuals who identify as pansexual can be attracted to a wide variety of genders and are not limited to the gender binary (i.e., men and women), including non-binary people and gender-queer people as well as cis and trans individuals. Even questioning one's sexual orientation and identity can be included under the umbrella of queer because questioning whether one is completely heterosexual can cause a heteronormative society to read them as gay.

In its formal grammatical etymology, **homophobia** is the extreme or irrational fear of or aversion to homosexual people (Weinberg 1972), but in its current usage, it means dislike of or prejudice against gay people as well as any attitudes or actions that harm gay and queer communities. In 2012, the Associated Press Stylebook, the benchmark of language usage in journalism, determined that the term "homophobia" was not a good representation of the anti-gay stereotypes, attitudes, and prejudice that targeted the gay and queer communities because it foregrounded "a form of mental illness" which was speculative (Byers 2012).[5] Although both terms are used by different organizations, homophobia, either individually or institutionally, refers to a plethora of stereotypes, language, attitudes, behaviors, and policies that seek to dehumanize and marginalize people who are not heterosexual. *Throughout the rest of this book, the terms homophobia and anti-gay will be used interchangeably, but homophobia will largely be reserved for individual phenomena whereas anti-gay will be used for institutional phenomena.*

Satirizing Individual Homophobia

Although marginalization is about more than interpersonal treatment, the role of individuals attitudes toward gay people and gay communities cannot be overstated in the processes of gay and queer marginalization. As has already been described in Chapter 3, the experiences of queer people are driven by individual feelings of aversion and research has demonstrated that feelings of disgust reduce support for anti-discrimination policies that foreground gay and queer communities (Terrizi Jr. et al. 2010; Miller et al. 2017). Popular discourse tends to focus on individual homophobia because a single person's anti-gay stereotypes, prejudice, and discrimination are easier to identify, but institutionalized homophobia emerges from collective individual anti-gay attitudes, and individual anti-gay attitudes can inhibit institutional change.

As the gay rights movement of the 1970s and 1980s became a part of the national conversation, several popular television series featured **gay episodes**, which were

---

5 The organization eliminated "Islamophobia" for the same reason at the same time.

single episodes in long-running television series where a gay character is featured prominently but briefly for the purpose of triggering an emotional and personal epiphany in the main straight character. This strategy mocks the "loveable homophobe," a specific form of the lovable bigot (see Chapter 1), as a person who is holding onto outdated prejudices despite a changing world. Prominent gay episodes during this time include episodes of *Sanford and Son* ("The Piano Movers," 1972), *The Mary Tyler Moore Show* ("My Brother's Keeper," 1973), *The Bob Newhart Show* ("Some of My Best Friends are..." 1976), *The Jeffersons* ("Once a Friend," 1977), and of course, *All in the Family*.

Judging Books by Covers (*All in the Family*, S1E5, CBS 1971)
In the episode "Judging Books," Archie expresses his disgust with Roger, Gloria and Michael's friend who has recently returned from Europe. Roger is slim and wears glasses and an ascot. He is cultured with expensive tastes. These visible characteristics lead Archie to refer to him as "sweetie pie Roger" and a "strange little birdie" who is "queerer than a four-dolllar bill" and threatens their "decent home." As was the standard approach of the show, Gloria and Michael attempt to push back on Archie's absurd statements, insisting that Roger is straight, and that Archie is applying faulty outdated stereotypes to their friend. Furthermore, they acknowledge that it doesn't matter if Roger is gay because what people do in their personal lives is none of their business.

When Roger arrives, Archie is visibly uncomfortable and continues to make inappropriate and implicitly homophobic remarks in his presence. Frustrated with Archie's ignorance and incessant mocking, Michael reveals that his friend Steve, who Archie considers to be an exemplary man because he plays football, is tall and muscular, and drinks beer, is actually gay. The episode comes to a climax when it is revealed that Steve and Roger know each other through Steve's camera store:

> ARCHIE: Let me ask you something. How long you known this kid, Roger, that was in with Mike?
> STEVE: Ooh. A couple of years since he started coming to shop.
> ARCHIE: Couple of years. Now you're a man of the world. You must know that this kid is kind of a la-de-dah (gestures with his hands), right?
> STEVE: Is that what Mike thinks of Roger?
> ARCHIE: Forget about what Mike thinks. I can't even tell you what he thinks.
> STEVE: What does Mike think, Arch?
> ARCHIE: He thinks that friend of his, Roger, is straight. And for another thing, Steve. You're going to want to bust him wide open when I tell you this. I don't know where he gets these brainstorms. But he thinks you're a—. I can't even say, Steve.
> STEVE: He's right Arch.
> ARCHIE: Huh?
> STEVE: He's right.
> ARCHIE: You mean about he's right about his friend, Roger?
> STEVE: About everything.
> ARCHIE: Aw. Come on. You wanna joke about it. All right. Come on, get off it guy.

> STEVE: Arch. How long you known me? 10, 12 years? In all that time, did I ever mention a woman?
> ARCHIE: What difference does that make? You're a bachelor! Bachelors are always acting kind of private.
> STEVE: Exactly.

Suddenly, Archie's world is turned upside-down when he realizes that his friend is gay. Furthermore, Steve, comfortable in his own sexuality, forces Archie to reconsider how he associates gender presentation and sexuality. The audience is directed to laugh at Archie's inability to process how his friend Steve (a real "man's man") can be gay but Roger, who he perceives to be effeminate, can be straight, revealing the absurdity association between gender-based stereotypes and sexuality. The episode reveals that the traditional approaches to sexuality are futile and the lovable bigot must adapt. However, neither Roger nor Steve are featured in subsequent episodes, allowing Archie to return to his bigoted world views unabated.

Other popular sitcoms, including *Cheers, Roseanne, Golden Girls, Friends*, and *Seinfeld*, also have their own flagship gay episodes. The strategy was effective when recurring gay characters were rare. Often considered to be one of the most prominent satirical outlets of the late twentieth (and into the twenty-first century), *The Simpsons* features Wayland Smithers, a recurring closeted gay character whose sexuality is most frequently mocked because he is afraid to come out to his boss, C. Montgomery Burns, to whom he is intimately, and unrequitedly, attracted. However, in 1997, *The Simpsons* received critical praise for its gay episode featuring John Waters, prominent independent filmmaker and queer icon.

Homer's Phobia (*The Simpsons*, S8E15, FOX 1997)
Homer befriends John, the owner of a kitschy shop in the mall that sells classic pop culture trinkets without realizing that John is gay. When Homer learns of John's sexuality, he becomes extremely agitated; Homer panics that he "danced with a gay," that the property value would drop because they can no longer say that "...only straight people have been in this house," and that John would "give [his family] gay." Throughout the episode, Homer begins to question his own identity as well as his son's sexuality, particularly when Bart behaves in ways that can be interpreted as not masculine, like singing karaoke and eating pink desserts. In a desperate attempt to ensure that Bart does not "turn gay," he takes Bart on hyper-masculine field trips that repeatedly and hilariously backfire:

- Homer leaves Bart in the middle of a freeway for two hours to stare at a cigarette billboard featuring two attractive women pillow-fighting. After watching the billboard, Bart announces he wants a cigarette, but to Homer's frustration, he echoes a feminized advertising message: "anything slim!"
- Homer takes Bart to a steel mill to show him "real all-American Joes doing what they do best" only to find out that it is a "gay steel mill" a commentary on the metaphorical association between steel production and masculinity in the United States (Balay 2014).
- Homer, Barney, and Mo take Bart deer hunting to ensure that he grows up "straight." On their way to the campsite, Bart makes an ironic observation when he admits he's never been hunting before: "Something about a bunch of guys alone together in the woods seems kinda gay."

This episode frames Homer as the "lovable homophobe" whose antiquated ways are out of step with the rest of the family. The episode received critical acclaim and an Emmy for Outstanding Animated Program as well as the Gay and Lesbian Alliance Against Defamation (GLAAD) Media Award for Outstanding TV (Individual Episode) in 1997. However, after teaching this episode for years, I have witnessed students become deeply hurt by the repetition of homophobic and anti-gay rhetoric. They miss the satire or do not see satire as a sufficient rationale for the rampant homophobic lines. Furthermore, students who are not *Simpsons* fans may lack the essential knowledge that Homer is a bad husband, father, neighbor, employee, and friend, and audiences are expected to laugh at his antics (see lovable bigot in Chapter 1) even though he is the main character. Although quality entertainment is in the eye of the beholder, it is essential to consider *how* the show, not just the individual episode, shows viewers what to laugh at and reveals why something is absurd. In this episode, the rest of the family likes spending time with John, and Marge actively pushes back on Homer's homophobic attitudes and actions, repeatedly calling his perspective on gay communities ridiculous.

Although these episodes were considered to be progressive for the time, the characters are often featured as a collection of simple stereotypes and their fleeting nature inhibited audiences from seeing these characters as fully fleshed individuals. In addition, audiences are left to hope that the lovable homophobe will change their homophobic ways (spoiler: they don't). This episode actively addresses these tropes.

Activity 4.2 Camp as Satire

Gilad Padva (2008) describes this episode as a celebration of queer counterculture and an embrace of camp, which is defined both as "…affected, theatrically exaggerated; effeminate; homosexual" (Oxford Dictionary, 1996 via Padva 2008, p. 61) and "…ironic but playful exaggeration and subversion of expected sex role behavior" (Fejes and Petrich 1993, p. 397). The systematic repression of a group of people results in two primary media-related strategies: resistance, or not engaging with problematic media content, and subversion, or reinterpreting mainstream content through a queer lens (Gross 1991). Over the course of the twentieth century, an over-the-top approach to heteronormative content elicited a culture that simultaneously embraced and spoke back to social norms, inviting those with a keen eye to see messages that went unnoticed to the larger heterosexual audience.

Camp itself is satire because it points to the absurdity of what is considered "normal." Its subversive qualities often served as a wink and a nod to those who were already in on the joke. In this case, satire was a way of coping with one's own oppression as a way to laugh at the world one was forced to navigate. In 2019, the Met Gala featured the theme "Camp." The invitation came with a guide to camp by Susan Sontag, who defined the term in 1964 as "…an aesthetic 'sensibility' that is plain to see but hard for most of us to explain: an intentional over-the-top-ness, a slightly (or extremely) 'off' quality, bad taste as a vehicle for good art" (Werthein et al. 2019). This very public event was the outcome of decades of camping by the gay and queer communities as a means of inclusion. *Search for examples of camp online and consider how they draw attention to heteronormative tropes through exaggeration.*

John does not adhere to gay stereotypes and is written as a fleshed but fleeting character with diverse interests. Furthermore, John dispassionately reveals the humor of singular gay episodes in which the main character is changed for the better through some interaction with this gay person. After he saves Homer's life in the wake of a hunting trip gone bad, John highlights the counterproductivity of this tokenistic trope: "Well, Homer, I won your respect. And all I had to do was save your life. Now if every gay man could just do the same, you'd be set."

Stereotypes of Sexuality

As with all the social categories featured in this book, identifying with a sexuality is completely independent from one's personality, demeanor, and life choices. Where we find intimacy has nothing to do with the way we dress, behave, or think. Despite this fact, we regularly use people's sexuality to determine their individual characteristics and vice versa. Men who are not strong, muscular, and assertive and women who

---

Jaboukie Young-White Explains Why Guns Are Gay (*The Daily Show with Trevor Noah* 2019)

By Sophia Digiantommaso, Ashley Laird, Cedric Middleton

The piece starts out with Trevor Noah explaining the issue of gun violence in America. He is then joined by Jaboukie Young-White, and they discuss what could be done to address the issue. Jaboukie essentially declares that the easiest way to decrease gun ownership in America without reformed gun regulation is to "make guns gay." To support his idea, he explains that a recent study shows that men don't recycle out of fear of looking gay. Jaboukie claims, "We just have to harness that same toxic masculinity and just direct it toward guns… you know, sweet, gay guns." Jaboukie explains that guns are gay because they're "long, hard, the best ones are Black" and they are all "kept in the closet." He makes a play on "the right to bear arms" as the "right to bare arms" and goes on to discuss how gun laws sound so gay that they could be used as Grindr usernames and Kelly Clarkson gay anthems.

The skit also drives home the hyper-masculine notions of homophobia by talking about how a study shows men don't recycle out of fear of looking gay. Jaboukie leverages such an absurdity when he claims that this same toxic masculinity should be directed toward guns, so men are apprehensive to use them out of the phobia of seeming gay. The bit where he explains that guns are gay because they're "long, hard, the best ones are black" and they are all "kept in the closet" is similar to a bit in "Homer's Phobia," an episode of *The Simpsons* that confronts Homer Simpson's bias against gay people. In the episode, Bart Simpson tells Homer Simpson that a bunch of men hunting together in the woods "sounds gay" (Groening et al. 1997). This pattern across more than one satirical text highlights the widespread social absurdity that though heterosexual men may perceive gay culture as being repulsive, practices that heterosexually men take part in such as sports and hunting can easily be related to the gay clichés.

Though the interview between Trevor Noah and Jaboukie Young-White may appear to be a professional, news-like interview discussing the controversies of

(Continued)

> (Continued)
>
> guns, it really satirizes the absurdities of masculine ideals toward gun use and queer identity. Trevor's role within the piece is to act as a typical, heterosexual male news anchor, i.e., a reflection of masculinity. He asks straightforward, serious questions, to which Jaboukie relentlessly gives outlandish responses, peppered with stereotypes of how gay men are socially perceived. This dichotomy is intentional because its purpose is to be satirical. If this isn't clear enough to the viewer, when asked "How do you decrease gun ownership without gun regulation?" Jaboukie responds, "Oh Trevor, Trevor, Trevor you silly little bitch… easy! We just have to make guns gay" as a rainbow with AK-37s in the clouds is displayed above the posing Jaboukie. This eccentric addition to the piece, in conjunction with Jaboukie's outlandish responses to questions, reveals that it isn't a serious news interview and provides context to the satire for the viewer. Overall, this artifact from *The Daily Show* does a wonderful job at satirizing the absurdities of widespread hegemonic masculinity.

are not slender, effortlessly attractive, and demure are presumed to be gay. A man who works in occupations dominated by women, such as childcare or nursing, is assumed to be feminine and subsequently gay; women who are accomplished or career-driven are deemed masculine and assumed to be lesbians. By extension, stereotypes associated with intimate behaviors are also gender specific: Men who are attracted to men are assumed to be promiscuous, an amplified version of the stereotypically masculine drive for sex with multiple partners; women who are attracted to women are assumed to be overly emotional and therefore fall into relationships quickly.

The expectations of gendered presentations and behaviors outlined in Chapter 3 are heteronomative. Even the terms "effeminate," "fairy," "mannish," and "dyke" are used as anti-gay insults for men and women who do not adhere to gendered norms in their presentation and behavior. Regardless of social category, stereotypes are absurd because they rely on and foster limited thinking, but stereotypes of sexuality are uniquely detrimental because they build on and reinforce gendered stereotypes, thus negatively impacting queer and straight people alike (see toxic masculinity in Chapter 3).

These stereotypes are further fueled by the under-representation and misrepresentation of gay and queer individuals in American media. Across decades of American media, gay people have been constructed as sexually deviant and predatory. The Catholic-inspired Motion Picture Production Code (1934–1968), also referred to as the Hays Code, argued that cinema should "maintain social and community values" and that movies should uphold the sanctity of marriage and the home. Included within the last point was the line that, "…sex perversion or any inference to it is forbidden" (Shurlock, 1947), capturing a collective attitude toward homosexuality that continues to this day: Homosexuality is a "perversion, sickness, or crime" that can infiltrate and corrupt others. The aforementioned stereotypes, including feminine behavior among men and masculine behavior among women, are often used to establish villains in content targeting both adults (Fejes and Petrich, 1993) and youth (Putnam, 2013; Sharmin and Sattar 2018). The stereotype of queer people as inherently deviant, evil, and ultimately malicious and destructive is pervasive and impacts societal institutions.

Satirizing Anti-Gay Institutions

As is the case with pervasive discrimination, mocking individuals who hold these beliefs is often easier than satirizing centuries-old systems that maintain these disparities. **Institutionalized homophobia** happens when anti-gay attitudes and behaviors become the basis of policy, often in line with and reinforcing stereotypes. Similar to the issues about gender raised in Chapter 3, heteronormativity eliminates a nuanced understanding of humans' diverse lives in the interest of a single cisgendered, heterosexual, monogamous norm, which actively impedes the ability of those who are not "straight" to thrive. For decades, non-heterosexual interactions were framed as perverse and deviant according to production codes adopted by the Hollywood film industry, same-sex relations were illegal and punishable by vice squads that raided spaces where gay men were rumored to congregate, and gay and queer people could legally be fired from their jobs simply for their sexuality and gender presentation.

Furthermore, discourse that focuses on the individual, including predictors of homosexuality or lifestyle trends, inhibits larger discussions about the widespread discrimination targeting gay and queer communities (Wilcox 2003) and support for institutional change (Garretson and Suhay 2016). We never get to discussions about unequal treatment in healthcare (Thoreson 2018), education (Casey and Levesque 2018), the workplace (Bussewitz and Pisani 2020; Galupo and Resnick 2016), and the legal system (Davidoff and Nadal 2013; Jones 2021a). Although individual homophobes may not directly contribute to the institutional disparities, they rely on and reinforce these discriminatory practices. In a particularly perfect line from "Homer's Phobia," Homer explicates his attitudes toward gay people when John asks him what he has against gay people: "You know! It's—. It's not usual. If there was a law, it would be against it." The irony of this line is that there *have* been laws, and they *have* been against gay people.

This gay-as-societal-threat described above is repeated through instructional videos of the 1950s, in which young people were taught how to spot a homosexual and the supposed associated dangers. The classic 10-minute propaganda film *Boys Beware* (1955) warns viewers of the dangers of homosexuality and define a "homosexual" as "...a person who demands an intimate relationship with members of their own sex." The film features four vignettes about young boys being kidnapped, assaulted, or murdered and informs boys to be wary of men who are "...too friendly, or try to win your confidence too quickly" because they were sick. They had "...a sickness that was not visible like smallpox, but no less dangerous and contagious; a sickness of the mind." The film is a harmful but essential part of American history, and satirical outlets like *Family Guy* have pointed to the absurdities of dehumanizing gay people through supposedly educational media.

You've Got a Gay! (*Family Guy*, S4E25, FOX 2006)
In the *Family Guy* episode, "You May Now Kiss the...Uh...Guy Who Receives" (2006; S4E25), there is a brief 42-second parody educational video entitled "The Homosexual and You; Produced by Pat Robertson Industries," which provides tips to tell "when you've got a gay." The film cuts to two men on the couch. One asks the other, "What's your favorite Madonna album?" to which the off-camera narrator replies, "If his answer is anything but 'I've never bought one 'you've got a gay!'" The scene freezes and the offending man is stamped with red text reading, GAY. The film then cuts to a man in a

Figure 4.3 This brief but spectacular cutaway requires the audience to be aware of a wide array of historial trends This brief but spectacular cutaway. Stills from You've Got a Gay (*Family Guy* 2006).

doctor's office having blood taken. The off-camera narrator says, "If instead of human blood, you find a deadly corrosive acid, you've got a gay!" An alien then bursts from the patient's chest and attacks the doctor, who shoots it dead with a shotgun.

The scene repeats homophobic and anti-gay stereotypes and then amplifies and exaggerates these sentiments to reveal their extreme ridiculousness. Making assumptions about sexuality from taste in music is commonplace but is one end of a spectrum of assumptions and that reinforce the perception that gay people are inherently different. By jumping from musical preferences to corrosive acid for blood and a massive bloodthirsty alien, the brief clip plays on historical trends about the dehumanization of gay people that were embedded in social guidance videos, like *Boys Beware*, highlights the spectrum of anti-gay stereotypes that build on each other, and mocks institutionalized homophobia.

From 1945 to 1955, there was an effort to systematically purge all gay and lesbian individuals from the State Department, Civil Service, and any public office because their sexuality made them vulnerable to blackmail by foreign powers, making them a threat to national security. This period is now known as the "Lavender Scare" (Johnson 2009) and used the existing biases to rationalize further discrimination: Society did not accept gay people and that social ostracism allowed them to be turned by foreign powers. This policy remained in place until 1973 when a federal judge ruled that a person's sexual orientation cannot be the sole reason for termination from federal employment.

This discriminatory chapter in American history is part of the same social moral panic of McCarthyism. However, McCarthyism and the Red Scare of the 1950s, which led to public congressional hearings and infamous blacklists that prevented people from working in various industries because they *might* have ties to communism are discussed more frequently. We rarely hear about the Lavender Scare even though this instance of institutionalized homophobia serves as important outcome of anti-gay attitudes of the time, and charted the trajectory of anti-queer rhetoric for decades to come. Although the 1973 ruling prevented explicit discrimination based on sexuality, Bill Clinton implemented "Don't Ask, Don't Tell" in 1995, which forced queer people to remain closeted to work in the military for almost two decades. This supposed compromise reinforced homophobic attitudes and an institutional expectation of keeping one's sexuality secret to work and live without retribution.

In recent years, religious exemption laws around the United States have also curtailed the advances of queer communities and sexual minorities. The **Religious Freedom Restoration Act (RFRA)** was established in 1993 to protect religious minorities from being penalized for religious practices that were against federal law (e.g., traditional Indigenous celebrations on federal land). It has since been deployed to protect *dominant* religious groups from anti-discrimination laws that largely seek to curtail anti-gay trends. The case of *Masterpiece Cake Shop v. Colorado Civil Rights Commission*, which pitted a bakery that refused to make a cake for a same-sex wedding against the Civil Rights Commission tasked with determining whether the company had broken the state's anti-discrimination law, garnered mainstream coverage in 2018, but "License to Discriminate" laws have had a much wider impact. These efforts seek to establish blanket exemptions for discrimination under claims of religious beliefs, allowing child welfare agencies,

Figure 4.4 Religious Objections (2019); *Source*: Berge, P. (1 May 2019) / Q Syndicate.

adoption agencies, and health providers to refuse service to gay and queer communities[6] (Human Rights Watch 2018).

This so-called "conscience rule" argues that a business can deny service based on firmly held religious beliefs, largely undermining the purpose of anti-discrimination laws in the first place.[7] In the above cartoon, the ambulance driver refuses to help a person in serious medical need because of his sexuality as indicated by a rainbow shirt. The driver then rationalizes this discrimination with market economics, ignoring the fact that they are the first responders on the scene. This cartoon is one of many at the time drawing attention to how legalizing interpersonal discrimination would continue to specifically harm gay and queer communities.

Satirizing Erasure: What about the Ls and the Bs?

Markedly absent through much of this conversation has been the representation of lesbians and bisexuals (the L and the B in LGBTQ). A content analysis of media prior to 1993 reveals an emphasis on gay men when addressing issues pertain to the gay and lesbian community, including in journalism, entertainment, and advertising (Fejes and Petrich 1993). In 2016, a similar analysis of film and television revealed a continued focus on White gay men, with an absence of women, people of color, and non-heterosexual sexualities other than gay (Smith et al. 2016).

Historically, gay men have threatened a hegemonic patriarchy that advantages cisgendered heterosexual men through very traditional (hegemonic) masculinity (see Chapter 3). In the wake of the 1970s, advertisers and brands became increasingly aware of the gay community as viable consumers but focused specifically on middle-class to upper-class White men (Badgett 2003), furthering the representation of this group while ignoring other sexual identities, such as lesbian and bisexual people. This lack of representation in media effectively limited the general public's awareness of diversity within the gay community, complicating the process of satirizing their experiences.

For lesbians, the lack of representation in mainstream media has been amplified by the misrepresentation of women in American media. Women's culture, from the mystique of what happens in the bathroom to the intimacy of relationships between women, has always been largely shrouded from the mainstream audience (read: heterosexual men). Whereas gay male desire has been framed as disgusting and sinister to heterosexual men, physical relationships between women have repeatedly been shown for the excitement of the same audience in line with the male gaze (see Chapter 3). In this space, lesbian satire has been largely framed as a feminist

---

6 This also includes women seeking medical services like birth control or abortions.
7 Racial discrimination was also rationalized using firmly held religious beliefs. Biblical stories like the "Curse of Ham" from the Book of Genesis was deployed to explain why people with darker skin should be systematically punished through slavery for the wrongdoings of their ancestors, and in the 1965 the judge who refused the appeal of Richard and Mildred Loving said, "Almighty God created the races white, black, yellow, malay and red and he placed them on separate continents... [showing] that he did not intend for the races to mix" (*Loving v. Commonwealth*, 1966).

endeavor. That is, the absence of lesbians and gay women in media is seen as a part of the mediated misrepresentation of women in general and lesbian satire is often considered feminist satire despite its unique intersectionality.

The Rule (*Dykes to Watch Out For*, Bechdel 1985)
The strip features two women, ostensibly on a date, walking past a movie theater, debating whether to see a movie. One turns to the other and outlines her "rule" for seeing movies. It must satisfy three basic requirements: "ONE, it has to have at least two women in it who, TWO, talk to each other about, THREE, something besides a man." Ultimately, they realize that movies that meet these basic requirements are rare and opt instead to go home and make popcorn.

Meeting the "Bechdel Test," as is it now known, has historically been a major hurdle for Hollywood films. Although films from the 1930s and 1940s pass the test (bechdeltest.com), patterns in the media industry have amplified content that reinforces stereotypes, stunting conversations about different groups. Fewer than half of Oscar-nominated Best Picture films from 1929 to 2017 pass the test (BBC.com). Furthermore, entire categories in the 2020 nominations lacked films that met this low bar despite widespread coverage of the issue. Many eked out a pass with characters whose names were not mentioned in the dialogue itself (e.g., *Joker*), indicating a greater issue with female representation in media writ large: Fewer than one-third of named characters (i.e., not "woman #2) were female (Smith et al. 2016). In addition, even movies that are considered progressive on issues of class, sexuality, and race (e.g., *Moonlight, Slumdog Millionaire*) fail the test demonstrating that the intersectionality of women is often missing in mainstream culture.

Figure 4.5 The Rule comic established what has come to be known as the "Bechdel Test" for gender representation in movies (*Dykes to Watch Out For*, Bechdel 1985).

The issue of gender disparity goes beyond simply gender visibility. The pervasive problem is that single female characters exist in a world of men, commonly referred to as the *Smurfette problem*. This problem limits movies' ability to talk about women, and the diversity of womanhood, with honesty and nuance. Women in films are more likely to talk about men on screen, reiterating assumptions of heterosexuality. As a result, women are not framed as dynamic individuals with sexualities beyond heterosexual relationships. This absence impacts all women but is uniquely problematic for queer women who have been woefully underrepresented in the mediated fights for queer rights. The strip itself, drawn from a larger queer comic series, inadvertently reveals that queer marginalization processes have affected queer and non-queer people alike.

Similarly, conversations regarding bisexuality and pansexuality, or being emotionally or physically attracted to more than one gender, have been largely absent from mainstream media, causing many to question whether bisexuality and pansexuality are stable or valid identities (Burke and LaFrance 2018). Discussions regarding bisexuality and pansexuality are further complicated given the assumption that sexual identity ends when one is in a monogamous relationship and thus not actively engaging in relationships with multiple partners of different genders. Both straight and gay people describe bisexual people as indecisive, confused, focused on sex, and prone to promiscuity (Burke and LaFrance 2018). These stereotypes persist even though approximately 3% of Americans identify as bisexual, which is technically more than half (54.6%) of LGBTQ adults in the United States (Jones 2021b). The absence of bisexuality and pansexuality in cultural discussions regarding sexuality also allows these negative stereotypes to flourish despite a relatively progressive shift in attitudes toward gay communities.

Because conversations about bisexuality and pansexuality have been so nonexistent, satirists cannot reliably count upon audiences to have an awareness about the complexity of this identity. Artifacts run the risk of being misinterpreted by audiences, a major concern for risk-averse industry-generated content. Refreshingly, this concern applies less to user-generated content shared via digital and social media. Bisexual and pansexual content creators have shared and amplified their own experiences independent of industry gatekeepers in recent years, producing intriguing and valuable content satirizing the process of bisexual marginalization.

Bisexual Makeup Tutorial (Amy Geliebter 2015)
Amy Geliebter describes all of these stereotypes and more in a 2015 YouTube beauty tutorial parody that was covered in several mainstream media outlets. In the four-minute video, Amy takes the viewer through her daily makeup ritual, highlighting each featured product for the camera. A voiceover elaborates how each component serves as a metaphor for bisexual discrimination experienced from the gay and straight communities, interpersonal interactions, and media representations.

> The first thing I'm going to do is start with a nice, clean, moisturized face. This is to simulate the clean slate that we're all born with before homophobia and societal gender norms are shoved down our throats.

Figure 4.6 Social media provides a space for new genres (e.g., makeup tutorial video) and marginalized discussions (e.g., experiences of bisexual people) to enter the mainstream sphere. Geliebter's litany of absurdities is magnified by the genre's quick editing and direct to camera address. Thumbnail from Bisexual Makeup Tutorial (Amy Geliebter 2015).

For my foundation, I'll be applying straight passing privilege. And you can repeat this myth using either the straight community or the LGBTQ community. That's what's so great about being bisexual, you're just not accepted anywhere!

Next, I'll be using a contour kit that has about as many different shades of powder as there are sexual identities and gender identities within the queer community, but we don't want equal representation so we're going to use a very select few.

I'll be highlighting right underneath my brow bone and in the inner corners of my eye. This is primarily to draw attention to my eyes so that I can better seduce men and women and ruin the relationships of both straight and lesbian couples.

The last step is to apply a nice nude lip gloss. I'll be using the shade Taboo. What's great about this color is that it ensures the taboo word "bisexual" never leaves your lips. You can find this shade of lip gloss most frequently used in the show Orange is the New Black where the main character is bisexual, but the word "bisexual" is never actually used.

Each line reveals Geliebter's frustration with anti-bisexual stereotypes. The pattern quickly becomes evident: Show the product, describe the experience of being bisexual, then sarcastically underline how these experiences reveal and reinforce the dehumanization of bisexual people. By doing so in the format of a makeup tutorial, the audience learns how to create a face that is acceptable in public while being walked through misunderstandings of this sizable community. The video was shared widely and featured in prominent mainstream media outlets including HuffPost and

> **Activity 4.3 Satirizing Social Media Erasure: Creating Representation via Visibility**
>
> "Whereas visibility refers to the extent to which a group is present, representation refers to the extent to which the needs of the group are actively addressed in other societal institutions. Just because a group is visible in culture does not mean that they are accurately represented politically, economically, or socially via media" (L'Pree 2014).
>
> Visibility is the first step to representation, and events like National Coming Out Day every October 11 and concepts like Gay Pride are political. They are designed to bring attention and visibility to a community that has been historically repressed and made invisible, thereby honing a cohesive voice through which to demand representation, political and social. In the twenty-first century, an opportunity for visibility has been defined by social media, allowing historically marginalized people to speak out. However, if you are not sensitized to this content or do not actively seek it out, it will most likely not appear in your social media feed given the deployment of algorithms to provide content to users that adhere to their beliefs and preferences.
>
> Search online for prominent bloggers, vloggers, influencers, and comedians who identify with sexualities you are not familiar with or do not receive attention in the mainstream media. These might include asexual, lesbian, bisexual, and polyamorous sexualities. In their artifacts, what are they laughing at? How do they make evident the marginalization processes to which they are subjected, either dispassionately or satirically?

Cosmopolitan because it addressed a common experience that bisexual people continue to share on social media (Patil 2017; Hope 2021).

Laughing at Sexuality in the Twenty-First Century

Through platforms including industry-generated content in legacy media and user-generated content on social media, the twenty-first century has seen greater awareness of the full spectrum of sexuality and a much broader conversation about sexuality and intersectionality. For decades, the most frequent representation of sexual minorities was that of White gay men, which is repeated in many of the featured examples. Even as the larger society has become more intersectionally aware, White gay men contine to be overrrpresented in popular media. A 2016 study on diversity and entertainment in industry-generated film and television by Smith, Chouieti, and Pieper revealed that, of more than 11,000 speaking characters, only 231 identified as LGBTQ or 2% of the overall sample. Of these 231 characters, 72.1% were male and 78.9% were White showing a continued prevalence of White men in overall queer representation.

Despite this continued focus on White men in representations of the gay community, other segments of the community have made their voices heard and presence felt. They have spoken out about issues pertaining to sexuality, race, class, socioeconomic status (SES), religion, and ability to draw attention to unique marginalization processes, past and present. Recalling Daniel Loftus' essay X analyzing "Gay Wedding" from *Key and Peele*, the sketch's cast features prominent Black actors including Lance Riddick, Romany Malco, Vernee Watson-Johnson, and Gary Williams. The satire works regardless of whether the viewer is Black or aware of the unique homophobia within the Black (largely church-going) American community. But for viewers who are sensitized to this struggle, seeing actors that are known for their family roles (e.g., Vernee Watson-Johnson played Will Smith's mother on *The Fresh Prince of Bel Air*), the satire hits differently; one's family may be theoretically willing but also incapable of understanding that gay people are people.

Similarly, the socioeconomic struggles within the gay community have also received greater attention. As described in Chapter 2, complex SES and class issues are often absent from mainstream media due to the class-based disparities within the entertainment industry. But in recent years, nuanced stories of gay individuals in diverse economic strata have emerged on social media, fostering a robust conversation about the intersection of sexuality and socioeconomic status.

> "My name is Dewayne Perkins. I am a poor, gay, Black man. Technically, if I were to prioritize it, it'd be Black first, because that's what you see when you see me. And I would put poor before gay, simply because I would pretend to be straight for money. Love d*ck, but love financial stability more!"
> – Comedian Dewayne Perkins (Comedy Central 2019)

These stories have combatted the **myth of gay affluence** or the pervasive belief that gay people occupy an "affluent, well-educated, professional elite" with greater expendable income to spend on luxury goods (Badgett 2003). This myth is contrary to the lived experiences of gay and queer people, who are more likely to be rejected from their families, kicked out of their homes, and experience poverty at a higher rate than their non-gay counterparts. A greater percentage of gay (20.5%) and bisexual (25.5%) men live at or below the federal poverty line compared to heterosexual (15.3%) men, (Badgett et al. 2013), 27% of LGBT adults expeirenced food insecurity compared to 17% of non-LGBT adults (Brown et al. 2016), and LGBTQ youth aged 18–25 experience a 120% greater chance of encountering homelessness (Gibbard Kline 2018). Furthermore, lower-SES gay individuals may experience more anti-gay hostility in their communities as well as classism from the mainstream gay community, resulting in riskier behaviors than their higher-SES counterparts (McGarrity 2014).

These conversations are still largely shrouded from large parts of the population and mainstream media even though social media features more voices telling more honest stories. This, combined with the fact that a greater percentage of younger Americans identify as something "other than completely straight" (Ingraham 2015), has prompted a surge in gay-positive and queer-positive online communities (Jenzen 2019) that use humor to address systematic oppression: Check out the hashtag #bisexual on TikTok, which is populated by young people simultaneously commenting on and laughing at changing world. However, there are important things to remember when creating satire that focuses on issues of sexuality.

What we don't understand about sexuality is still much bigger than what we understand or think we understand. The individuated nature of sexuality, i.e., sexuality is something that we experience as individuals, encourages solipsistic approaches to the sexuality of others, for example, the sense of disgust regarding sexual activities in which we do not personally participate in some cases or the sheer disbelief that someone could experience intimacy in a manner that we do not. This solipsism may seem ridiculous, but it forms the basis of institutional discrimination against sexual minorities. The broad range of sexuality has existed since the dawn of mankind, but our awareness and our language is changing, and the absurdity of this cultural lag is ripe for satire.

Gay people are still denied equal treatment in many institutions because they are not heterosexual. Although the fight for marriage equality was the benchmark for years, attaining it does not signal the end of the fight. One of the major "culture wars" of the twenty-first century is a clash between conservative religious ideologies and inclusive, progressive secular ideologies. Being gay is not easy or fun even though it may appear so in certain media content. Learn, explore, and then consider your own awakenings to recognize that the sexual norms you have been exposed to are a limited subset of the human condition. Understanding and helping others to understand complex disparities and discrimination should be the goal of a good satirist.

Sexuality is not a choice, but a willingness to explore oneself is. Self-exploration is hard, as is changing one's perspective of the world. Left to our own devices, we may choose to remain oblivious to many of our own emotional and physical desires. When we become more attuned to ourselves and the world around us, we may come to realize that we can attain satisfying intimacy in spaces and with people we had not considered before, or we may realize that the intimacy we have been seeking all along is the most satisfying. When satirizing sexuality, or specifically the marginalization processes regarding sexuality, making fun of people for their sexuality is lazy and can perpetuate a discriminatory history. Instead, consider the choices being made by everyone involved: The choice to be happy and proud of one's sexuality; the choice to deny goods and service to people because of their sexuality; and the choice to acknowledge, accept and learn from people whose intimate experiences are different.

Additional Activities

Activity 4.4 Marriage Equality: What's left to laugh at?
Marriage equality, the legal recognition of dyadic unions between consenting adults regardless of gender, has been a flagship issue for civil rights during the late twentieth and early twenty-first century. Although the Supreme Court determined in 2015 in the case of *Obergefell v. Hodges* that the fundamental right to marry is guaranteed to all couples according to the Fourteenth Amendment. However, this ruling emerged only after decades of back and forth at the state and national level. Arguments centered not just on marriage but all of the advantages that come with marriage, like spousal employment benefits, right to care, and tax exemptions.

(Continued)

> (Continued)
>
> Review a timeline of marriage equality in the United States and consider how these issues are still at play even though government-sanctioned marriages are legal for gay and queer people. This is an issue that we will return to regarding race in the next chapter, but the idea that discrimination is over can make it difficult if not impossible for people to realize that major disparities still exist. *How do we satirize the plight of gay people when there is a pervasive sense that the issues have been solved?*

> **Activity 4.5 Recurring Gay Characters**
>
> Although the lovable homophobe continues to be a classic American media trope designed to address issues of anti-gay prejudice and discrimination, there was a dearth of recurring gay characters for the better part of the twentieth century. Billy Crystal played Jodie Dallas on *SOAP* (1977–1981), the gay son of a wealthy family in a satirical soap opera. The role was met with praise by some for creating a gay lens through which Americans could see the effects of homophobia and anti-gay discrimination. Others saw the stereotypical tropes of closeting and conversion as well as role being played by a straight actor.
>
> The 1990s brought several gay characters into American homes: Pedro in *The Real World: San Francisco* on MTV (1994), Rickie Vasquez in *My So-Called Life* on FOX (1994–1995), Ellen in *Ellen* on ABC (1994–1998), and eventually, Will Truman and Jack McFarland in *Will and Grace* on NBC (1998–2006). Today, gay characters can be found across network, cable, and streaming platforms. *Choose a current recurring character on one of your favorite programs and assess how the character deals with anti-gay stereotypes, prejudice, and discrimination. When is humor used? Does it point to the absurdity of the treatment, or does it downplay the severity of the event? What makes this perspective unique compared to guest gay characters dealing with the same issues? How?*

References

American Experience. (n.d.). Boys Beware – 1955 [video]. PBS. www.pbs.org/wgbh/americanexperience/features/stonewall-boys-beware.

Badgett, M.L. (2003). *Money, Myths, and Change: The Economic Lives of Lesbians and Gay Men*. University of Chicago Press.

Badgett, M.V., Durso, L.E., and Schneebaum, A. (2013). New patterns of poverty in the lesbian, gay, and bisexual community. https://williamsinstitute.law.ucla.edu/publications/lgb-patterns-of-poverty (accessed 16 May 2022).

Balay, A. (2014). *Steel Closets: Voices of Gay, Lesbian, and Transgender Steelworkers*. UNC Press Books.

Bechdel, A. (1 October 1985). *Dykes to Watch Out For*. Firebrand Books.

References

Brown, T.N.T., Romero, A.P., and Gates, G.J. (2016). Food insecurity and SNAP participation in the LGBT community. https://williamsinstitute.law.ucla.edu/publications/lgbt-food-insecurity-snap (accessed 16 May 2022).

Burke, S.E. and LaFrance, M. (2018). Perceptions of instability and choice across sexual orientation groups. *Group Processes & Intergroup Relations* 21 (2): 257–279.

Bussewitz, C. and Pisani, J. (18 June 2020). Even with ruling, workplace still unequal for LGBTQ workers. https://apnews.com/article/6a8e597cedff63f21f1646da90c8f2a9 (accessed 5 May 2022).

Byers, D. (26 November 2012). *AP Nixes 'Homophobia', 'Ethnic Cleansing'*. Politico.

Casey, L. and Levesque, E.M. (2018). LGBTQ students face discrimination while Education Department walks back oversight. Brookings.

Clarkson, J. (2008). The limitations of the discourse of norms: Gay visibility and degrees of transgression. *Journal of Communication Inquiry* 32 (4): 368–382.

Comedy Central. (22 September 2014). Key & Peele – Gay wedding advice. YouTube. https://www.youtube.com/watch?v=rtgY1q0J_TQ.

Comedy Central Stand-Up. (12 November 2019). When you're turned on by "scared straight" – Dewayne Perkins – Stand-up featuring [Video]. YouTube. https://www.youtube.com/watch?v=TGXS5rjuy-c (accessed 5 May 2022)

The Daily Show with Trevor Noah. (4 September 2019). America endures another mass shooting & Jaboukie explains why guns are gay | The Daily Show [video]. YouTube. www.youtube.com/watch?v=dCf4_qQOKgQ.

Davidoff, K.C. and Nadal, K.L. (April 2013). LGBT issues in the criminal justice system. Divison 44 Newsletter. www.apadivisions.org/division-44/publications/newsletters/division/2013/04/lgbt-issues.

Fejes, F. and Petrich, K. (1993) Invisibility, homophobia and heterosexism: Lesbians, gays and the media. *Critical Studies in Mass Communication* 10 (4): 395–422.

Galupo, M.P. and Resnick, C.A. (2016). Experiences of LGBT microaggressions in the workplace: Implications for policy. In: *Sexual Orientation and Transgender Issues in Organizations* (ed. T. Köllen), 271–287. Springer.

Garretson, J. and Suhay, E. (2016). Scientific communication about biological influences on homosexuality and the politics of gay rights. *Political Research Quarterly* 69 (1): 17–29.

Geliebter, A. (15 February 2015). Bisexual makeup tutorial [video]. YouTube. www.youtube.com/watch?v=YHwdLZldThU.

Ghaziani, A. (10 June 2018). Op-Ed: What we really mean when we talk about acceptance of gay people. Los Angeles Times.

Gibbard Kline, M. (12 February 2018). *Centering Youth of Color and LGBTQ Youth People in Efforts to End Homelessness*. United States Interagency Council on homelessness.

Groening, M., (Writer), Brooks, J., (Writer), Simon, S., (Writer), and Anderson, M., (Director) (16 February 1997). Homer's Phobia [Television series episode]. In: *The Simpsons* (ed. J. Brooks et al.). 20th Century Fox Television.

Gross, L. (1991). Out of the mainstream: Sexual minorities and the mass media. *Journal of Homosexuality* 21 (1–2): 19–46.

HBO. (1 February 2010). Wanda Sykes: I'ma Be Me – Gay vs. Black (HBO). YouTube. www.youtube.com/watch?v=1_wWJ-_4uSY.

Hope, S. (24 February 2021). 30 jokes about being bisexual that low-key are basically me. Buzzfeed.

Ingraham, C. (24 August 2015). One third of millennials now say they're less than 100% straight. Washington Post.

Jenzen, O. (31 January 2019). LGBTQ teenagers are creating new online subcultures to combat oppression. https://theconversation.com/lgbtq-teenagers-are-creating-new-online-subcultures-to-combat-oppression-110848 (accessed 5 May 2022).

Johnson, D.K. (2009). *The Lavender Scare: The Cold War Persecution of Gays and Lesbians in the Federal Government*. Chicago, IL: University of Chicago Press.

Jones, A. (2 March 2021a). Visualizing the unequal treatment of LGBTQ people in the criminal justice system. Prison Policy. www.prisonpolicy.org/blog/2021/03/02/lgbtq.

Jones, J. (24 February 2021b). LGBT identification rises to 5.6% in Latest US estimate. Gallup.

Lear, N., (Writer), Styler, B., (Writer), Speight, J., (Writer), and Rich, J., (Director) (9 February 1971). Judging books by covers. In: *All in the Family* (ed. N. Lear). Tandem Productions.

Loving v. Commonwealth, 206 (V.A. Sup. Ct. 6163).

L'Pree, C. (12 October 2014). Visibility and representation. The Media Made Me Crazy. https://charisselpree.me/2014/10/12/visibility-and-representation.

MacFarlane, S., (Writer), Zuckerman, D., (Writer), Goodman, D., (Writer), and Polcino, D., (Director). (30 April 2006). You may now kiss the... uh... guy who receives [Television series episode]. In: *Family Guy* (ed. S. MacFarlene and C. Sheridan). 20th Century Fox Television.

Marlens, N., (Writer), Black, C., (Writer), Rosenthal, D., (Writer), and Junger, G., (Director). (30 April 1997). The Puppy Episode [Ellen]. American Broadcasing Company.

Martin, K.A. and Kazyak, E. (2009). Hetero-romantic love and heterosexiness in children's G-rated films. *Gender & Society* 23 (3): 315–336.

McGarrity, L.A. (2014). Socioeconomic status as context for minority stress and health disparities among lesbian, gay, and bisexual individuals. *Psychology of Sexual Orientation and Gender Diversity* 1 (4): 383–397.

Miller, P.R., Flores, A.R., Haider-Markel, D.P., Lewis, D.C., Tadlock, B.L., and Taylor, J.K. (2017). Transgender politics as body politics: Effects of disgust sensitivity and authoritarianism on transgender rights attitudes. *Politics, Groups, and Identities* 5 (1): 4–24.

Moore, P. (20 August 2015). A third of young Americans say they aren't 100% heterosexual. YouGov.

Padva, G. (2008). Educating The Simpsons: Teaching queer representations in contemporary visual media. *Journal of LGBT Youth* 5 (3): 57–73.

Patil, A. (24 May 2017). 22 Tweets for bisexuals who are just tired of the bullshit. Buzzfeed.

Putnam, A. (2013). Mean ladies: Transgendered villains in Disney films. In: *Diversity in Disney Films* (ed. J. Cheu). Jefferson, NC: McFarland & Company, Inc.

Russell, G.M. and Bohan, J.S. (2006). The case of internalized homophobia: Theory and/as practice. *Theory & Psychology* 16 (3): 343–366.

Sharmin, T. and Sattar, S. (2018). Gender politics in the projection of "Disney" villains. *Journal of Literature and Art Studies* 8 (1): 53–57.

Shurlock, G. (1947). The motion picture production code. *The Annals of the American Academy of Political and Social Science* 254 (1): 140–146.

Smith, B. A., Murib, Z., Motta, M., Callaghan, T. H., and Theys, M. (2018). "Gay" or "homosexual"? The implications of social category labels for the structure of mass attitudes. *American Politics Research* 46 (2): 336–372.

Smith, S., Choueiti, M., and Pieper, K. (2016) Gender bias without borders. Geena Davis Institute on Gender in Media. seejane.org/wp-content/uploads/gender-bias-without-borders-full-report.pdf.

Smith, S.L., Choueiti, M., and Pieper, K. (2016). Comprehensive Annenberg report on diversity in entertainment. USC Annenberg. https://annenberg.usc.edu/sites/default/files/2017/04/07/MDSCI_CARD_Report_FINAL_Exec_Summary.pdf.

So who's the boy in the relationship? The whole point of Lesbianism is that there are no boys. (October 2020). imgflip. https://imgflip.com/i/4kq1xh.

Spiegelhalter, D. (5 April 2015). Is 10% of the population really gay? https://www.theguardian.com/society/2015/apr/05/10-per-cent-population-gay-alfred-kinsey-statistics.

Terrizzi Jr, J.A., Shook, N.J., and Ventis, W.L. (2010). Disgust: A predictor of social conservatism and prejudicial attitudes toward homosexuals. *Personality and Individual Differences* 49 (6): 587–592.

Thoreson, R. (23 July 2018). You don't want second best. Human Rights Watch.

Travis Nuckolls. (14 Feb 2008). When Did You Choose to be Straight? YouTube. https://www.youtube.com/watch?v=QJtjqLUHYoY.

Weinberg, G. (1972). *Society and the Healthy Homosexual*. New York: St. Martin's Press.

Werthein, B. et al. (4 May 2019). What is camp? The Met Gala 2019 theme, explained. New York Times.

Wilcox, S.A. (2003). Cultural context and the conventions of science journalism: Drama and contradiction in media coverage of biological ideas about sexuality. *Critical Studies in Media Communication* 20 (3): 225–247.

5

Satirizing Race

> *"To be a Negro in this country and to be relatively conscious is to be in a rage almost all the time."*
> —James Baldwin

Race is one of the most contentious topics in American discourse. This is due in part to the extended racialized (racist) history of the United States coupled with a desperate desire to deny and disavow that history. Race is largely a salient characteristic that has an automatic effect on cognition, meaning that race impacts every interaction, but our collective refusal to discuss race means that we often don't understand *how* race impacts every action. Everyone has an opinion regarding race but few of those opinions are grounded in science, psychology, history, or reality because of a collective lack of understanding about how race operates. This chapter will describe the construction of race, the operationalization of White and the absurdity of trends in racialized discourse.

Black, White, Red, Yellow, Purple, Green: Defining Race

A **race** is a group of people who have been clustered for social, economic, and legal purposes according to a set of shared characteristics. Although related and often used synonymously, race is different from ethnicity. Whereas **ethnicity** refers to one's cultural upbringing and the social practices of the group in which one was raised, race is a category involuntarily imposed on people because of some characteristic. People who share a race may not always share an ethnicity. For example, Black Americans are ethnically distinct from Black Brits, Black Brazilians, or Black Caribbeans, despite all of these groups being categorized as Black. Similarly White Americans are ethnically distinct from White Brits, White Brazilians, or White Caribbeans. A shorthand way to distinguish race and ethnicity is to define ethnicity as *internal* categorization, related to one's social experiences growing up. By comparison, race is an *external* categorization by others that aggregates people for social, economic, and legal purposes. So, if race is not a reliable indicator of one's ethnicity or experiences, why do we rely on it so heavily?

Diversity and Satire: Laughing at Processes of Marginalization, First Edition.
Charisse L'Pree Corsbie-Massay.
© 2023 John Wiley & Sons, Inc. Published 2023 by John Wiley & Sons, Inc.

Starting in the sixteenth century, a social need emerged to distinguish people based on their geographic origins to determine their value (and superiority) as global migration increased. In 1775, Johann Friedrich Blumenbach proposed five races of "man" in his book *On The Natural Varieties of Mankind*: Caucasoid (of European ancestry), Ethiopian or Negroid (of African ancestry), American Indian, Mongolian (of East Asian and Polynesian descent, as well as some parts of the Americas like indigenous Alaskans), and Australoid, which included Australian Aboriginals and other people of South Asian descent. Along with the theory of **polygenism**, the defunct theory that different races of humans evolved independently of each other, these categories were considered scientific fact and deployed to rationalize discriminatory treatment. People of African origin were deemed to be intellectually and socially inferior to people of European origin, a distinction that was then used to rationalize their enslavement.

The idea that one's ability, personality, and value are associated with a given geographic region still impacts our understanding of people today. One's **phenotype** (the set of observable characteristics of an individual resulting from the interaction of its genetics with the environment, e.g., hair color, height, muscular structure) does not automatically or reliably indicate where people are from or their culture. It is often said that race is a social construct because the categories that we use to define race emerge through historical social conflict. However, the fact of this social construction does not temper its implications and impacts. We categorize others based on characteristics that *we* deem to be important even though these characteristics may be inconsequential to the person we are categorizing.

What Kind of Asian Are You? (Ken Tanaka 2013)

Figure 5.1 A man of European descent approaches a woman of East Asian descent to strike up a conversation; small talk about the weather quickly devolves into racial stereotypes. Still from What kind of Asian are you? (Ken Tanaka 2013).

In this 2013 YouTube video by Ken Tanaka, a woman of East Asian descent and a man of European descent are running along a trail. He approaches her and strikes up a conversation. After discussing the weather, he asks, "Where are you from? Your

English is perfect." She replies, "San Diego. We speak English there." He brushes off her response, and repeats his question slower and with exaggerated hand gestures: "Where... are you... *from*?"

> SHE: Well, I was born in Orange County, but I never actually lived there.
> HE: No, I mean before that.
> SHE: [incredulously] Before I was born?
> HE: [clarifying] Where are your people from?
> SHE: Well, my great grandma is from Seoul.
> HE: [excitedly] Korean! I knew it! I was like, she's either Japanese or Korean. But I was leaning more towards Korean.
> SHE: [exhausted] Amazing.
> HE: [presses hands together and bows slightly] Ahm-sha-SEE-nah.[1] There's a really good teriyaki barbeque place near my apartment. I actually really like kimchi!
> SHE : Cool....

This brief interaction reveals an all-too-common experience in the United States, which was constructed as a European colony in the sixteenth century. Therefore, those who are not of European descent are often interpreted as *recent* immigrants (i.e., one or two generations removed). In the video, the woman answers his question "where are you from" truthfully, it becomes clear that he is interested in her ancestors' heritage, not her personal identity. When he finally learns that her family is of Korean descent, he excitedly shares his limited knowledge of Korean culture: He makes a small bow, mentions a Korean barbeque place near his home, expresses his love of kimchi (a traditional Korean dish of pickled cabbage) and delivers a formal greeting in mispronounced Korean. The small piece of information about one of her distant ancestors leads him to focus on her Korean-ness, ignoring clear similarities, like residing in the same geographic region (Southern California) and engaging in a similar activity (jogging). He substitutes his own assumptions about her even after she explains those assumptions are incorrect and illogical (i.e., where she is from *before* she was born).

Throughout the interaction, the camera cuts between closeups of the man and the woman. The audience sees his pride in being able to rattle off Korean trivia and her resulting disbelief and frustration. The full absurdity of his question "Where are you *really* from?" is revealed in the second half of the clip when she flips the question and asks him, "What about you? Where are you from?"

> HE: San Francisco.
> SHE: [slower with exaggerated physical gestures] But where are you— from?
> HE: Oh. I'm just American.
> SHE: Really? You're Native American?
> HE: No. Just regular American.
> SHE: [stares in silence]
> HE: Oh, well, I guess my grandparents are from England.
> SHE: Oh, well— [in exaggerated cockney accent] 'Ello Guv'nah! What's all this then?! Top o' the mornin' to ya! Let's get a spot o' tea, a spot o' tea.

---

1 Annyeonghaseyo is a formal greeting in Korean, but his pronunciation is incorrect.

Double, Double, Toil and Trouble! Mind the gap!! Beware Jack the Ripper. BLOODY HELL!!! Pip Pip Cheerio! [returning to an American accent but still exaggerated] I think *your people's* fish and chips are *amazing*!
HE: You're weird.
SHE: Really? I'm weird? Must be a Korean thing.

Much like the segment "When did you choose to be straight" from Chapter 4, which flipped the question to reveal its underlying implications, he is stumped when faced with the same question he so casually asked her. She then goes into a tirade of British trivia, referencing warnings on the London subway, British phrases in an over-the-top accent (e.g., "Hello Governor!"), and traditional British food, mimicking his actions from earlier but which makes him uncomfortable and confused. Her response reveals how simply repeating catchphrases and cultural dishes as a way of communicating with people or connecting with their (assumed) culture is lazy, stereotypical, and ultimately offensive. These cultural affiliations from generations back are only a small part of her current identity, but dominated the interaction because she exhibited racialized features, or features that are assumed to signify ethnic information.

Activity 5.1 Who is a "Regular American"?

In the clip, "What kind of Asian are you," the man of European descent self-identifies as a "Regular American" but the woman of East Asian descent cannot be a "regular" American, revealing the conflation between race, ethnicity, and nationality. Regardless of her place of birth and upbringing, she is a *perpetual foreigner*, a phrase used to describe the inability of some groups to be fully integrated into American culture because of the social stereotypes associated with their characteristics. She explicitly says that her great-grandmother was from Seoul whereas his grandparents are from England, a brief interaction that reveals her family has been in the United States longer than his.

It is clear the categorization of who is "American" and by extension who deserves citizenship, rights, and ultimately respect is impacted by race more than time spent within the confines of the United States. Using the IAT (See Activity 1.4), Devos and Banaji (2005) revealed that Indigenous Americans are not associated with "American" as compared to European Americans even though most people explicitly consider Native Americans to be "more American" than European Americans. Revisit your examples from Activity 2.5 and consider how race plays into the rhetoric of the American Dream. How is the rhetoric of the American Dream interpreted by those who are not considered "regular Americans?"

The extent to which certain features are considered racialized is connected to the phrase "race is socially constructed." Over time, certain characteristics are determined by a society to indicate that a person is different from the dominant group, a process of othering, and changes between societies depending on current social, political, and economic contexts. A characteristic is **raced** when it is used to define whether a person belongs to a racial category that has been established independent of individual experiences. Racialized characteristics include relatively small external differences among people (e.g., skin tone, facial features, name, or accent) to make determinations about their individual qualities (e.g., intelligence, personality, or work ethic).[2] This process of **racialization**, using a single piece of information to "understand" a whole person,[3] perpetuates false notions of mental, emotional, and intellectual difference. This process relies on the same basic psychological tendencies that cause us to rely on heuristics or stereotypes as described in Chapter 1.

In 1968, Jane Elliott wanted to teach White third-grade children in Randall, Iowa, about race and discrimination in the wake of the assassination of Martin Luther King, Jr. She developed an exercise that manifested stereotypes, prejudice, and discrimination using eye color. Children were told that blue-eyed children were smarter than brown-eyed children. She effectively turned eye color into a racialized characteristic. Within minutes, the children began to make judgments about their classmates based on their eye color despite knowing each of them personally for years. The following day, she informed the children that she was mistaken, and the brown-eyed children were actually smarter. Their stereotypes, prejudice, and discrimination quickly reversed in line with the artificially constructed hierarchy. Elliott's exercise became national news, was featured in the 1970 news documentary *Eye of the Storm*, and has been repeated countless times since. Most importantly, this simple exercise reveals how quickly we can adopt and deploy racialized thinking around seemingly arbitrary characteristics without historical precedent.

Auto Erotic Assimilation (*Rick and Morty*, Adult Swim 2015)

Rick and Morty are a grandfather and grandson duo who, much like *Gulliver's Travels*, go on adventures around the universe and encounter different worlds that often satirize situations plaguing humanity. In this episode, they visit a world where everyone's consciousness is controlled by a singular entity named Unity. Summer, Morty's sister, argues that collective consciousness is wrong, and people should have their own agency even though all inhabitants treat each other with respect and work to solve problems, ensuring the world functions as best as possible for all. Eventually, Unity's control over the population is destroyed. As individuals awake from their collective stupor and regain their self-awareness, Summer asks, "Do all of you remember who you are?"

> RON: Yeah. My name is Ron Benson and I'm an electrical engineer, father of two, and as you can see from my flat concentric nipple rings, [rips open his button down shirt] I'm a member of this planet's top race!
>
> DEREK: I'm Derek Jefferson, I'm a landscaper, and I'll be damned if that ripple nipple bitch's race is superior. [pulls off his shirt] The cone nipple people will rule this world!
>
> RON: You shut your mouth you dirty knife-nipple bastard!
>
> DEREK: What did you say to me you target-chested piece of shit?!
>
> UNKNOWN PERSON: [runs screaming] RACE WAR!

---

2 Skin tone is an infinite spectrum, and constructing cohesive groups around skin tone is a futile task; people who are categorized as "Black" (i.e., of African descent) can be very light and people who are very dark may not be of African descent (e.g., South Asian or Indigenous). Clearly race is not simple, but we try to construct it as simply as possible.

3 Entire groups of people, or people who are members of a given group, or people who simply exhibit the characteristic even if they are not a member of the group. There are several examples of White people who have names that are considered to be Black: My Name is Jamal, I'm White (NPR Staff 2015); What it's like to be a white woman named LaKiesha (Blake 2019).

At this point, the entire population descends into a planet-wide brawl, reviving a long-standing feud that was suspended by Unity's collective control. Summer begs for calm, "Why are you fighting? Can't you see you're all the same?" To which Morty laughs, "Ah Summer! First race war, huh?" This moment reveals the ridiculousness inherent in which characteristics we racialize. Skin tone and other phenotypic features are the most salient **racial signifiers**, indicators of racial categories, but this choice is largely arbitrary. By building race around something as inconsequential as nipple shape, *Rick and Morty* demonstrate that the racialization of skin tone (and the subsequent racial strife on earth) is just as as silly. The last line from Morty ("First race war, huh?") also highlights that the process of racialization, making something from nothing and using it to attack others, is unfortunately standard human behavior.

When Religion is Raced

Religion is closely associated with ethnicity because it is an often important cultural component. A **religion** is a social group defined by shared ideology that invokes the sacred through the nature of existence, moral practices, and customs. Thus, those associated with a given religion share a system of beliefs that explicate what is moral and our grand purpose on this earth. A religion becomes raced when the followers of that religion and their families (including those who are non-practicing) are assumed to exhibit homogenous individual characteristics and stereotyped accordingly. Ken Tanaka's "What Kind of Asian Are You" (the first artifact in this chapter) could easily be deployed to comment on simplistic understandings of Muslims (e.g., "As-salamu alaykum") or Jewish people ("I really like bagels"). Similarly, the flip would be just as effective ("I think your people's ham is amazing").

The hegemonic religious hierarchy in the United States emerged alongside its racial hegemony and these parallel processes led to the racialization of religious groups. The United States was founded by Puritan Separatists who fled Europe to escape persecution from the Church of England and to establish the United States as a Christian nation. Early colonizers of the New World effectively escaped life at the bottom of the religious hierarchy in the Old World (i.e., Europe) to become the top of the religious hierarchy in the New World, perpetuating hegemony by persecuting those who did not adhere to their religious beliefs. "Puritans not only made it difficult for the people who lived among them, they made it impossible for anyone living alongside them" (Cullen 2004, p. 12). For example, Indigenous people were considered heathens because they did not adhere to a Christian god, which was used to justify their systematic genocide (Nunpa 2020). Despite rhetoric of religious freedom written into the nation's founding documents, the dominance of one religious group established a cultural environment where this religion is framed as normal. Other religions are marginalized or erased from the public sphere.

Consider the treatment of Muslims in the United States during the 20th century. Edward Said's 1978 book *Orientalism* documents the long-standing fascination of the West (i.e., United States, Western Europe) with the Middle East and the Muslim World. His concept of "orientalism" captures the lens through which we see that part of the world and the people who are associated with it. However, there are almost two billion Muslims worldwide. Not all people from the Middle East are Muslim, and not all Muslims are from the Middle East. However, this stereotypical association has dominated American understanding of this religious group along with popular culture stereotypes of people from the Middle East as backward, uncivilized (e.g., *Lawrence of Arabia*, 1962; *Aladdin*, 1992; *Dune*, 2021), and innately violent.

"Halal in the Family" (Funny or Die 2015)

This four-episode web series[4] by Assaf Mandvi parodies the classic American family sitcom with an over-the-top father, a well-meaning mom, and a couple of teenage kids who are trying to fit in at school. In the first episode, "B'ully" (Mandvi et al. 2015) daughter Whitney is being bullied online by a girl in her school, who posted a photoshopped picture of Whitney wearing a turban driving a taxi. Assif is outraged and says "That is terrible! We are not Sikhs!" Fatima, the mom, pushes back and reminds her husband that being miscategorized as a different religion is not the crux of the problem. Rather, the problems stems from the girl posting crude stereotypes online, to which Aasif responds, "Fine! But if you're gonna stereotype us, at least get it right. We don't wear turbans!" Later, Aasif tries to teach the girl from school how to be a better bully by showing her nuanced racist stereotypes of religions: Muslims are "terrorists," Sikhs are "towelheads," and the Amish are "sheep shaggers." The girl is outraged at the caricatures and acknowledges they are very offensive. Aasif agrees and tells her she has to be ready to go the distance with her racism. He then flips the board to reveal a picture tweeted by Barry West, a Nashville county commissioner, pointing a gun at the camera with the caption, "HOW TO WINK AT A MUSLIM" (2013). The girl is appalled.

This brief clip connects many different issues regarding racism, including stereotypes and prejudice, and reveals how they are deployed with respect to religion. More importantly, Mandvi highlights the spectrum of problematic discriminatory rhetoric, from simple caricatures to public posts from elected officials, in the

Figure 5.2 Assif Mandvi parodies the well-meaning but absent-minded father popular in eighties' sitcoms who teaches the next generation about bigotry through a hyper obsessive desire to assimilate into American mainstream (read: White) culture. Stills from "B'ully" *Halal in the Family* (2015).

---

4 The original pilot for the series was called *The Qu'osby Show* (Comedy Central, 2011) but was renamed post-production after the allegations against Bill Cosby gained national attention although many of the jokes including the ugly sweaters remained.

lighthearted and easily understood format of the American family sitcom and parodying the lovable bigot.

"Racist" is an Adjective

Racism is the ideology that all members of a given race possess common characteristics or abilities, which are used to distinguish them as inferior or superior to another race or races. Public discourse tends to focus on **individual racism**, or how individuals racialize others through their stereotypes, prejudices, and discrimination, but this focus on individual instances of racism are one small manifestation of racial disparities. **Institutionalized** (or systemic) **racism** refers to the larger social effects of these stereotypes, prejudices, and discriminatory behaviors when the belief that all members of a given race possess certain characteristics becomes the basis of policy and institutional decision-making. Much like individual and institutional homophobia as described in Chapter 4, individual and institutional racism work together to upload racial hierarchies and disparities and are therefore inseparable. As described earlier, race and racism are historically situated to establish and maintain power structures. Therefore, something is racist if it peptuates racial disparities by advantaging people who have been historically advantaged or disadvantaging people who have been historically disempowered.

It is important to consider the term "racist" as an adjective (an attribute of something else that perpetuates a racial hierarchy, e.g., racist attitudes, racist policies, racist language) and not a noun (e.g., a racist). When racist is used as a noun to refer to attitudes of an individual, these accusations can be easily denied by people claiming that they do not "hate" people of certain racial group or exhibiting a specific racialized characteristic, which is ultimately a distraction from the larger effects of racism. Instead, it is helpful to recognize that the collective actions of individuals exhibiting racial stereotypes, prejudice, and discrimination lead to institutional policies that reinforce racial disparities. Therefore, the focus should be on these institutional disparities, rather than debating whether an individual is or is not "a racist." Through this lens, understanding race means exploring the impact that race has and continues to have on human interactions.

Racist Timeout (*The Daily Show with Jon Stewart*, Comedy Central 2012)

On February 26, 2012, George Zimmerman pursued and shot 17-year-old Trayvon Martin in a gated community in Florida. Zimmerman claimed self-defense because he felt threatened and was not arrested according to Florida's Stand Your Ground (SYG) law. The case gained national attention and became a polarizing moment in national politics. In this 2012 clip from *The Daily Show with Jon Stewart*, Senior Black Correspondent Larry Wilmore talks about the real racism present in the case. Stewart acknowledges that the case is difficult to discuss because it devolves into people leveling or defending themselves against charges of racism. Wilmore then proposes a solution:

> WILMORE: That's why we are going to have a racist timeout. America, for the next five minutes no matter what is said, nobody is racist[5].... If we

---

[5] Stewart seems over the moon by the prospect of talking about race without immediately being called a racist. Wilmore tells him to calm down. At the end of the segment after time has run out, Stewart says, "I was gonna ask about cornrows!".

> remove accusations of racism, we can finally talk calmly about the racial elements of this story.
> STEWART: So, there is some racial elements in this story. Some racism in this story—.
> WILMORE: Are you kidding me Jon? We got a Hispanic guy with a Jewish name killing a Black guy?! It's gotta be in there *somewhere!*

Wilmore then proceeds to lay out the racial elements of the case without fear of being called racist. "Zimmerman sees a Black guy in a hoodie, but Black guys in hoodies have been reportedly breaking into homes, so noticing him is not racist, but maybe a little race-y..." Zimmerman then shot Martin and the police let him go but the police were following the law in Florida, which allows Zimmerman to use lethal force if he felt threatened.

> WILMORE: With this defense, you don't even have to go in front of a jury. You tell the cops at the scene of the crime that you were standing your ground and they'll give you the benefit of the doubt. That's the culprit!
> STEWART: Ah ha! The benefit of the doubt is racist!
> WILMORE: Exactly Jon.
> STEWART: [incredulously] Wait? Black people don't get the benefit of the doubt?
> WILMORE: In shooting cases?! It's the one entitlement that Black people can't get from the government! [audience groans] Oh shut up.
> STEWART: So, you think White people get more benefit of the doubt in shooting cases?
> WILMORE: Maybe not even consciously, Jon. But when Vice-President Cheney shot his friend in the face, 'Oh! it was just two White guys having fun with guns! Hey! You pumped your buddy full of birdshot? You didn't mean that! I give you the benefit of the doubt.' Come on Jon. Can you imagine if Obama shot Eric Holder in the face? Trust me. One of those n****rs would be going to jail. The only thing in doubt would be the length of the sentence.
> STEWART: [hesitantly] Did you just call President Obama the n-word?
> WILMORE: Of course not Jon. Give me the benefit of the doubt! [slyly] I was referring to Eric Holder.

The idea that the benefit of the doubt could be racist seems ridiculous until one digs deeper into the phenomenon. The *benefit of the doubt*, "a concession that a person or statement must be regarded as correct or justified, if the contrary has not been proven" (Oxford Languages), relies on how much one trusts and believes that another individual did not have nefarious intentions. The benefit of the doubt benefits members of groups already in power making it an apparatus of propagating (racial) power.[6] Majority and dominant groups are less stereotyped because of historical positions of power and diverse representations in media, resulting in a inferential bias in their favor. In a 2014 interview with the author, Wilmore described this segment as an

---

[6] Multiple analyses demonstrate that the implementation of SYG laws disproportionally align with pre-existing racial bases; whereas 45% of homicides featuring White shooters and Black victims were considered justified, only 11% of homicides featuring Black shooters and White victims were considered justified (Southern Poverty Law Center 2020).

example of inferential racism or the unquestioned assumptions regarding race. "The benefit of the doubt is racist.... Why would [Zimmerman] get the benefit of that?"

Race and racism have been built into the systems that continue to impact us today. Failing to recognize how this racialized history manifests in our interactions can also be considered racist. Consider the long history of racial segregation and **redlining**, the economic practice of outlining certain areas of a city to indicate the land circumscribed is undesirable or a bad investment (Hillier 2003). Desirability was highly correlated with the racial and ethnic composition of the community. Thus, redlining created neighborhoods organized by race, a segregation that persists even though the practice was largely outlawed in the 1970s. The impacts of segregation by socioeconomic status (SES) and race are still apparent, especially in the quality of life available within these districts. They are more likely to have lower-quality schools, worse air quality, fewer grocery stores, and an increased police presence.

The Talk (Steve Sack 2013)

By Cairo Spencer

The cartoon is split into two halves and it's titled "The talk." On the left side, under the words "White Americans," we see a White father and his son are sitting on a bed. In the father's speech bubble, we see a bird and a bee, symbolizing that the father is explaining to his son where babies come from. On the right side, under the word "African-Americans," we see a Black father and his son having a talk as well. In the Black father's speech bubble, we see a picture of a gun and lady justice with a sign that reads the "U.S. Justice System." These symbolize that the father is explaining to his son how his life is unequal, how he could be harmed at any moment, and that the U.S. justice system will not have his back.

To understand this piece, you must understand that "the talk" is usually the nickname for a dreaded conversation parents have with kids about how sexual intercourse works. You also have to understand the history of injustice against African Americans. There is so much injustice that they have another version of "the talk," and it's a crucial conversation because it affects children as soon as they walk out of the door. If you're African American, too often you are considered a suspect in the eyes of the law, and you don't get breaks in the U.S. Justice System because it is systematically created to put Blacks at a disadvantage in life and in the court of law.

The cartoon is satirizing the differences between the lives of White families and African American families. Though White families discuss the niceties of life, African Americans are on the other side warning their children about the close proximity of death and unfairness. White Americans don't have to worry about being stopped and frisked because the system is designed to help them and them only. The cartoon is satirizing the differences of the two groups and depicting them as opposites in the way they talk about life and what they have to discuss with their children to allow them to make it through life as informed and safe as possible.

This is a great piece of satire in my opinion. It highlights a very real subject, "the talk," that people who aren't Black may be unaware of. It is something I think about daily meaning that it is very current and it is a very relatable problem amongst African-American males. It is especially relevant considering all of the Black males that have been killed for doing nothing wrong by male and female police officers. It puts the two races as opposites though that can help the viewer see the difference in lifestyles and how unfortunate those differences truly are when looked at side-by-side.

Figure 5.3 "The Talk" Steve Sack. *Source*: Steve Sack / CAGLE CARTOONS, INC.

Satirizing Whiteness

Although racism is regularly discussed when it disadvantages people of color in the United States, the inverse is the fundamental root of this phenomenon: Racism in the United States (and the larger colonized world) advantages whiteness or people considered to be White. For example, the government-sanctioned forced displacement of Indigenous Americans allowed for the homesteading of White Americans. Other racialized phenomena, like voting restrictions, access to property and education, and even the ability to profit from one's own labor a described in Chapter 2, disadvantaging people of color while advantaging White people.

This ideology of whiteness is more than the state of being light-skinned or of European descent: It advantages certain ethnic constructs and disadvantages others to maintain a racialized power structure that advantages people considered White, allowing White people to avoid the nuanced experiences of those who are not White.[7] Our simple understanding of race as skin tone emerged from the economic and social need to aggregate European countries and colonists during the Age of Discovery/Colonization. Europeans arrived in the Americas (the "New World") seeking to capitalize on the resources available, and populations that did not possess European features were exploited or destroyed to guarantee opportunities for Americans of European descent. In this environment, skin tone and other features indicated that some people were of European descent and eligible for certain opportunities while others were not.

---

7 I have not capitalized "whiteness" because, unlike Blackness or the essence of being Black, whiteness is a way of looking at the world through a dominant solipsistic lens. Not all people considered White adhere to an ideology of whiteness, and not all people who adhere to an ideology of whiteness are considered White. Similarly, I have not capitalized white when referring to white supremacy or white privilege as they are extensions of whiteness as an ideology.

Peter's Progress (*Family Guy*, S7E16, FOX 2009)
The final episode of *Family Guy*'s seventh season, entitled "Peter's Progress" (2009) tells the story of the founding of Quahog, the Rhode Island town where *Family Guy* takes place, as told by Griffin Peterson (Peter Griffin in a previous life). When Peter, Joe, and Quagmire land on the shores of Rhode Island, Peter presciently describes the paradox of freedom in America by race as well as the complexity of Whiteness itself:

> We're gonna build a new settlement. We'll have a happy new life, and we'll have equal rights for all. Except Blacks, Asians, Hispanics, Jews, gays, women, Muslims—. Um—. Everybody who's not a White man. And I mean "White" White, so no Italians, no Polish. Just people from Ireland, England, and Scotland. But from only certain parts of Scotland and Ireland. Just full-blooded Whites. No, y'know what? Not even Whites. Nobody gets any rights. Ahhhh. America.

Figure 5.4 In classic Family Guy fashion where present-day characters are reimagined in historical fiction, Peter learns that he was the founder of Quahog in a past life, inviting commentary about the founding of the United States, satirizing current phenomena via trends in our past. Still from "Peter's Progress" (Family Guy 2009).

The brief monologue dissects the trajectory of America's ideological roots, from "equal rights for all," to the actual implementation of this ideology, effectively saying the quiet part out loud. Peter reveals very quickly who "all" refers to, or more importantly who it does *not* include: "Blacks, Asians, Hispanics, Jews, gays, women, Muslims." He then goes on to describe what he means by White: "Just people from Ireland, England, and Scotland," excluding people from Italy, Poland, Ireland, and Wales. Establishing who is "White" which seemed so simple at the top of the monologue, quickly falls apart as he lists the groups that were were not considered White during the Age of Discovery/Colonization. Ultimately, the construct of "full-blooded Whites is an impossible metric, leading to the final line: if freedom in America is for White people and being White is defined by purity, then "Nobody gets any rights. Ahhh. America."

In addition to the legal and economic opportunities, being considered White also confers social advantages. In racially and ethnically **pluralistic** societies (where there are many races and ethnicities present, as arguably equal citizens), to be White is to *not* be raced (Dyer 2005). This protection from being raced and, by extension stereotyped, is an advantage. People who are categorized as White will not experience greater scrutiny by the police, will experience less rejection from civic institutions, and will not be subjected to systematic dehumanization in the wake of European colonization.

Arbitrary constructs of blood quanta like the **one-drop rule** meant that anyone with any non-European ancestry would automatically categorized as not White; this is also referred to as the practice of **hypodescent,** which is to assign people with any "subordinate" racial group in their heritage to the subordinate group.[8] Whereas being White is constructed as an exclusive category where people are excluded from advantages and opportunities, being Black is constructed as an inclusive category where anyone who is

---

Black No More (George S. Schuyler 1931)

By Patty Terhune

Inner "lurking" being Black is a repeated theme in the 1931 novel by George S. Schuyler titled *Black No More*. Throughout the entire novel, Schuyler is satirizing the way people discuss race in America. From the way that Foster talks about Mrs. Crookman, the reader can assume that the book is making a claim that appearing White is different than really being White. It is likely that this book is a commentary on attitudes at the time surrounding White people versus Black people. According to the book, just because people may appear to be White does not mean that they possess the systemically decided-upon traits of what being White and Black really entails; rather, the traits could be factors of education, economics, personality, etc.

In the book, after Black Americans have undergone the Black-No-More treatment and become White, their children still ended up being born Black even though neither parent aesthetically appeared to be black. Schuyler portraying being Black as an invisible trait that lies dormant until a child is born is likely mocking the way that being White is usually discussed. White is seen as invisible because it is viewed in society as hegemonically dominant and built into society's power structures as neutral or good. Schuyler's use of Black identity is almost more silent than invisible. Blackness seems to be lurking, waiting to make an appearance. This likely is a commentary as well. Even when being Black is so common that it is actually the underlying majority, it is still considered a plague in the book. Having mixed babies was still socially unacceptable even though they could easily get the Black-No-More treatment to become White if it was just the tone of the skin that was deemed the problem and not the existence of being Black in and of itself.

There was also an incredibly popular and influential eugenics movement going on in America around the time this book was published. It was an entire racial minority and disabled persons cleansing movement to sterilize individuals that the American Eugenics Society deemed unfit to reproduce. Methods they used included forced sterilization of those with physical or mental disabilities and stopping inter-racial marriage through legal methods or strong-arming. The eventual goal was to have more strong White babies and less "others." Given this context, it becomes clear that Schuyler was mocking this movement with the Black babies being born to seemingly White individuals. Though the society

(Continued)

---

8 Conversely, hyperdescent assigns people with multiple groups to the group that is most superior; by this defintion, people mixed with White heritage would be defined as White.

> (Continued)
>
> in his novel had tried its own methods of racial cleansing to make more strong, White, able offspring, it did not work.
>
> Present-day, the national identity or national normal is still the idea of White. This is perpetuated through media in casting choices, rhetoric, and representation behind screen or page. Yet, more than 44% of Millennials are part of a minority race or ethnicity. This is nearing half and will only grow in future generations.

not White experiences discrimination, dehumanization, and a lack of opportunity (Corsbie-Massay, Riley, de Carvalho 2022). Categorizing some people as White and some people as Black literally separated the haves (or could haves) from the have nots.

An ideology of **white supremacy**, in which White people are believed to be better than other racial or ethnic groups, results in characteristics associated with (Western) European descent (e.g., light skin, straight hair, narrow features) being perceived as more desireable. Those who exhibit these characteristics are considered more civilized, attractive, intelligent, capable, and valuable. This **colorism**, or prejudices against individuals with darker skin tones and for individuals with lighter skin tones manifests in social, economic, and even legal disparities: Men with darker skin and Afrocentric features received harsher sanctions in a reveiw of Black and White offenders in Minnesota (King and Johnson 2016).

As a result, people are willing to spend a lot of money to achieve a European appearance. In South America, Asia, and Africa, continents that feature a diversity of skin tones and hair types, lighter skin and straight hair are still held in higher esteem. The skin lightening industry is estimated at $8.6 billion in 2020, with $2.3 billion spent in the United States alone (Hall 2021). Similarly, the human hair trade was worth $7 billion in 2020 (MacLeod 2020) and the hair straightening industry was valued at just under $600 million in 2018 (Allied Market Research). Centuries of scientific racism, a pseudoscience that claimed there was evidence for the biological superiority of certain races over others as described earlier in this chapter, continue to impact race relations today (Saini 2019).

> **Activity 5.2 Experiences of Blackness**
>
> What is Blackness? Establishing Blackness, or what it means to be Black, is inherently difficult because of its fluidity, contingency, and overall complexity (Asante et al. 2016). For centuries, Blackness was defined by White people because of their positions of power in institutions and the systematic prevention of literacy among Black people. However, Emancipation, Civil Rights, and social media have allowed Black people to define what it means to be Black, showcasing the wide range of Black experiences in the United States and around the world. In these narratives are stories of suffering and triumph, pain, and perseverance.
>
> Although Blackness has historically been constructed as a discriminatory catch all, Blackness is also a sense of self-assuredness that comes from experiencing systematic discrimination (Corsbie-Massay, Riley & De Carvalho, 2022). This journey of self-actualization has been captured in many documentaries including Chris Rock's *Good Hair* (2009), *Dark Girls* (2012), and *Dark Girls 2* (2020), all of which document the impact of anti-Black beauty aesthetics on Black people. Watch one of these films or any of the user-generated content online that addresses these topics and consider how the a European beauty standard impacts the experience of Blackness today.

White Like Me (*Saturday Night Live*, S9E10, NBC 1984)
The classic 1984 routine by Eddie Murphy on *Saturday Night Live* satirizes whiteness by focusing on the fact that some people are afforded opportunities because of their features. It parodies the 1961 book, *Black Like Me* by by John Howard Griffin, where a White journalist in Blackface goes to the South to experience anti-Black discrimination first hand.[9] The book became a bestseller and changed the conversation regarding race and racism among White Americans. In the six-minute segment, Murphy dons elaborate "whiteface" makeup, including a wig and prosthetics, to achieve a European appearance. To learn how to "act White," he reads a "whole bunch of Hallmark cards" and watches *Dynasty*, a popular primetime drama that featured the tribulations of a rich White family in Texas.

When his facade is complete, the camera follows Murphy through New York City as a White man, experiencing exaggerated privileges. First, a "White" Murphy enters a corner shop and attempts to buy a newspaper. The clerk is shocked and refuses his money, telling him, "There's no one around, just take it." Murphy (and the audience) is confused but after prompting from the clerk, he takes the newspaper and leaves the store. A voiceover features Murphy saying, "Slowly, I began to realize, when White people are alone, they *give* things to each other *for free*." Murphy then boards a city bus. When the only other Black man on the bus disembarks, the bus quickly turns into a speakeasy-like environment with upbeat music, a cocktail waitress with a tray full of drinks, and dancing in the aisle.

Figure 5.5 Unlike the trope of blackface, which features non-Black actors donning makeup and costumes in order to "perform" Blackness as a means of mocking and ultimately dehumanizing Black people, whiteface often features non-White actors donning makeup and costumes to satirize the insidious invisibility of whiteness. Still from "White Like Me" featuring Eddie Murphy in "whiteface" (Saturday Night Live 1984).

---

9 Griffin was not the first to write about the Black experience using this approach; another journalist named Ray Sprigle had published a series of articles entitled, "I Was a Negro in the South for 30 Days," which were later adapted into a book entitled, *In the Land of Jim Crow* (1949).

In the penultimate scene, Murphy, using the name "Mr. White," tries to get a loan from a bank with no collateral, no credit, and no identification. Shocked at his application, the Black loan officer says, "This is not a charity. This is a business," before being cut off and dismissed by his White boss. Laughing at the Black loan officer's oblivious adherence to the rules, the White bank officer rips up Murphy's application and hands over stacks of cash. "Just take what you want Mr. White. Pay us back any time. Or don't! We don't care!"

The sketch flips the interaction from *Black Like Me* to feature the experiences of someone parading as White and provides the polar opposite of the experience of Blackness in the South: Whiteness in the North, in which an "underground" White world works to make the lives of other White people more enjoyable and easier. Being White is often framed as invisible, which enables an ideology of whiteness as the norm, the clip makes salient the associated advantages of being White. In an interview with *The A.V. Club*, Neal Brennan, co-creator of *The Chappelle Show*, said that watching this sketch was probably the first time he thought, "Oh. Being Black is different. That is a totally different experience" [from being White] (Eakin 2017).

Satirizing White Panic

A response to an increasingly multicultural and diverse society is to claim that the dominant group is now a threatened minority. This sentiment is evident in statements that elicit social panic, such as, "DIVERSITY IS WHITE GENOCIDE" (Culpepper 2014; Kiefaber 2014), "White people will be a minority by 2042" despite still being the largest racial group at 49% (Colby and Ortman 2015),[10] and the "great replacement theory," an increasingly mainstream conspiracy theory that claims White Americans are being purposefully made extinct and replaced by non-White immigrants (Obaidi et al. 2021). Phrases like these which imply (or explicitly state) that White people are becoming extinct triggers an existential fear known as mortality salience, or awareness of one's own death, which impacts one's self-esteem and view of the world (Burke et al. 2010) even though acknowledging racial diversity is not the same as systematically killing White people.

Satire frequently targets this existential fear, that the presence of non-White people is directly related to the demise of White people, because it is baseless and absurd yet still has power. Public and social policy was driven by a fear of thriving communities

---

The Day Beyoncé Turned Black (*Saturday Night Live*, S41E13, NBC 2016)

By Kathleen Ahearn

This sketch is satirizing the response Beyoncé received after releasing an unapologetically Black music video to her song "Formation." Critics of the music video accused Beyoncé of being anti-police since her video includes nods to the Black Lives Matter movement. There is a shot of graffiti on a wall reading "Stop Shooting Us" as well as an image of a young Black boy dancing in front of a line of armed policemen. The day after she released the video, she performed "Formation" at the Super Bowl Halftime Show, surrounded by Black backup dancers wearing outfits reminiscent of the Black Panthers.

(Continued)

---

10 In the words of Hari Kondabolu, "49% White only makes you the minority if you think the other 51% are exactly the same. That only works if you think: 'Well, it's 49% White people and 51% you people'" (Waiting for 2042, 2014).

> (Continued)
>
> Through satire, the goal of this text is to make people realize that maybe the reason they're so outraged by "Formation" isn't because it's Beyoncé speaking on behalf of the Black Lives Matter movement – it's that she's Black and she's written this song for Black people to relate to.
>
> The SNL sketch is structured as a horror movie trailer. The premise of the sketch is that it's the day that White Americans learned their beloved Beyoncé is Black, and it follows society as it implodes from this new knowledge. As the narrator explains, "It was the day they lost their damn White minds."
>
> WOMAN   "I don't understand this song"
> MAN   "Hot sauce in my bag, swag?...What does that mean?"
> MAN 2   "Maybe this song isn't for us?"
> WOMAN   "But usually everything is!"
>
> At 1:13, a scared White woman approaches her friend, explaining they have to leave America because Beyoncé is Black. Her friend responds, "Amy, I'm Black." The White woman goes, "No you're not, you're like, 'my girl.'" As her friend explains that she can still be Black and that there's Black people all over the world, she points out to a man on the street and remarks that he too is Black. The White friend goes, "Well I know HE'S Black," alluding that his Blackness is more obvious because of his attire.
>
> A news clip at 1:50 shows that this developing story is getting even more serious as they're learning that Beyoncé ISN'T the only Black celebrity; in fact they have just discovered Kerry Washington is Black too! A distraught woman is seen crying under her desk, as she mutters, "No… it can't be! She's on ABC!" There are Black people watching White people's world implode who are confused. "Do they not realize I'm Black too?"
>
> SNL's satire of post-racialism addresses the absurdity of not seeing race. Once people in the sketch realize "their" Beyoncé is Black, the world implodes into a post-apocalyptic disaster zone. They simply can't fathom this news, and it's making them question everything. "Is Taylor Swift still White," a little boy asks his mother. The idea that White people have any right to be outraged at Beyoncé for expressing her own opinion and accepting and furthering the cause for Black Americans is inherently absurd, and the video is trying to draw attention to this. Beyoncé is a singer, an actress, designer, activist, icon, wife, mother, and woman. She is also Black, and has been the whole time.

of color for centuries, which allowed them to be decimated without recourse. In recent years, videos of White people calling 911 or otherwise overreacting to people of color simply existing go viral almost weekly, revealing that this fear is still present and still has power. The adjective "unapologetically" before a non-White ethnic or racial group (e.g., Asian, Black, Indigenous, Latino) refers to a disregard for the White lens and approval from the mainstream White audience. Yet, simply discussing one's own history and one's own experiences are frequently interpreted as an attack on White people because of the absurdity of whiteness.

This is evident in the rhetorical backlash to the phrase "Black Lives Matter," a phrase designed to draw attention to the fact that Black lives have not mattered for the better part of American history. Through centuries of slavery, Black people were tortured, sold, and murdered as a matter of policy because they were the property of White slave owners. When Black people were no longer enslaved, their lives (and deaths) were still perceived as less valuable than White lives. This is evident in both the discourse about Black lives (see *Key and Peele Super Bowl Special* in Chapter 1) and concrete socioeconomic metrics: In 2020, the net worth of a typical White American family was $171,000, almost 10 times greater than that of a typical Black American family at $17,000 (McIntosh et al. 2020), and White lives are insured at median of $150,000, three times that of an median Black life insurance policy at $50,000 (Egan and Danise 2020). Independent of monetary value, the life expectancy for Black people is three to four years shorter than that of White people, a gap that has been exacerbated by COVID (Andrasfay and Goldman 2021), Black people are more likely to be killed by the police than most other racial groups[11] (Males 2014), and homicides with Black victims are significantly less likely to be solved than homicides with White victims (Chiwaya et al. 2021). However, the phrase "Black Lives Matter" is met with responses like "White Lives Matter" and "All Lives Matter" to avoid focusing on the systematic disadvantages suffered by Black people and reiterate a narrative that rhetorically demands equality without a recognition of centuries of inequality and subsequent inequity.

"All Lives Matter"

Figure 5.6 "All Lives Matter" Matt Bors (2015); *Source*: Matt Bors.

---

11 Native Americans are most likely to be killed by police.

Although the phrase "All Lives Matter" feels morally righteous, it serves as a retort to "Black Lives Matter," not to advocate for the equal treatment for all lives. As will be discussed in the next section, this "colorblind" approach emphasizes a sense of equality without a recognition of past disparities (West et al. 2021; Yancy and Butler 2015). When other lives are in the balance, "All Lives Matter" proponents do not emerge as a cohesive unit to draw attention to violations of human rights. The last panel makes clear that not all lives matter, and more egregiously, Muslim people do not even qualify as "lives."

Similarly, structural efforts to rectify racial disparities, such as affirmative action in higher education and government positions, foregrounding minority-owned businesses, or simply amplifying content and perspectives from historically marginalized groups, are framed as "anti-White discrimination" or "reverse racism." In a 2008 survey, White Millennials were more likely to agree with the statement that

---

Activity 5.3   What is Reverse Racism?

If racism is anything that reinforces racial disparities, then reverse racism in theory would be anything that disrupts racial disparities. This sounds pretty good! But this is not how the phrase "reverse racism" is deployed. Instead, it is used to malign efforts to disrupt historical racial disparities by calling these restorative actions racism. Racism has been built into society over centuries of human interactions post-colonialism through systems designed to disadvantage groups and reinforce the ideology that certain groups are inferior.

Consider Aamer Rahman's take on Reverse Racism from his 2013 special, *Fear of a Brown Planet*. He says that to be a reverse racist:

> All I would need would be a time machine. And now what I do is I get in my time machine and go back in time to before Europe colonized the world, right? And convince leaders of Africa, the Middle East, Central and South America to invade and colonize Europe. Just occupy them, steal their land and resources, set up some kind of like, I don't know, trans-Asian slave trade where we exported White people to work on rice plantations in China. Just ruin Europe over the course of a couple of centuries so all their descendants would want to migrate out and live in the places where Black and brown people come from. Of course, in that time, I'd make sure I set up systems that privileged Black and brown people at every conceivable social, political, and economic opportunity. So, White people would never have any hope of real self-determination. And every couple of decades, make up some fake war as an excuse to blast them back to the Stone Age, say it's for their own good because their culture's inferior. And, just for kicks, subject White people to colored people's standards of beauty so that they end up hating the color of their own skin, eyes, and hair. After hundreds and hundreds and hundreds of years of that, I got on stage at comedy show and said, 'Hey, what's the deal with White people? Why can't they dance?' That would be reverse racism.

Have you heard the term "reverse racism" before? When was it used and what did the speaker intend to accomplish by deploying this phrase? How did this deployment of the term "reverse racism" maintain and reinforce historical racial hierarchies?

"Discrimination against Whites has become as big a problem as discrimination against Black people and other minorities," whereas Black Millennials and Millennials of Latin American descent were more likely to disagree (Hutchings 2009). Yet, White people are less likely to live in low-quality neighborhoods, more likely to have access to healthy food and good schools, less likely to go to jail for the same crimes, and more likely to be hired because of their race. Therefore, refusing to disrupt, and thereby exacerbating, these disparities is racist.

Instead, *feelings* of discrimination have come to dominate the conversation. In 2019, Tennessee lawmaker Warren Hurst said, "White men in America have very few rights.... You'll hear them stand on stage and say, 'Oh, I'm for the poor and the Black.' You've never heard any one of them say, 'I believe White people have rights, too'" (Chistian 2019). This feeling of being left out of a conversation is not the same as lacking rights. All rights in the United States were originally established to protect the opportunities of wealthy, landowning White men. They have had property rights, the right to vote, the right to free speech and religious freedoms, and the right to *not* be subjected to unlawful search and seizure from the inception of these rights. Civil rights movements occur when people fight, protest, and agitate to gain these rights. The claim that any attempt to equal the playing field is "reverse racism" or "anti-White discrimination" is devoid of a greater understanding of the history that resulted in current racial disparities.

Colorblindness is a Medical Condition, Not a Solution for Racism

Race exists because we have collectively constructed and deployed race, causing race to impact every aspect of human life. In the United States, race has impacted who could vote, who was in control of their own bodies, and who could gain access to the benefits of citizenship and humanity. These disparities reverberate today despite the implementation of laws intended to stymie effects of racial discrimination, causing many to feel a sense of hopelessness regarding the overwhelming and seemingly infinite issue of race in the United States. As a result, many have adopted a colorblind perspective, claiming that they "don't see race" in hopes that this will free them from individual accountability regarding racial dynamics.

In his 2003 book, *Racism without Racists*, Eduard Bonilla-Silva outlines the rhetorical phenomenon of **colorblindness**, or the process of disregarding racial and ethnic characteristics when selecting who will participate in activities and will receive services. As an individual ideology, colorblindness is often deployed to avoid addressing one's own contribution to a problematic racial past, present, and future, and it is considered to be a form of racism. Although it may feel good to deny one's own personal involvement in processes of racial marginalization, colorblindness maintains racial hierarchies. Furthermore, refusing to see color also means refusing to acknowledge how race impacts the lives of others. "Colorblindness creates a society that denies their [people of color's] negative racial experiences, rejects their cultural heritage, and invalidates their unique perspectives" (Williams 2011).

"I Don't See Race" (College Humor 2017)
The three-minute clip opens with four people sitting around a table at work. The conversation begins when Zac expresses excitement over the "super diverse movies"

that came out in the past year. Katie responds with confusion, saying "I never really thought about that." Her colleagues seem to be in disbelief as she goes on.

KATIE: Call me crazy, but I just don't see race. I guess I'm just the least racist person here.
ZAC: Race is like often like a pretty obvious thing to observe. It's not like racist to notice.
KATIE: Ha! I had to laugh, Zac. Oh my goodness, I only see one race.
GRANT: Ugh.
KATIE: The human race.
GRANT: Such bullshit! You're only telling yourself that so you don't have to think about racism or confront your own prejudices.
KATIE: No, I'm not prejudiced! Okay? I don't even judge (Mike) Trapp for being a woman!
MIKE: I'm a man, Katie, you know that.
KATIE: No, honestly, I just guessed. This is gonna sound nuts, but I don't see gender and I don't see sex, I just see people.

The clip continues as Katie doubles down on her colorblindness by saying that she doesn't see gender, disabilities, or age. Her inability to see the individual differences becomes increasingly ridiculous as she claims that she is unable to see people who are pregnant and she has never seen a wheelchair. She refuses to recognize that her siblings and parents are different ages. Her co-workers point out that by not seeing differences, it is impossible to respect people and their unique needs. Katie continues to claim that her inability to see individuals as individuals is what makes her a true believer in "equality," to which Zac replies, "That's. Not. What. Equality. Means!" Eventually after being pressed, Katie slams her hands on the table and reveals the impetus behind this approach, "Guys! Come on, okay! I just want to be able to do and say whatever I want, whenever I want, and I don't want to have to think about the world's problems!" To which Zac, Grant, and Mike nod in understanding, "That actually sounds pretty good.... I guess I can understand that...good way to live."

The video as a whole reveals the absurdity of the common but flawed phrase "I don't see race" by applying it to other categories like gender, disability, and age, much like the Wanda Sykes monologue in Chapter 4. Each character dispassionately explains how ignoring demographics makes it impossible to be a good person (e.g., in response to not being able to see wheelchairs, Mike says, "...if someone were in a wheelchair, you would not install a ramp in your building?" to which Katie says, "I would refuse"). Ignoring individual differences prevents us from moving through the world as prosocial agents of change. The idea of ignoring the unique needs of overtly disadvantaged individuals (e.g., pregnant or disabled) demonstrates the nonsensical nature of colorblindness through exaggeration. In the final line, the other characters that originally demanded Katie be more cognizant of individual and institutional discrimination hilariously acknowledge that *not* being aware of the world's problems feels good. However, it is ultimately very problematic because the capacity to *not* be aware of the issues plaguing disadvantaged racial groups is in itself a unique advantage of being White and a manifestation of whiteness.

One of the most insidious outcomes of individual colorblindness is the deliberate disregard of history. Agreement with a colorblind approach to race relations has been correlated with pro-White and anti-minority attitudes (Richeson and

Nussbaum 2004), condoning and encouraging race-themed parties (Tynes and Markoe 2010), and reduced recognition of discrimination (Offerman et al. 2014). Alternatively, a greater belief in **multiculturalism**, which is the belief that that cultural and ethnic differences should be celebrated and integrated, has been correlated with reduced racial bias in the workplace as reported by racial minority employees (Plaut et al. 2009).

Assimilation vs. Appropriation

A colorblind approach also impacts how we think and talk about the relationships and power differentials between racial groups. When two groups come into contact, a new cultural product can emerge that synthesizes the two cultures, referred to as **acculturation**. However, when a dominant group meets a marginalized group, the resulting cultural interaction tends to reinforce the pre-existing power dynamic through assimilation or appropriation.

Assimilation is the adoption of the dominant or majority culture by minority or marginalized individuals, while minimizing or discarding the original minority or marginalized cultural practices. Members of a minority group are expected to look and act like the majority group as a means of acceptance in the dominant culture. Immigrants to the United States are expected to learn English, participate in American customs, and minimize their ethnic signifiers, such as by adopting an American adaptation of their name. Assimilation is not just a top-down process enforced by those in dominant positions. The desire to fit in can lead marginalized individuals to voluntarily repress their own culture and remove their own ethnic signifiers. Expectations of assimilation rely on the same processes as colorblindness; newcomers will adopt majority cultural practices and effectively conceal their ethnic differences, thereby allowing those in the dominant to ignore group differences. Although colorblindness and assimilation are framed as processes of integration, they implicitly reinforce the majority culture as more normal, valuable, or superior, and marginalized cultures as abnormal, worthless, or inferior.

Ching Chong (Means I Love You) (Jimmy Wong 2011)

In 2011, UCLA student Alexandra Wallace posted a video on YouTube entitled "Asians in the Library," in which she complains about "...the hordes of Asian students they let into our school every year." She is frustrated with their failure to "learn American manners" and how they fill the dorms with "...their mothers and their brothers and their sisters and their grandmas and all the other people they brought along from Asia with them." She directs her ire at international students in the library who talk on the phone while she is studying and mocks them: "OOOH. Ching chong ling long ting tong! OOOOH," deploying *yellow-speak* historically used to mock people of East Asian descent. The video went viral within a matter of days, prompting apologies from Wallace and UCLA. The event was a clear manifestation of "...a 'new racism' by foregrounding students who speak Asian languages and have different family traditions, as it insidiously groups and attacks UCLA's American-born as well as our international students of Asian ancestry" (Statement by the Asian American Studies Department and Center at UCLA, 2011).

The video was polarizing and prompted conversations about anti-Asian racism in the twenty-first century. But Jimmy Wong, an aspiring actor in Los Angeles, drew the most attention to the issue with his response posted to YouTube. The song, "Ching Chong (Means I Love You)" is a classic singer-songwriter love song in which Wong translates Wallace's yellow-speak into a hilarious ballad. He sarcastically explains that everything she claims to be wrong with Asian students is really an expression of desire. "What my family is doing on those Friday nights, is teaching me how to cook and dress, 'cause baby I want to take you out and blow your freaking mind." Most of the song is a joke at Wallace's expense, with Wong expressing his love for her despite her stereotyping of and prejudice toward Asian and Asian American students. In several sections, he switches to make dispassionate statements about her attitudes to ensure that the audience does not mistake his message for anything but satire. In the second verse, he says:

You ain't that polite nice American girl your mama raised you to be.
So when you reach that epiphany...
Wait! Are you freaking kidding me? If you have an epiphany every single time you study that means you're probably doing something wrong...
But like it when you're wrong...

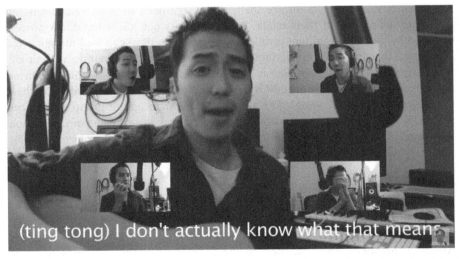

Figure 5.7 There was collective public outrage regarding Wallace's racist rant, Wong's satirical love song addressed (and diffused) many of the issues; the video also helped launch Asian American voices on YouTube. Still from "Ching Chong (Means I Love You) Jimmy Wong featuring Wong singing and performing all components of the song with captions for emphasis.

Similarly, **appropriation** is sampling cultural artifacts from minority groups by the majority, often discounting the nuanced context with which they were originally created. Cultural sampling is inevitable when cultures mix, but it rises to appropriation when the history and story of the people whose culture is being sampled is ignored, manipulated, or changed. In the case of marginalized groups, this process reinforces a form of cultural annihilation, or the systematic elimination of a group's culture. This is part of **cultural genocide** or "...acts and measures undertaken to destroy nations' or ethnic groups' culture through spiritual, national, and cultural destruction" (Armenian Genocide Museum, nd); it is the elimination of a culture by ignoring or obfuscating cultural meaning. The process of cultural annihilation begins with removing or changing the meaning of a cultural artifacts.

Columbusing: Discovering Things for White People (College Humor 2014)
In this clip, Bernard, who is Black, meets Brian, who is White, at a bar in the Bedford-Stuyvesant neighborhood of Brooklyn. When Bernard arrives and compliments the spot, Brian says, "Thanks! I just discovered it." Bernard is immediately frustrated saying that he frequents the bar all the time. To which Brian corrects himself; "Yes. Sorry. I didn't discover it. I Columbused it.... I discovered it for White people."

Brian then explains the term "Columbusing." As its name would suggest, it describes when a White person "discovers" something from non-White people and cultures. When Brian shows Bernard his most recent tweet, "Just unearthed a hidden gem. #columbus #idiscoveredbedstuy," Bernard objects: "My parents live in Bed-Stuy!" Brian expresses that Columbusing is a fact of life and then lists off artifacts that have been Columbused:

> Nobody said Columbusing was fair. I mean just ask the Native Americans or Mary Lambert, the lesbian songwriter whose gay rights anthem didn't get popular until it was remixed by a straight dude. Macklemore Columbused same-sex marriage just like Gwyneth Paltrow Columbused Eastern medicine... and Sublime Columbused reggae... Hummus... Columbused from the Middle East by health-conscious Whiteys. Zumba classes... Columbused from Columbia. Boating shoes... [are] practically moccasins which we Columbused from the Native Americans among other things....

This brief satirical video demonstrates the everyday things that White American culture has appropriated from world cultures while erasing the original source material. Deploying the term "Columbusing," which had been defined in Urban Dictionary about a year earlier, instead of "appropriation," also bypasses the traditional triggered responses people have around this cultural buzzword. It replaces it with a hilarious recognition that the nation as a whole was appropriated from the people who first lived here. Furthermore, Brian catches Bernard misattributing twerking to Miley Cyrus 10 years after the Ying Yang Twins released a song "Whistle While You Twurk," revealing that "Columbusing" is a common practice and anyone can succumb to this misattribution. This context helps the viewer be honest with themselves in how they too have perpetuated appropriation or "Columbusing."

Discussions about appropriation emerge in response to people sampling artifacts from a culture outside of their own. This sampling can include food, fashion, music, and language. Although the issue of appropriation is much bigger than any given instance, these moments trigger anger and conversation, often from marginalized groups. Adding insult to injury, when appropriated artifacts are commodified to enable members of the majority (appropriating) group to profit, the originators of the artifact are eliminated from this source of revenue, further disempowering them as a group. In the process, we also risk overlooking the trials and tribulations in the history of the minoritized group as well. From ethnic costumes at Halloween and on the fashion runway to race-themed parties, from sports mascots drawn from Native American imagery to the mainstream popularity of African American Vernacular English (AAVE), each of these instances of cultural appropriation disadvantage the group whose culture is being appropriated while enhancing or financially advantaging members of the majority group. Assimilation and appropriation reinforce pre-existing power structures by encouraging the repression or annihilation of the minority or marginalized culture while ensuring that the majority or dominant culture is maintained and enriched.

Laughing at Race in the Twenty-First Century

For many, race is the unfinished business of the United States. The genocide, enslavement, and dehumanization of racial and ethnic groups were essential to the founding of this nation. This racist past continues to reverberate through every aspect of life, despite national rhetoric that we are in a post-racial society. This absurdity is ripe for satire, given our difficulties in directly tackling race.

The United States is often referred to as an ethnic **melting pot**, a collection of different cultures that all contribute to the larger culture. With every new ethnic group, the overall melting pot of the United States becomes more diverse and ultimately more exciting. However, this rhetoric conflicts with the actual lived reality of many: In addition to chattel slavery which was legal from the inception of the United States through the Emancipation Proclamation of 1863, government-sponsored Indian Residential Schools removed Native children from their families from the seventeenth to the twentieth century in order to "civilize" and assimilate them into European-American culture, Alien Land Laws of the nineteenth and twentieth centuries prohibited people of Asian descent from settling in the United States, and the Mexican Deportation/Repatriation systematically deported between 400,000 and two million people of Mexican descent in the United States to Mexico between 1929–1936. In recent years, multiple lawmakers have introduced various legislation seeking to make English the official language of the United States and require an English proficiency test for citizenship, again seeking to codify the majority culture and further marginalize minority languages and cultures.

Despite a litany of past and present injustices, many believe that any discussion of race is racist, making it impossible to address the effects of the past. The colorblind ideology that it is at the heart of American rhetoric is and has always been problematic because it allows individuals to avoid addressing how we perpetuate racial disparities, making it impossible to achieve a more egalitarian future. In the past few decades, scholars have focused on the effects of racial disparities on our currently lived experiences, an area of study commonly referred to as **critical race theory**.

However, fear of this conversation and anger about an unadulterated accounting of our own past has led many to decry this approach, going so far as to pass legislation making it illegal to discuss in classrooms (Kim 2021; Ray and Gibbons 2021; Schwartz 2021). Critiquing policies in an environment where the absurdities of reality are actively maligned or legally prohibited is the precise goal of satire. So, what do we need to remember when laughing at race in the twenty-first century?

We are the outcome of the past, therefore it is impossible to "get over" the past. Almost everything has been impacted by race. When people say "This has nothing to do with race," they are denying these facts and instead demonstrating that they would rather ignore how race might impact the issue at hand. Race may not always be the cause, but it is almost always a catalyst. It amplifies pre-existing phenomena as has been described throughout the book (e.g., class disparities, gender disparities). In this scenario, the job of the satirist is to reveal the role of race when people do not want to believe that race continues to impact the present, thereby helping the collective face the past to improve the future.

Something is a race because we treat like one. When it comes to race, discourse is the definition. When a group is racialized, that is, some characteristic becomes the primary means of understanding and engaging with all members of said group, the group becomes a race. Today, groups that do not fit into the simplistic racialized boxes described by Blumenbach and others of the time are actively racialized. People of Latin American descent (i.e., Latinos, Latinx, Latiné) are connected through a culture that combines Hispanic conquistadors, conquered Indigenous populations in the Americas and enslaved Africans, thereby establishing a collective ethnicity, but they are treated as a race. Individuals with "Latin-sounding" names will be subjected to specific stereotypes, prejudices, and discrimination. Similarly, Muslims are connected by a religion (Islam) regardless of race. But people who are assumed to be Muslim (e.g., have a Middle-Eastern name or wear a headscarf) are targeted with stereotypes, prejudices, and discrimination associated with Muslims (khan et al. 2021).

Appreciating a group or being an ally is more than having a marginalized friend or sampling marginalized cultures. Repeatedly, people try to defend themselves against accusations of racism by claiming they have a racially marginalized friend. This response reveals a woeful lack of understanding of the meaning of racism and its pernicious effects.[12] Much like colorblindness, this approach centers on individual prejudices and attitudes while denying larger social phenomena. This is the opposite of **appreciation**, or the practice of learning about a culture that is not your own with a serious and meticulous interest. We come to different cultures in different ways, including sampling of music, food, fashion, or language, but appreciation is more than simple fascination with cultural artifacts. It is essential to see and satirize when marginalized cultures are sampled, appropriated, and used for profit, and then refocus the conversation to encourage audiences to empathize with the experiences and voices of people whose culture is being exploited.

---

12 Deploying one's marginalized friend is also dehumanizing as it turns the "friend" into defensive object instead of a whole person with thoughts and opinons regarding the issue at hand.

Additional Activities

Activity 5.4   So, What's *Actually* Racist?

This chapter focused on the processes of race and racism, describing in detail groups that have been historically advantaged to help readers recognize how race and racism work. However, the chapter has not addressed in detail the stereotypes of marginalized and racialized groups, which is essential to recognizing the absurd treatment of race in American media and culture. Consider a racial, ethnic, or religious group of which you are not a member and review the stereotypes that have been associated with this group. How did this stereotype emerge? How is it used to marginalize the group both individually (i.e., how do these stereotypes affect the way out-group members interact with members of the marginalized group) and institutionally (i.e., how do these stereotypes impact policy that impacts the marginalized group)? Now that you are aware of the historical stereotypes, can you think of any media artifacts that reinforce these stereotypes either purposefully or inadvertently?

Activity 5.5   Is it Appropriation?

Accusations of appropriation are commonplace. Celebrities, non-celebrities, and even brands are constantly being called out on social media for instances of appropriation, often without explanation. Consider one of these instances and analyze how it is (or is not) appropriation using the following questions:

1) Are the accused individuals a part of the culture from which they are sampling? If not, how familiar are they with the culture? Have they vacationed or have they spent extended periods of time with members of the group from which they are sampling?
2) What is the history of the artifact that is being sampled? Is this history incorporated in the accused individual's use of the artifacts or has it been erased? How does this inclusion or erasure disrupt or perpetuate historical hierarchies?
3) Has the artifact been used to discriminate against the original culture? If so, then how does detaching it from long-standing discrimination privilege the accused and discriminate against the culture being sampled?
4) Are the accused individuals the only people profiting from sampling this artifact? Or are they actively incorporating and amplifying members of the original culture?
5) Ultimately, does this sampling create something new that incorporates dominant and marginalized cultures (i.e., acculturation), or does it encourage the dominant culture to fetishize aspects of a group that has been historical marginalized (i.e., appropriation)?

References

Andrasfay, T. and Goldman, N. (2021). Reductions in 2020 US life expectancy due to COVID-19 and the disproportionate impact on the Black and Latino populations. *Proceedings of the National Academy of Sciences* 118 (5).

Asante, G., Sekimoto, S., and Brown, C. (2016). Becoming "Black": Exploring the racialized experiences of African immigrants in the United States. *Howard Journal of Communications* 27 (4): 367–384.

Blake, J. (15 June 2019). What it's like to be a white woman named LaKiesha. CNN.

Bonilla-Silva, E. (2003). *Racism without Racists: Color-Blind Racism and the Persistence of Racial Inequality in the United States*. Rowman & Littlefield Publishers.

Bors, M. (30 December 2015). All lives matter. TheAlmightyGuru.

Burrell, T. (2010). *Brainwashed: Challenging the Myth of Black Inferiority*. United States: Smiley Books.

Burke, B.L., Martens, A., and Faucher, E.H. (2010). Two decades of terror management theory: A meta-analysis of mortality salience research. *Personality and Social Psychology Review* 14 (2): 155–195.

Chistian, T. (23 October 2019). Tennessee Lawmaker claims white men in America have 'very few rights'. Essence.

Chiwaya, N., Hersher, M., Tambe, A., and Ramos, E. (25 June 2021). *Interactive: What solved murder data says about homicides in the U.S.* https://www.nbcnews.com/news/us-news/track-solved-murder-rates-united-states-n1271928 (accessed 5 May 2022).

Colby, S.L. and Ortman, J.M. (March 2015). Projections of the Size and Composition of the U.S. Population: 2014 to 2060. https://www.census.gov/content/dam/Census/library/publications/2015/demo/p25-1143.pdf (accessed 5 May 2022).

College Humor. (7 July 2014). Columbusing: Discovering things for White People [Video]. YouTube. https://www.youtube.com/watch?v=BWeFHddWL1Y

College Humor. (8 April 2017). I Don't See Race [Video]. YouTube. youtube.com/watch?v=5qArvBdHkJA

Corsbie-Massay, C.L., Riley, B.K., and de Carvalho, R. (2022). Examining the unprofitability of authentic Blackness: Insights from Black media professionals. *Journal of Applied Communication Research* 50 (3).

Cullen, J. (2004). *The American Dream: A Short History of an Idea that Shaped A Nation*. Oxford University Press.

Culpepper, B. (15 March 2014). Racially-charged banners reading "diversity = white genocide" taken down by Birmingham police. https://abc3340.com/archive/banners-taken-down-by-birmingham-police.

The Daily Show with Jon Stewart. (4 April 2014). Racist Timeout [Video]. Comedy Central.

Devos, T. and Banaji, M.R. (2005). American= white? *Journal of Personality and Social Psychology* 88 (3): 447–466.

Dyer, R. (2005). The matter of whiteness. White privilege: Essential readings on the other side of racism, 9–14.

Eakin, M. (24 January 2017). Neal Brennan on why white dog shit is the funniest kind of excrement. AV Club.

Egan, J. and Danise, A. (2 November 2020). Survey Exposes Gaps in Black Ownership of Life Insurance. https://www.forbes.com/advisor/life-insurance/black-ownership/ (accessed 5 May 2022).

Fear of a Brown Planet. (28 November 2013). Aamer Rahman (Fear of a Brown Planet) - Reverse Racism [Video]. YouTube. https://www.youtube.com/watch?v=dw_mRaIHb-M

Hall, R. (22 February 2021). It's 2021 and skin bleaching is still a billion-dollar industry. Mic.

Hillier, A.E. (2003). Redlining and the home owners' loan corporation. *Journal of Urban History* 29 (4): 394–420.

Holocaust Museum shows effort to develop "master race". (21 April 2004). TODAY.

Hutchings, V.L. (2009). Change or more of the same? Evaluating racial attitudes in the Obama era. *Public Opinion Quarterly* 73 (5): 917–942.

Khan. et al. (June 2021). Missing & Maligned: The Reality of Muslims in Popular Global Movies. USC Annenberg Inclusion Initiative.

Kiefaber, A. (15 March 2014). 'pro-white' group hosts rally in Florence. https://www.cincinnati.com/story/news/local/florence/2014/03/15/florence-white-man-march/6460529/ (accessed 5 May 22).

Kim, R. (2021). Under the Law:'Anti-critical race theory'laws and the assault on pedagogy. *Phi Delta Kappan* 103 (1): 64–65.

King, R.D. and Johnson, B. D. (2016). A punishing look: Skin tone and Afrocentric features in the halls of justice. *American Journal of Sociology* 122 (1): 90–124.

Kondabolu, H. (5 February 2014). Hari Kondabolu- 2042 & the White Minority [Video]. YouTube. www.youtube.com/watch?v=85fr6nbiMT4 (accessed 16 May 2022).

MacFarlane, S., (Writer), Zuckerman, D., (Writer), Wild, W., (Writer), and Iles, B., (Director). (17 May 2009). Peter's Progress [Television series episode]. In Family Guy, 20th Century Fox Television.

MacLeod, C. (20 December 2020). The economics of the human hair trade. The Hustle.

Males, M. (26 August 2014). Who Are Police Killing? http://www.cjcj.org/news/8113 (accessed 5 May 2022).

Mandvi, A., (Writer), Kahn, M., (Writer), and Kah, M., (Director). B'Ully. In Halal in the Family, Sweet180. (2015).

McIntosh, K., Moss, E., Nunn, R., and Shambaugh, J. (27 February 2020). Examining the Black-white wealth gap. https://www.brookings.edu/blog/up-front/2020/02/27/examining-the-black-white-wealth-gap/ (accessed 5 May 2022).

NPR Staff. (6 May 2015). 6 Words: 'My Name Is Jamaal … I'm White'. NPR.

Nunpa, C.M. (2020) *The Great Evil: Christianity, the Bible, and the Native American Genocide*. Tuscon, AZ: See Sharp Press.

Obaidi, M., Kunst, J., Ozer, S., and Kimel, S. Y. (2021). *The "Great Replacement" conspiracy: How the perceived ousting of Whites can evoke violent extremism and Islamophobia.* Group Processes & Intergroup Relations.

Offermann et al. (2014). See no evil: Color blindness and perceptions of subtle racial discrimination in the workplace. *Cultural Diversity and Ethnic Minority Psychology* 20 (4): 499–507.

Plaut, V.C., Thomas, K.M., and Goren, M.J. (2009). Is multiculturalism or color blindness better for minorities? *Psychological Science* 20 (4): 444–446.

Ray, R. and Gibbons, A. (November 2021). Why are states banning critical race theory? Brookings https://www.brookings.edu/blog/fixgov/2021/07/02/why-are-states-banning-critical-race-theory/ (accessed 17 May 2022).

Richeson, J.A. and Nussbaum, R.J. (2004). The impact of multiculturalism versus color-blindness on racial bias. *Journal of Experimental Social Psychology* 40 (3): 417–423.

Roiland, J., (Writer), Harmon, D., (Writer), Ridley, R., (Writer), and Newton, B., (Director). (9 August 2015). Auto Erotic Assimilation [Television series episode]. In Rick and Morty, Starburns Industries.

Sack, S. (17 July 2013). Sack cartoon: The Talk. Star Tribune.

Said, E. (1978). *Orientalism*. Pantheon Books.

Saini, A. (2019). *Superior: The Return of Race Science*. Boston: Beacon Press.

Saturday Night Live. (15 December 1984). White Like Me - SNL [Video]. YouTube. https://www.youtube.com/watch?v=l_LeJfn_qW0

Saturday Night Live. (14 February 2016). "The Day Beyoncé Turned Black" - SNL. YouTube. www.youtube.com/watch?v=ociMBfkDG1w

Schuyler, G. (1931). *Black No More*. New York City: Macaulay Co.

Schwartz, S. (11 June 2021). Map: Where critical race theory is under attack. EducationWeek. https://www.edweek.org/policy-politics/map-where-critical-race-theory-is-under-attack/2021/06 (accessed 17 May 2022).

Southern Poverty Law Center. (July 2020). "STAND YOUR GROUND" KILLS: How these NRA backed laws promote racist violence. https://www.splcenter.org/sites/default/files/_stand_your_ground_kills_-_how_these_nra-backed_laws_promote_racist_violence_1.pdf (accessed 5 May 2022).

Tanaka, K. (23 May 2013). What kind of Asian are you? [Video]. YouTube. https://www.youtube.com/watch?v=DWynJkN5HbQ

Tynes, B.M. and Markoe, S.L. (2010). The role of color-blind racial attitudes in reactions to racial discrimination on social network sites. *Journal of Diversity in Higher Education* 3 (1): 1–13.

West, K., Greenland, K., and van Laar, C. (2021). Implicit racism, colour blindness, and narrow definitions of discrimination: Why some White people prefer 'All Lives Matter' to 'Black Lives Matter'. *British Journal of Social Psychology* 60 (4): 1136–1153.

Williams, M. (27 December 2011). Colorblind ideology is a form of racism. Psychology Today.

Yancy, G. and Butler, J. (2015). What's wrong with 'all lives matter'? *New York Times* 12: 156.

6

Satirizing Atrocities

> *You cannot hope to build a better world without improving the individuals.*
> – Marie Curie

Although marginalization satire is rarely "lighthearted," I have tried to keep the conversation moving throughout this book without exploring some of its darkest manifestations. However, the processes of processes of marginalization result in atrocities through systematically dehumanizing certain groups of people. This final chapter will address some of the most egregious outcomes of marginalization and discrimination, but the atrocities featured here are not exhaustive. Readers are encouraged to consider how processes of marginalization has resulted in past and current atrocities as well as how they can and should be satirized. These atrocities include, but are not limited to:

- The witch trials of the late sixteenth and early seventeenth centuries, where upwards of 40,000 women were killed on suspicion of being a witch (Hoak 1983).
- Gynecological experimentation without anesthetics on enslaved women by the "father" of gynecology in the mid-nineteenth century.
- Separation of Indigenous families throughout the United States and the housing (and torture) of Indigenous children at "residential schools".
- The Tuskegee Syphilis Study between 1923 and 1972, which purposefully withheld diagnoses and lifesaving treatment from Black men.
- Ongoing systematic violence toward queer and trans people (Waldron and Schwencke 2018).
- Separations of families at the Southern border from 2017 to 2020 (Kellaway 2015).

What are Social Atrocities?

An **atrocity** is "An extremely wicked or cruel act, typically one involving physical violence or injury." **Social atrocities** are cruel acts involving physical violence or injury that impact a society or a social group wherein (1) victims are targeted for their membership in a given social group, (2) the victims are targeted by an organized collective of perpetrators and enablers, and (3) there is a power differential between the perpetrators and the victims of these crimes. Social atrocities are not singular instances of atrocious behavior. Rather, they are characterized by the systematic, widespread vicious acts against a group of people based on their affiliation with a marginalized group. The atrocity of slavery placed Black people in danger *because* they were Black, and witch hunts did violence against women *because* they were women who did not adhere to the social expectations of femininity.

The United Nations explicitly identifies atrocity *crimes*, which are international crimes that "affect the core dignity of human beings" and are considered to be "the most serious crimes against humankind" (UN Framework of Analysis for Atrocity Crimes 2014). Atrocity crimes include genocide and ethnic cleansing, crimes against humanity, and war crimes. Consider the 1949 Geneva Convention, which outlines four categories of people against whom violence is considered a war crime: (1) wounded or sick armed forces in the field, (2) wounded, sick, or shipwrecked armed forces at sea, (3) prisoners of war, and (4) civilians. In each case, those who commit these crimes are in a more powerful position than their victims and the targeted individuals are powerless *because of* their situation.

People who are not marginalized or vulnerable can still be victims of atrocious violence, but they are not systemically targeted or victimized as a group in the same manner. Statistics easily demonstrate one social group systematically suffering from a pattern of cruel acts involving physical violence or injury whereas other groups are not. People living in low-income neighborhoods are less likely to have access to medical care (Thomas 2018) and quality education (Camera 2018); women are more likely to be sexually assaulted compared to men (National Sexual Violence Resource Center 2015); queer youth are more likely to be ostracized by their families and suffer from homelessness (Kline 2018), Black children and children of Latin American desscent are more likely to be cited for behavioral problems as early as kindergarten, leading to a greater chance of incarceration in a phenomenon known as the school-to-prison-pipeline (Okunafua and Eberhardt 2015). Each of these statistics reveal that these groups are suffering disproportionately and systematically in ways that their counterparts are not.

Social atrocities manifest from a confluence of social forces intimately related to the constructs presented in Chapter 1: Social atrocities rely on ideologies to rationalize cruel and violent discrimination against those without power, thus allowing those in power to retain power. Consider the procedural patterns leading up to **genocide**, or the systematic eradication of a racial, ethnic, or religious group. Gregory Stanton, professor of genocide studies, established eight stages of genocide in 1996, which has since been expanded to 10 stages: (1) classification, (2) symbolization, (3) discrimination, (4) dehumanization, (5) organization, (6) polarization, (7) preparation, (8) persecution, (9) extermination, and (10) denial (Stanton 2013).

The processes of marginalization are evident at each of these stages; people are first categorized as different (classification) and marked with symbols to indicate their difference (symbolization), effectively stereotyping the targeted group through ideology and discourse, which allows and encourages people and institutions to marginalize them. This process of discrimination is then amplified by stripping them of their humanity and associating them with inhuman animals and insects to ensure widespread prejudice against the targeted group. This dehumanization, amplified through polarizing propaganda, rationalizes and demands organized eradication (organization). These social efforts come to fruition as the group is separated from the larger community (preparation), persecuted, and exterminated. Given the atrocious nature of these crimes, the common response over the course during this extermination is to deny that genocide is happening until it is unavoidable; then when it becomes unavoidable, to deny the causes and outcomes of these actions.

As described in earlier chapters, focusing on individual actions and attitudes can prevent people from recognizing atrocities when they are happening or mustering outrage, even when one becomes aware of systematic cruelty or violence. Although in hindsight, we acknowledge that the concentration of specific ethnic groups in camps or another restricted geographic space is an atrocity, people often deny that ethnic groups are being targeted and systematically dehumanized in the moment (e.g., Indigenous people in North America, Uyghur Muslims in China) because we may not envision something as "cruel." This subjective component of acknowledging atrocities is deeply problematic because it allows our flawed perceptions of humanity to dictate whether an atrocity is happening; we work to ignore the indicators that an atrocity is occurring until the persecution and extermination have transpired, making it impossible to ignore.[1]

The next section will describe three strategies for satirizing atrocities that target patterns in discourse, ideology, and hegemony, and avoid punching down, or mocking those impacted by atrocities.

Strategies for Satirizing Atrocities

The only way to prevent history from repeating itself is to ensure that people are ready, willing, and prepared to call out these trends when they occur and Stanton's stages demonstrates that this path follows a consistent pattern. One person making disparaging remarks against a group may not seem atrocious, but these sentiments can affect institutional policies that can result in targeted cruelty and violence if these sentiments are taken as normal or as truths by a critical mass in the population or among those in power.

Artifacts satirizing atrocities tend to target the primary figure head largely seen as responsible for coordinating the atrocity, but this strategy distances the audience from the marginalization process by blaming a single person for the atrocity instead of recognizing how the atrocity itself is an outcome of multiple social processes. In the case of social atrocities, marginalization satire should help the audience see how they contribute to the marginalization of certain groups as well as how they can be part of the solution, regardless of whether they believe they are personally impacted by the group's marginalization. The following three strategies are important when creating satire that disrupts the progression of social atrocities.

1. Draw attention to the absurdity that led to the atrocity.
Stanton explains that the early stages of genocide (and by extension, social atrocities) involve the othering of groups (actively exclude, ostracize, alienate, and discriminate

---

[1] Outrage ensues when these atrocities are committed in the context of race, ethnic, or religious genocide (e.g., rape as a systematic weapon to threaten and terrorize a marginalized group in the midst of a genocide, systematic starvation and the taking of resources causing the further suffering among marginalized groups in the midst of a genocide), but these atrocities independent of genocide are often collectively ignored.

against a given group that is already marginalized), which ensures that we do not collectively see the commonalities between people and groups and instead classify *them* as different from *us*. Othering is rooted in stereotypes or strategies that we deploy to avoid thinking about people as complex, nuanced human beings in the same way that we think about ourselves and our own groups. This component of the atrocity is so integrated in discourse, hegemony, and norms, it can be difficult to discern while it is occurring.

Our Transgender Siblings Have Heartbeats (Clackamas United Church of Christ, 2020)
The suffering of transgender people can be traced to discrimination rooted in dehumanization, driven by the socially entrenched idea of a gender binary (see Chapter 3) that considers humans as inherently cisgendered. Trans people are people, and the repeated framing of trans people as "things" or "monsters" denies their humanity. At the same time, the rhetoric among anti-abortion activists is that fetuses become humans when they have a heartbeat, which is first discernible less than two months after conception. The sign "OUR TRANSGENDER SIBLINGS HAVE HEARTBEATS" underscores that if the metric of a human is a heartbeat, then it is absurd that we do not see trans folks as humans. The satire is even more striking given its location: On the public board of the Clackamas United Church of Christ in Milwaukie, Oregon; a church that has gained popularity for its social justice statements (Prior 2019).

2. Draw attention to the absurdity that prevents us from acknowledging the atrocity.
Dehumanizing individuals alleviates a major cognitive hurdle in the process of social atrocities: We need not concern ourselves with individuals who are not human. This dehumanization alleviates individuals from the guilt and shame associated with the

Figure 6.1 Marquee outside Oregon church reading "Our Transgender Siblings have Heartbeats." *Source*: Clackamas United Church of Christ / Facebook.com.

systematic destruction of human life. Atrocities are collectively ignored because we often do not consider these individual acts as atrocious, or we do not consider the people to whom they are being inflicted as equals. Therefore, artifacts that effectively satirize atrocities must draw attention to how the public and people in power refuse to recognize acts of cruelty and violence.

Dr. Seuss and the American Response to the Holocaust (1941–1943)
In a series of political cartoons, Theodor Geisel, publishing as Dr. Seuss, commented on the growing threat of nationalism in early 1940s Europe. Many cartoons depicted caricatures of European dictators Hitler and Mussolini as evil monsters committing atrocities (Gritz 2013), but other cartoons targeted Americans' refusal to pay attention to the events in Europe. In one cartoon, a man is peddling selling "Ostrich Bonnets" that are guaranteed to "Relieve your Hitler Headache!" Men line up to be fitted with hats that resemble long-necked birds that cover the wearer's face. The placard reads, "Forget the terrible news you've read, your mind's at ease in an ostrich head!" On the right side of the frame is a row of men with their ostrich bonnets buried in the sand, tuning out the world around them and relieving themselves of any responsibility to act against the oppression. Although we often discuss atrocities via the individuals who are actively committing atrocious acts (e.g., Nazis), social atrocities are defined by a collective organized group of perpetrators and enablers; without enablers, perpetrators cannot perpetrate without recourse.

3. Draw attention to the ongoing impact on those who suffered from the atrocity.
The last stage that Stanton describes is denial, which "…is among the surest indicators of further genocidal massacres" (Stanton 2013). Denial is endemic to our inability to recognize or acknowledge the atrocity as it is happening, as is evidenced in the Dr. Seuss panel. We also deny atrocities by ignoring the stories of survivors and ongoing effects. Atrocities do violence to victims as well as their larger associated group, including those that may not have been subjected to immediate physical injury. To understand the absurdity of atrocities, we must willing to listen to those who have suffered and allow them to cope with their pain in the best way that they see fit, including through laughter. Centering the stories of victims helps avoid denial and ideally more atrocities.

Welcome to Hell (*Saturday Night Live*, S43E7, NBC 2017)
Just seven weeks after the hashtag #MeToo went viral in 2017, *Saturday Night Live* cast members Cecily Strong, Kate McKinnon, Aidy Bryant, and Melissa Villaseñor were joined by Saoirse Ronan for a parody song called "Welcome to Hell." It looks and feels like a classic over the top bubble-gum pop music video with bright colors, catchy lyrics, women in cute dresses acting like pubescent girls, but the lyrics addressed something much darker: The experiences of women who live in perpetual fear of being sexual harassed and assaulted.

> STRONG: Hey there, boys. We know the last couple months have been frickin' insane.
> BRYANT: All these big, cool, powerful guys are turning out to be, what's the word? Habitual predators?

MCKINNON: Cat's out of the bag, women get harassed all the time!
BRYANT: And it's, like, 'Dang, is this the world now?'
RONAN: But here's a little secret that every girl knows.
STRONG: Oh, this been the damn world!

The song was directed at those who were surprised at the sheer size and virality of the necessary conversation about sexual assault. The SNL cast members explain what women do to *not* get sexually assaulted, like using keys as a weapon, acting mentally unstable to deter would-be attackers, and avoiding rideshare cars. They also discuss the impact of having one's pleas and calls for help be ignored. In a brief interlude, Leslie Jones enters the stage and reminds the (all White) ensemble, "You do know that it's, like, a million times worse for women of color, right?" to which the other women vehemently agree before continuing to sing with Jones now part of the ensemble.

These three strategies ensure that satire focuses the attention of the audience on the marginalization processes common to social atrocities. Furthermore, they avoid punching down by targeting collective sentiments that perpetuate atrocities and amplifying the experience of victims. It is tasteless to make fun of trans people when they are four times more likely to live in poverty (Movement Advancement Project 2014), mock Jewish people when discussing the Holocaust, or laugh at women in an environment of pervasive sexual terror. Hegemonically disadvantaged individuals have historically been the punchline, creating a discriminatory loop that inhibits audiences from recognizing atrocities that target these groups given that their dehumanization is framed as funny. Ultimately, jokes that "punch down" perpetuate pre-existing power dynamics because they reflect both the outcome *and* the antecedent of social atrocities. Therefore, they are not satire.

Figure 6.2 "House of Cards is ruined, and that really sucks. Well here's a list of stuff that's ruined for us: Parking and walking and Uber and ponytails, bathrobes and nighttime and drinking and hotels and vans. Nothing good happens in a van!" Thumbnail from "Welcome to Hell" *Saturday Night Live* (2017).

The rest of this chapter will describe social atrocities and analyze artifacts that effectively satirize these atrocities, including poverty and homelessness, sexual assault, the HIV/AIDS crisis during the late 20th century, slavery, and genocide.

Satirizing Extreme Poverty and Homelessness

Chapter 2 described the absurdities of socioeconomic status (SES) and class, but did not address **extreme or absolute poverty**, which is "…a condition characterized by severe deprivation of basic human needs, including food, safe drinking water, sanitation facilities, health, shelter, education, and information" (United Nations 1995).

Globally, approximately 700 million people or 9% of the world's population live in extreme poverty, which is defined as less than $2/day, and it is anticipated that COVID will add another 150 million people (World Bank 2020). In American discourse, the term "extreme poverty" is usually applied to other countries (see "If it happened here" by *Slate* in Chapter 1), not the situation of people living in the United States even though a United Nations Human Rights investigation found that 18.5 million Americans (5.6%) lived in extreme poverty (2018). According to Catherine Flowers, a scientist investigating hookworm[2] in rural Alabama, "Our billionaire philanthropists like Bill Gates fund water treatment around the world, but they don't fund it here in the United States because no one acknowledges this level of poverty exists in the richest nation in the world" (Pilkington 2017). This lack of awareness regarding the situation of extreme poverty in America highlights a little-known social atrocity happening at home.

The United Nations (UN) states explicitly that extreme poverty is defined by low income *and* an inability to access basic essential services. However, there is an intractable focus on income when extreme or absolute poverty is discussed in the public sphere. Researchers, politicians, and pundits argue ad nauseum about what qualifies as "poverty" and different metrics manifest very different numbers. The aforementioned numbers from the UN are based on the number of Americans who had a yearly income lower than half the national poverty line, or approximately $16 per day for a single individual and $33 per day for a family of four. In response to the UN report, the United States government countered that only about 250,000 people in the United States live in extreme extreme (or "deep") poverty, which they defined as living on less than $4 per day (Stein 2018). However, the focus on what qualifies as "extreme poverty" avoids discussing the experience of those living in atrocious conditions, including the fact that two million Americans don't have access to running water and basic plumbing (Jagannathan 2019).

Eight Million Americans Rescued from Poverty with a Redefinition of Term (*The Onion* 1999)

> WASHINGTON, DC–Approximately eight million Americans living below the poverty line were rescued from economic hardship Monday, when the

---

[2] A 2017 study found 34% of residents in a rural Alabama county tested positive for hookworm, a parasite that thrives in raw sewage and a condition that is commonly associated with extreme poverty and a lack of basic sanitation (McKenna et al. 2017).

U.S. Census Bureau redefined the term. "We are winning the war on poverty," said bureau head James Irving, who lowered the poverty line for a four-person family to $14,945. "Today, millions of people whose inflation-adjusted total household income is less than $16,780 are living better lives." Said formerly poor Jackson, MS, motel housekeeper Althea Williams: "I never dreamed I'd ever become middle-class. America truly is the land of opportunity."

At first glance, mocking the policy decisions that define poverty may not seem like drawing attention to the absurdity that caused the atrocity. But showcasing how a change in defintion can reduce the number of people in poverty without actually improving their quality of life reveals how the atrocity of poverty is ignored. Phrases like "rescued from economic hardship," "winning the war on poverty," and "living better lives," remind readers that the lives of people who are struggling and living on $1400 a month have not changed; even if the rhetoric regarding poverty sounds more optimistic. The final quote from a housekeeper in Missouri underscores the absurdity of arbitrary socioeconomic lines, reiterating the idea that America is the land of opportunity because policymakers have determined her to be middle class. The reader knows her situation has not changed; rather, she is simply reacting *as if* her situation has changed. This ridiculous twist ends the artifact on a joke about the expense of class mobility rhetoric in the United States.

One of the most identifiable and evident outcomes of these disparities is **homelessness**, or being without somewhere to sleep at night. According to the Department

Figure 6.3 "Faces of Homelessness" Phil Hands 2020. *Source*: Phil Hands/ Madison Media Partners Inc.

of Housing and Urban Development (HUD), approximately 580,000 people in the United States (2.2%) experienced homelessness on any given night (2021). This figure includes both people who are **sheltered**, meaning in homeless shelters, transitional housing, hotels and motels paid for charitable organizations, and are **unsheltered**, meaning staying in cars, parks, and encampments. Mediated representation of homelessness are grossly skewed; the Center for Media and Social Impact revealed that major television programs and newspapers misrepresented housing issues in 2018 (CMSI, 2019). The most popular newspapers in the nation, "grossly underreported issues of homelessness, affordable housing, and gentrification, oversimplified and isolated housing stability issues, primarily represented homelessness as a policy story, and rarely acknowledged the existence of gentrification in American life."

In figure 6.3, political cartoonist Phil Hands reveals the diversity of people who qualify as homeless and invites the audience to consider their own understanding of the term. In the top left quadrant, we see the stereotypical representation of a homeless person: A grizzled man begging for money on the street. In each subsequent panel, we see people who are suffering from homelessness who are often ignored: An unemployed mother living out of her car, a young child attending school, and a woman working as a server. Each of these panels showcases how homelessness can manifest but may not trigger collective awareness or action: People living out of their car, attending school, or working. The cartoon draws attention to the factors that keep us from recognizing the atrocity, specifically, our stereotypes of homelessness and (extreme) poverty.

Though 61.8% of Americans will suffer from poverty in their lifetime (Rank and Hirschl 2015), twice as many Americans as those with Bachelor's degrees (32%) (Nietzel 2021), the pervasive shaming of those in poverty may prevent people from revealing this part of their life. Poverty is framed as an individual shortcoming as described in Chapter 2 and not as an institutional problem, thus preventing people from asking for help. In the case of the top-left panel, the man begging on the street adheres to our stereotypes of poverty and explicitly implores passers-by for their assistance. Hands then replicates his sign "HOMELESS PLEASE HELP" for the other three individuals, amplifying the issue to make audiences see what they have (implicitly or explicitly) denied. Homelessness impacts a wide swathe of the population, including people who do not meet the collective stereotypical representation of homelessness, and all are suffering.

Poverty and homelessness are social atrocities because cruel acts resulting in starvation and death are based on a social category: Socioeconomic status (SES). Furthermore, this cruel treatment is the result of an organized collective of perpetrators and enablers who work to inhibit a living wage (see Activity 2.2), collective bargaining, and universal healthcare. A 2011 study attributed approximately 4.5% of American deaths to poverty (Galea et al. 2011), but the American public does not generally discuss extreme poverty and homelessness as atrocities. Prior to the pandemic, the United States had one of the starkest class gaps in life expectancy of all wealthy countries (Leonhardt and Thompson 2020), a disparity that was only heighted by the pandemic. This disregard for the health and well-being of those at the bottom of the income spectrum is an affront to the rhetoric of the American Dream and the idea that anyone with hard work and a little bit of luck can advance in the United States.

Satirizing Sexual Violence

Sexual violence, sex acts attempted or achieved through violence or coercion, including rape and sex trafficking, is pervasive and well-documented. In the United States alone, about one-third of American women report being the victim of sexual assault (Rabin 2011). These numbers vary according to the group being polled; over half of Indigenous women and over 40% of Black women report that their intimate partners have been physical violent toward them (Institute for Women's Policy Research 2011). This is the definition of a social atrocity: One group disproportionately experiences cruel acts of violence or injury because of their membership in a given social group.

Rape and sexual assault are rooted in individual and interpersonal gendered expectations. The combination of female **objectification** and **male entitlement** ensures women's bodies are seen as objects to which men have free and unfettered access (Griffin and Phillips 2019; Nettleton 2019). This interlocking gendered puzzle also fosters a **rape culture** where rape and sexual violence are normalized. As described earlier in this chapter regarding "Welcome to Hell," women come to expect sexual assault as extremely likely, inevitable, or even normal. Rape culture is perpetuated by glorifying sexual violence with positive feedback. This normalization is then furthered by **rape myths**: False but persistent beliefs and stereotypes regarding forced sexual intercourse, perpetrators, and their victims (Lonsway and Fitzgerald 1994). Rape myths include the ideas that women fabricate rape accusations when they regret their sexual choices or to harm men, all women fantasize about being raped, and only promiscuous women or women who dress provocatively are raped, all of which are false. Furthermore, television use has been correlated with rape myth agreement; the more television one watches, the more likely one is to agree with these false beliefs about rape (Kahlor and Eastin 2011).

Majorité Opprimée (Translation: Oppressed Majority, Eleonore Pourriat 2010)

This short film by French filmmaker Eléonore Pourriat follows a day in the life of Pierre as he collects his mail, drops his child off at daycare, and makes his way to work. In the process, he gets catcalled and sexually assaulted by a group of women in an alley, then further traumatized when he tries to report the incident to the police. However, the satire does not come from the narrative or the progression of events. Rather, the satire emerges from the "flipped" world in which Pierre lives, in which women are cast as hegemonically superior to reveal the absurd disparities of gender. This flip manifests in every aspect of the film, from the opening shot where a woman jogs topless, to the man operating a daycare who shaves to appear more attractive to his wife. A gang of women curse at Pierre using the term "father*cker" and his wife accuses him of bringing on the attack with his "above-the-knee Bermuda shorts."

The film is deeply impactful on multiple levels. It helps the viewer see gendered power dynamics that we have been encouraged to ignore, or accept as natural. The film is not traditionally funny, but students often laugh out of shock and discomfort as they see patterns in their own life in a new light. The film invites the viewer to recognize that the culture of sexual violence stems from the coordinated degradation and objectification of women that means their bodies are seen as property of men. Brief interactions where Pierre is sexualized by passers-bys or told to cover up by

Figure 6.4 After Pierre's assault in an alley and being retraumatized by recounting it to a disbelieving detective (also a woman), his seemingly supportive partner arrives at the hospital long after his ordeal because she couldn't get away from work. Still from *Majorité Opprimée* (2010).

powerful women in his life (the detective and his wife), parallel the behaviors that women are subjected to in a patriarchal society. By flipping the power dynamics of gender without actually flipping gender (i.e., women still appear in "feminine" clothing in and men in "masculine" clothing), the film draws attention to the absurdities of gender that cultivates a culture that normalizes sexual violence.

Sexual violence is further enabled by institutions responsible for protecting victims and prosecuting perpetrators. In *Majorité Opprimée*, Pierre is forced to recount his assault to a female detective who questions his testimony ("Broad daylight... and no witnesses... Interesting huh?") while objectifying her male assistant by complimenting his jeans after dismissing his intelligence. The scene demonstrates why only 31% of sexual assaults are reported to the police: Victims experience trauma from repeating the story to unsympathetic individuals (Van Dam 2018). Furthermore, it is assumed that perpetrators will not be held accountable; about 18% of reported rapes are prosecuted, and less than 1% of rapes and attempted rapes end in a felony conviction (Lee 2014; RAINN 2020). For victims across genders, these numbers deter reporting, given the likelihood that nothing will happen. The failure to define rape and sexual assault as a pervasive social atrocity is rooted in the institutionalization of rape myths at every level.

Our tendency to believe the best in some people and the worst in others manifests in many stories where individuals accused and even convicted of sexual assault are given the benefit of the doubt. Institutions work to ensure that they do not experience long-term impact as their future and general well-being seems paramount, not holding them accountable for their actions. The "Stanford swimmer" is an important example of who receives the benefit of the doubt. A freshman at Stanford from a wealthy White suburban family with Olympic potential was caught sexually assaulting an unconscious woman behind a dumpster in 2015. He was sentenced to six months in prison after a jury unanimously found him guilty on three charges, a fraction of the six-year minimum requested by prosecutors. In rationalizing his sentencing, the judge (himself a graduate of Stanford) stated he believed the victim had given consent even though she was unconscious. He expressed concern for the impact of a prison sentence on the perpetrator (Levin 2016), drawing on his character statements from friends and family. The idea that some men, specifically young, upper-class, White men, simply do not *look* like sexual predators is a sentiment held even by attorneys who are otherwise committed to ending sexual assault (Small 2015). **Victimizing the perpetrator**, or framing the long-term well-being of the perpetrator on par with or more important than justice served for their actual victim(s), enables this atrocity especially when it occurs among a network of powerful figures.

Rapists Now Have Their Own Recovery Center (Above Average Productions, 2016)
The New York-based comedy production company Above Average Productions released a two-minute video in the style of an infomercial for a recovery center. Rather than helping people who are suffering, this recovery center helps people who have *caused* others to suffer. The video opens with founder of the center, Spencer Ayerly, in an office setting explaining the fear and loneliness experienced by people "affected by rape." The viewer is led to believe that the recovery center is for victims of rape, but it is quickly revealed that Second Chances Recovery Center is a place to support rapists; "The negative stigma associated with your little slip-up can make your life a total bummer, but your future doesn't have to be a poopsie because of one past oopsie" a direct reference to the father of the Stanford freshman, who referred to the assault as "20 minutes of action."

Similar to the language around the "Stanford swimmer" case, Ayerly repeatedly brushes off the implications of the atrocious act of rape to ensure that the perpetrator is alleviated of emotional and procedural guilt. The Second Chances Recovery Center offers post "oopsie" strategies repeatedly deployed by those accused or convicted of rape: Including crafting a vague non-apology, forming the right witch hunt narrative, finding that one celebrity who's weirdly willing to go to bat for you, and practicing deflection techniques, effectively "saying the quiet part out loud." The segment also underscores how these second chances are often reserved for those with socioeconomic

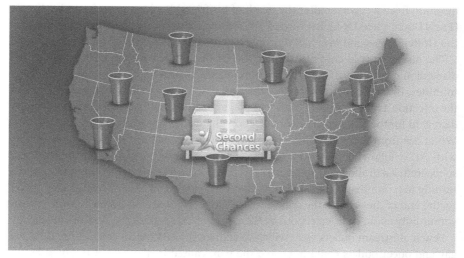

Figure 6.5 "Our location is equidistant from the countries biggest party schools, so our clients have access to world-class Greek life, where they can get back to being who they really are, just boys." Still from Rapists Now Have Their Own Recovery Center (2016).

privilege by featuring a testimonial from a young man who landed a cushy job at a bank where the CEO is his father's poker buddy: "Second chances are hard to come by, but when they do, they're strictly reserved for people who need them the least."

Although there is a rhetorical consideration for the victim, coverage that focuses on the perpetrators' perspective encourages the audience to empathize with the perpetrators because they are repeatedly invited to see through the perpetrators' lens. This, coupled with perpetrators who are hegemonically advantaged compared to the victim (because of class, gender, sexuality, or race), refocuses the argument away from the atrocity to humanize those who have actively dehumanized others. Such emphasis prevents a robust acknowledgment that an atrocity has been committed by arguing that holding the perpetrator accountable is an atrocity of equal standing. As described in "Racist Timeout" from *The Daily Show with Jon Stewart* in Chapter 5, the benefit of the doubt is racist, but it is also sexist and classist.

Satirizing the HIV/AIDS Pandemic

In the early 1980s, a wave of unexplained illnesses began to sweep through the United States, disproportionately impacting gay communities in New York, San Francisco, and Los Angeles. Although there had been similar cases among gay and heterosexual patients in the 1960s and '70s, the outbreaks in the in the 1980s began to trigger a nationwide conversation within the gay community. By the end of 1981, 131 people were confirmed to have died from the disease (Pickrell 2006), including men and women, as well children who were infected through blood transfusions or contracted in utero. This dire situation escalated rapidly and by the end of 1982, the Centers for Disease Control and Prevention (CDC) defined AIDS as a disease that can infect all people regardless of their sexuality. However, national leaders avoided publicly discussing the emerging epidemic for years; President Ronald Reagan made a public statement three years after the CDC's definition and only in response to a question from a reporter after the death of his friend Rock Hudson from the disease (Press Conference 1985). By the end of 1985, over 16,000 cases had been diagnosed in the United States and over 2,000 people had died of HIV/AIDS (CDC 2001).

The disease would continue to increase exponentially over the next few years but dispassionate conversations about prevention and treatment were isolated to gay communities. In the mainstream media, the lack of information and repeated mention of the infection as a "gay disease" or a "gay plague" activated homophobia and a collective disregard for the afflicted. The conversation changed when Ryan White, a 13-year-old White boy from Indiana with hemophilia who did not identify as gay, was diagnosed with AIDS following a blood transfusion from an HIV-positive donor in 1986. His school refused to allow him to return in response to pressure from parents and teachers, leading to a monthslong legal dispute that was widely covered in mainstream media. By the end of the decade, the American public recognized that people outside the gay community could be infected, but by then, over 50,000 Americans had already died.

Few mainstream outlets were wiling to address the HIV/AIDS crisis at the time, but gay and queer outlets could not avoid the pain caused by the lack of response by the government and society at large. Cartoonists within gay communities tackled this absurdity head on, including Danny Sotomayor (1958–1992), a Chicago-based cartoonist whose political cartoons about the AIDS crisis in the late 1980s were syndicated in gay outlets nationwide. His cartoons satirized the absurdities that led to the atrocity, including how homophobia and a lack of sex education affected leaders and everyday Americans and how refusing to recognize the national threat of HIV/AIDS allowed the disease to balloon out of control. In the first cartoon, First Lady Barbara Bush and President George H.W. Bush sit in bed as the president reads a newspaper with the headline: "100,000 DIAGNOSED WITH AIDS IN THE US," but he insists there is nothing important in the paper. The inability of the president to recognize an imminent national threat is by definition absurd and demonstrates a willful disregard for *certain* American citizens.

AIDS was officially declared a pandemic in 1993, leading to a coordinated international effort to address the disease. However, the infection rate among men who have sex with men was markedly sharper than those infected through intravenous drug use and heterosexual contact by this time. The stereotypes that gay men are inherently immoral, deviant, and undeserving of human rights (see Chapter 4) prevented the Americans at large from recognizing the impact of this unique atrocity. The rhetoric of AIDS as a gay disease in the 1980s had a catalyzing effect; it was disproportionately impacting gay men, but the public avoided discussing the disease and related science, which allowed it to spread unchecked and further devastate the gay community. This devastation reinforced the idea that HIV/AIDS was a "gay disease," feeding a cycle of marginalization. The procrastination and the resulting devastation to the queer community during this time still impacts this community and the nation at large. Survivors of this atrocity tell stories of watching their friends and loved ones die without government recognition, often while being ostracized by their family.

Ronald Reagan's death in 2004 triggered effusive praise across mainstream media, as is expected of a presidential passing. Yet many voices in communities

Figure 6.6 American Responses to AIDS (Danny Sotomayor, 1989). *Source*: Danny Sotomayor.

impacted by HIV/AIDS, including the gay community, remained stricken by the devastation that Reagan largely avoided. These contrasting messages surrounding his death were well synthesized in a cartoon by Mikhaela B. Reid, in which the cliché lines lauding Reagan are juxtaposed with the memories of survivors. Each panel features a speech bubble extoling Reagan with a thought bubble from a survivor that parodies the rhetoric and cadence to draw attention to their continued suffering (e.g., "Remember how optimistic he was!" is contrasted with "I remember the day I found out I was positive"). The style of the comic also satirizes the long-standing silencing of this community; whereas the praises of Reagan emanate from the televisions in black, bold, capital lettering, the survivors' responses are presented in smaller, lowercase words situated in thought bubbles. Furthermore, the televisions and broadcast messages get larger with each panel. In the penultimate panel, the mediated praise of Reagan ("He was the GREAT communicator") consumes more than half the panel, whereas the profiles of seven huddled survivors take up less than a quarter of the bottom of the panel as they collectively think, "We remember his silence."

HIV/AIDS continues to have a disproportionate impact on historically marginalized communities in the United States. In 2018, 41% of people with HIV in the United States were Black, significantly greater than their 13% representation in the national population.[3] Similarly, the rate of new infections infections among Black women is *13*

Figure 6.7 Silence + Death (Mikhaela B. Reid 2004). *Source*: Mikhaela B. Reid.

---

3 Similarly, 23% of people with HIV in the United States were of Latin American descent, greater than their 18% representation.

times that of White women (HIV.gov). The prevalence of HIV is highest among those at or below the poverty level (CDC 2011) and in a study of 23 high poverty neighborhoods in 2006 and 2007, the CDC found the incidence of HIV to be 2.4%, or one in 42, nearly six times that of households earning above the median of $50,000 annually (Denning and DiNenno 2010). Institutional policies regarding healthcare also exacerbate class-based disparities. Undiscounted lifetime medical costs for someone diagnosed with HIV at aged 35 was estimated in 2012 to be just under $600,000 ($326,000 with discounts; clinicalinfo.hiv.gov, 2021) and the average wholesale price for antiretroviral treatments (ART) continues to climb (McCann et al. 2020).

Tonsil Trouble (*South Park*, S12E1 Comedy Central 2008)
Although satirizing these disparities seems impossible, *South Park* tackled the absurdity of class and the HIV/AIDS crisis with their 2008 episode, "Tonsil Trouble". After contracting AIDS from a blood transfusion during a tonsillectomy, Eric Cartman purposely infects Kyle Broflovski, causing the two of them to visit Magic Johnson's house to look for a cure. Magic Johnson announced that he was HIV-positive in 1991 and since has lived with the disease. In the episode, Johnson claims that he does not have a cure but reveals that he sleeps on piles of cash every night, leading to the discovery that a concentrated dose of $180,000 shot directly into the bloodstream neutralizes HIV, the virus that causes AIDS. Although the larger episode received mixed ratings from critics, this moment explicitly satirizes the underfunding of AIDS research in the early days of the epidemic as well as the fact that those with money have a greater chance of survival.

Coverage of the HIV/AIDS crisis has diminished because its impact on White, male, middle to upper class Americans in positions of power has decreased. However, this ongoing global epidemic continues to ravage low-income and middle-income countries as well as marginalized populations in the United States. Furthermore, there is still a pervasive association of the disease with gay communities, which can

Figure 6.8 The boys are shocked to discover that Magic Johnson sleeps on piles of cash every night because he doesn't trust banks. Still from "Tonsil Trouble" (South Park 2008).

prevent people from getting tested for fear of being labeled "gay." It is estimated at 1.2 million people in the United States are living with HIV, and 13% are unaware of their serostatus (hiv.gov, 2021). In recent years, the acronym LGBTQ has been expanded to LGBTQ+ to denote those with HIV are subjected to stereotypes, prejudice, and discrimination similar to those targeting gay and queer communities.

Satirizing Genocide and Slavery

Genocide and slavery are considered two of the most heinous atrocities committed in the United States. Both of these atrocities entitled White Americans to use and abuse Indigenous and Black people freely as a matter of policy. Although these institutions are no longer legal, the ideologies and cultural strategies that preceded and rationalized both genocide and slavery are still present and are still used to dehumanize Americans of Indigenous and African descent, often through denial.

Denial manifests in many ways, including by appropriating the obliterated culture, thereby silencing the voices of survivors and descendants. Chapter 5 featured an extended discussion of appropriation and assimilation and how these two concepts perpetuate the marginalization of disadvantaged groups and bolster the status of the dominant group. One of the highest profile instances of genocide denial is the use of Native American caricatures, epithets, and stereotypes as sports mascots. In doing so, the history of these terms and images are actively decontextualized from their genocidal history.[4]

Outrage toward sports teams featuring Native American-inspired mascots is decades old. Dozens of professional, college, and high school teams changed their names and imagery during the twentieth century, including the Golden State Warriors (1969), Dartmouth College (1974), and Syracuse University (1978).[5] Despite these changes, some prominent professional teams retained these discriminatory images including the Cleveland Indians (changed to the Cleveland Guardians in 2021), the Atlanta Braves, and the Washington Redsk*ns (changed to the Washington Commanders in 2022), spawned by a wave of social media posts using the hashtag #changethename in 2014. Nonetheless, a 2020 analysis of MascotDB revealed that over 1,200 high schools nationwide featured Native American team names including 45 teams using the name Redsk*ns (Allchin 2020). This pervasive usage, from elementary school to professional sports, belittles the fact that approximately 12 million Indigenous people were killed from 1492 to 1900 to establish what is currently known as the United States (Stannard 1993; Thornton 1987).

Catching Racism (*The Daily Show with Jon Stewart* and The 1491s, Comedy Central 2014)
This segment is a pre-recorded package starring correspondent Jason Jones. It begins with a brief explanation of the public outrage regarding the name, Washington Redsk*ns, and a clip of the Washington Redsk*ns team owner Daniel Snyder defending the name: "The name of our team is the name of our team and it represents

---

4 European settlers killed 56 million Indigenous Americans in the sixteenth century alone in North, South, and Central America, causing the earth's climate to cool (Koch et al. 2019).

5 Although the title of "Orangemen" was not discontinued until 2004.

honor, it represents pride, it represents respect." Playing the naïve but interested journalist, Jones turns to a group of Native Americans for clarification. The group dispassionately describes the issues with the word, "It's a name that impairs, disables, [and] disenfranchises our population.... [It's] a dictionary defined racial slur.... Redsk*n is a bounty. It meant proof of Indian kill." Jones then turns to a group of Redsk*ns fans who claim that their culture and community is at risk if the name is changed. "If the Redsk*ns name is changed and I have children one day, what would I pass on to them? It'd be tough. It would be like losing a family member." They then go on to claim traces of Indigenous heritage ("one-twelfth Cherokee") to dismiss the public outrage. The clip ends with Jones asking, "If you brought a Native American, wouldn't they be a little upset?" To which one of the fans responds, "We need to be sitting down talking to the people that actually are offended." The group of Native Americans are then brought into the studio to do just that, but the interaction is muted. Instead, Jones provides a voiceover:

> It turns out these fans weren't comfortable having that conversation. In fact, afterward, they relayed to *The Washington Post* that they felt ambushed, in danger, and defamed.... In the end, they said they still would have gone on the show had they known there would be a debate but at least one of them 'wouldn't have worn his Redsk*ns jacket.'

The clip brilliantly demonstrates each of the three suggestions outlined at the top of this chapter. It draws attention to the absurdity of the systematic dehumanization of Indigenous peoples that caused the Indigenous genocide. It calls out the financial windfall that comes with sports and team-based identities in the United States that prevent us from acknowledging the long-standing impact of the Indigenous genocide. Finally, it singles out the ongoing impact that the genocide has had on Indigenous communities today. This last point is particularly relevant given the fact that the voices of Indigenous people, who were once 100% of the United States population and are now less than 1% of the population, are repeatedly dismissed, silenced, or co-opted, especially when people unaffiliated with Indigenous communities claim Indigenous heritage to dismiss their concerns.

Caucasians (2007, 2016, 2018)

In recent years, there has also been a satirical push to draw attention to the problematic nature of using Indigenous caricatures as mascots by flipping the message to create logos that feature stereotypical caricatures of White Americans. Two of these examples are featured in Figure 6.9. They are often met with outrage by White observers, arguing they are offensive and ridiculous, emotions that are not similarly activated when the target is a group of historically marginalized people. In a 2018 opinion piece in *USA Today*, author and entrepreneur Frederick Joseph describes the experience of wearing a "Caucasians" shirt on the street in Manhattan: "A man who had mistaken my shirt for an actual team shirt and said, 'Go Skins!,' to which I replied, 'Nah.' Upon his realization, he called me an 'a-hole'" (Joseph 2018).

Having an emotional response to being mocked is unsurprising, but the individuals described in Joseph's piece were also unable to recognize that their brief

168 | 6 Satirizing Atrocities

Figure 6.9 Logos that parody anti-Indigenous team logos using caricatures and stock images of White faces to flip the frame.

emotions are chronic among Indigenous and Native Americans. These featured logos are effective satire because they draw attention to what prevents us from recognizing the atrocity of genocide in the United States: These atrocities happened to people who were not White and the outrage comes only when the target is White. Furthermore, the artifact is brilliant in that it flips audiences' awareness of an atrocity through the simple medium of a t-shirt, much like "Poverty is Sexist" in Chapter 2.

Both of these artifacts foreground the humanity of those still suffering from the atrocity of genocide. Listening to those who have been affected by atrocity may be one of the most difficult satirical strategies especially for those not affected by the atrocity. Understanding this pain is deeply uncomfortable, and the inability to solve long-term effects from atrocities past may make one feel helpless.

Similarly, the practice of slavery continues to resonate today, regardless of those that would argue it was in the past. Many argue that slavery was resolved when Abraham Lincoln signed the Emancipation Proclamation, but the practice of slavery was buoyed by the ideology that people of African descent were less intelligent, more animalistic, and inherently more dangerous. Many argued that people descended from this group were best suited for physical labor and needed to be physically restrained because they were a threat to "civilized" society. They were referred to not as humans, but as "cargo," meaning non-human commodities that could be loaded upon ships and transported across the Atlantic Ocean and it is estimated that about 1.8 million people of African descent, about 14.5% of those who were captured and loaded upon ships, died during the Middle Passage. Casting Black people as inhuman evaded concern for their mental or physical well-being, and the worth of Black Americans was determined only by their value to White Americans, a sentiment that was also internalized by Black Americans (Burrell 2010; Du Bois 1897).

Number One Slave Draft Pick (*Saturday Night Live*, S39E9, NBC 2014)
On her first appearance on Weekend Update, Leslie Jones had a lot to say about Black beauty in response to People Magazine's recent cover announcing Lupita

Figure 6.10 Leslie Jones implores the audience to see how - despite being dismissed as unattractive and without value in the 21st century - her body type would be extremely valuable centuries earlier in a slavery economy. Still from Number One Slave Draft Pick (Saturday Night Live 2014).

Nyong'o as the "Most Beautiful Person Alive." After acknowledging and congratulating Nyong'o, Jones expressed her desire to be the most *useful* person alive. She pointed out that, as a six-foot-tall and strong woman, she is rarely the preferred choice at the bar but would undoubtedly be the first choice in the parking lot when facing a fight. She then goes on to describe that she would never be single in "slave days" because "Massa would have hooked me up with the best brother on the plantation. And every nine months I'd be in the corner having a super baby... Shaq... Kobe... Lebron..." The two-minute segment, a staple during her stand-up act prior to joining the cast, presented a not-so hypothetical world harkening back to an era of chattel slavery, when Jones would be valued because of how "useful" she was in her ability to reproduce offspring that were of value to "massa."

The routine was met with backlash from mainstream media outlets, which claimed that she was making light of slavery and devaluing herself as an independent woman. It is true that the rape and forced reproduction of enslaved people was in itself an abhorrent atrocity that continues to impact Black men and women today, but rather than idealize this atrocity, Jones' routine was an honest and open reaction about and by someone impacted by this atrocity generations later. In a piece for TIME Magazine, Roxane Gay (2014) explained the importance of the monologue and her own empathy with Jones in that moment:

> Beyond the surface of the joke, I see pain. I see rage. I see a woman speaking her truth. The "Black is beautiful" movement has worked to challenge damaging notions about Black beauty since the 1960s, but more than 50 years on, Black women rarely get to be beautiful. Black women get to be strong. We get to be imposing and intimidating. We get to be thick, hypersexual bodies. We get to be exotic. We get to be the dirty secret you won't take home to your family.... Look at Jones's face at the end of her monologue. See what is there. I am haunted by what I see. She was expressing a very specific loneliness I instantly recognized—having a big Black body that may never be seen as beautiful or desirable, while carrying so much desire that goes unsatisfied.

Calling artifacts created from the perspective of those who suffer from past and present atrocities offensive or tasteless is a reactionary response that avoids confronting the emotional baggage that this history elicits. Similarly, others may interpret the satire as reinforcing pre-existing hegemony instead of disrupting it (see The Inconsistent Effects of Marginalization Satire in Chapter 1). However, understanding the experiences of those who have suffered and those who continue to suffer is part of understanding the pattern of past atrocities and ensure that we are able to address future atrocities. Atrocities committed centuries ago still impact our intergroup and interpersonal interactions as well as the interactions that we have with ourselves (i.e., intrapersonal). To ignore or avoid discussions of an atrocity is to deny its very existence.

Satirizing Atrocities in the Twenty-First Century

Social atrocities are pervasive and ongoing. They impact the people that we care about even if we are unaware an atrocity is happening. Two-thirds of all Americans will experience poverty, but two-thirds of the people we encounter do not share stories about being poor. One-third of all women and one-sixth of all men in the United States will experience some form of sexual assault in their lifetime, but one-fourth of people we encounter do not share stories about suriving sexual assault. These ongoing atrocities are enabled in part *because* we do not encounter these stories.

The relationship between social atrocities and marginalization is circular. That is, cruel actions discriminate, dehumanize, disenfranchise, and destroy a group that is already at the margins of society. An action then becomes the defining characteristic of the group, making it difficult for others to see the group as a robust diverse set of people. This narrowing of the group's public presence thus reinforces stereotypes, prejudice, and discrimination toward the marginalized group. Furthermore, the group destruction inherent in social atrocities ensures that their stories will not be widely shared, feeding into a pattern of news media coverage that deems these stories not newsworthy. Gatekeepers may believe that such stories do not attract a sufficient segment of the audience to be profitable. By not recognizing or discussing these atrocities honestly and openly, the atrocities are allowed to repeat.

The role of marginalization satirists is to disturb this cycle. They draw attention to atrocities without perpetuating the marginalization of the group or dishonoring the memory of survivors and descendants of those impacted by the atrocity. It is a fine line to negotiate. We recognize social atrocities as the worst manifestations of our species and collectively seek to ensure they do not happen again. But as described at the start of the chapter, we don't always recognize the early indicators of these atrocities or the way these atrocities still impact us today, especially when we want to believe that we are better than our past selves. When satirizing atrocities, it is important to remember the following:

Explain how the atrocity reinforces pre-existing hierarchies. Atrocities are an outcome and an antecedent of marginalization processes. Audiences must be made aware of how atrocities connect with powerful hierarchies. Artifacts like Eight Million Americans, Rapists Now Have Their Own Recovery Center," and Number One Slave Draft Pick explicitly address hierarchies. They state who benefits from the atrocity, who is left behind, and how the atrocity continues to maintain this hierarchy. Respectively, these artifacts describe the sheer number of people suffering, the privilege inherent in bypassing accountability for one's atrocious actions, and the widespread devaluing of marginalized people. Because some of the audience will not understand the atrocity being satirized, as evident in the reaction to the Leslie Jones segment, satirists must take care when choosing to express this information.

Focus on the humanity lost in the atrocity. Atrocities requirethe dehumanization of the targeted group. Faces of Homelessness, Silence + Death, and Catching Racism humanize those suffering from these atrocities to underscore the impact of the collective negligence toward their situation. At the same time, actively committing or passively participating in an atrocity requires repressing one's own sense of empathy; we lose our humanity and learn to tolerate atrocities and this process deserves to be satirized. Artifacts like *Majorité Opprimée*, America Responds to AIDS, and "Our Transgender Siblings Have Heartbeats" reveal the slow but steady disregard of the targeted group from the general population, inviting audiences to consider how they contribute to a spectrum of behavior that leads to social atrocities.

Change the way people think about the atrocity. Good satire makes the audience see the world differently and laugh at the way that they used to see the world. Changing people's minds is essential when considering how to satirize the worst actions of humanity. Artifacts like Welcome to Hell, Dr. Suess' anti-Holocaust cartoons, and the Caucasian satirical logos demand that viewers realize the pervasive impact of rape culture, the way Americans enabled the Holocaust, and the feelings of widespread and unquestioned degredation. Saying that the satirist has the power to thwart an atrocity is an overstatement, but the satirist's ability to encourage others to *want* to thwart an atrocity is not.

Additional Activities

Activity 6.1 Spotting Social Atrocities

Given the complexity of social atrocities and their intimate association with stereotypes, prejudice, discrimination, and marginalization, spotting atrocities can be difficult. Today, we recognize the internment of the Japanese in the 1940s was an atrocity, but most Americans at the time were not outraged and even enabled their imprisonment. Similarly, Americans are largely unaware of the mass deportation of Mexican Americans from the United States a decade earlier. This social atrocity is referred to as the "Mexican Deportation/Repatriation," language that sanitizes the fact that hundreds of thousands of people (many of whom were American citizens by birth) were separated and deported based on their ethnicity. Large sections of the American public also still do not see the systematic separation and internment of refugee families at the southern border as an atrocity, even though it is uniquely cruel and violent. To this day, the public discourse serves to dehumanize these individuals and reinforce the idea that they do not deserve respect or human rights.

What atrocities are you aware of that are occurring today that target marginalized groups? Who is outraged about this atrocity and why? Who is *not* outraged about this atrocity and why? What do you think would happen if the same acts of cruelty and violence were happening to a different group?

References

Above Average. (2016). Rapists now have their own recovery center [Video]. YouTube. https://www.youtube.com/watch?v=abyNiPOnTQg (accessed 5 May 2022).

Allchin, H. (12 October 2020). Hundreds of schools are still using native Americans as team Mascots. FiveThirtyEight.

Black Man Blissfully Unaware His Name Going To Be Hashtag By End Of Week. (22 September 2016). The Onion.

Camera, L. (27 February 2018). In most statemay 19 2022s, Poorest school districts get less funding. USNews. https://www.usnews.com/news/best-states/articles/2018-02-27/in-most-states-poorest-school-districts-get-less-funding (accessed 19 May 2022).

Byers, D. (2012). *AP Nixes 'Homophobia,' "Ethnic Cleansing'*. Politico Magazine, 26.

CDC Fact Sheet: HIV Among Gay and Bisexual Men. (2016). The Centers for Disease Control and Prevention.

Centers for Disease Control and Prevention (CDC). (2011). Characteristics associated with HIV infection among heterosexuals in urban areas with high AIDS prevalence---24 cities, United States, 2006–2007. *MMWR. Morbidity and mortality weekly report* 60 (31): 1045–1049.

Centers for Disease Control and Prevention (June 2001). HIV and AIDS--United States, 1981–2000. *MMWR. Morbidity and Mortality Weekly Report* 50 (21): 430–434.

Comedy Central. (26 September 2014). The daily show - The Redskins' name catching racism (ft. Jason Jones) [Video]. YouTube. www.youtube.com/watch?v=loK2DRBnk24

Dam, A.V. (6 October 2018). Less than 1% of rapes lead to felony convictions. At least 89% of victims face emotional and physical consequences (Wonkblog). Washington Post.

Denning, P. and DiNenno, E. (July 2010). Communities in crisis: Is there a generalized HIV epidemic in impoverished urban areas of the United States. In *XVIII International AIDS Conference* (Vol. 1).

Du Bois, W.E.B. (1897). Strivings of the negro people. The Atlantic monthly 80 (August): 194.

Eight million Americans Rescued from poverty with redefinition of term. (10 November 1999). The Onion.

Explainer: Everything you need to know about pushing for equal pay. (14 September 2020). UN Women.

Framework of Analysis for Atrocity Crimes: A tool for prevention. (2014). United Nations.

Galea, S., Tracy, M., Hoggatt, K. J., DiMaggio, C., and Karpati, A. (2011). Estimated deaths attributable to social factors in the United States. *American Journal of Public Health*, 101 (8): 1456–1465.

Gay, R. (5 May 2014). SNL's Leslie Jones uses slavery to make a point about being black and beautiful (Opinion). TIME.

Glickman, L.B. (23 October 2019). Why President Trump used lynching as a metaphor. The Washington Post. https://www.washingtonpost.com/outlook/2019/10/23/why-trump-used-alynching-metaphor/ (accessed 24 May 2022).

Griffin, R.A. and Phillips, J.D. (2019). Eminem's "Love the Way You Lie" and the normalization of men's violence against women. In: Race/Gender/Class/Media (ed. R. Lind), 212–215. Routledge.

Gritz, J. (15 January 2013). When Dr. Seuss took on Adolf Hitler. The Atlantic.

Hands, P. (24 January 2020). Faces of homelessness [Comic Strip]. *Wisconsin State Journal*.

Hee Lee, M.Y. (9 December 2014). The truth about a viral graphic on rape statistics (Fact Checker). Washington Post.

History of Lynching in America. (n.d.) NAACP. https://naacp.org/find-resources/history-explained/history-lynching-america.

Hoak, D. (1983). The great European witch-hunts: A historical perspective. *American Journal of Sociology* 88 (6): 1270–1274. https://www.nytimes.com/2018/06/03/opinion/children-border.html (accessed 5 May 2022).

Jagannathan, M. (23 November 2019). 2 million Americans don't have access to running water and basic plumbing. MarketWatch.

Joseph, F. (2 August 2018). I wore a 'Caucasians' shirt to expose the hypocrisy of racist logos. I wore a 'Caucasians' shirt to expose the hypocrisy of racist logos. USA TODAY.

Kahlor, L. and Eastin, M.S. (2011). Television's role in the culture of violence toward women: A study of television viewing and the cultivation of rape myth acceptance in the United States. *Journal of Broadcasting & Electronic Media* 55 (2): 215–231.

Kellaway, M. (18 February 2015). REPORT: Trans Americans four times more likely to live in poverty. The Advocate.

Kline, M.G. (12 February 2018). United States Interagency Council on Homelessness: Centering Youth of Color & LGBTQ Young People in Efforts to End Homelessness. https://www.usich.gov/news/voices-of-youth-count-centering-youth-of-color-lgbtq-young-people-in-efforts-to-end-homelessness/ (accessed 19 May 2022).

Koch, A., Brierley, C., Maslin, M.M., and Lewis, S.L. (2019). Earth system impacts of the European arrival and Great dying in the Americas after 1492. *Quaternary Science Reviews* 207: 13–36.

Leonhardt, D. and Thompson, S. (6 March 2020). How Working-class life is killing Americans, in charts. New York Times.

Levin, S. (14 June 2016). Stanford sexual assault: Read the full text of the judge's controversial decision. The Guardian.

Lonsway, K.A. and Fitzgerald, L.F. (1994). Rape myths. *In Review. Psychology of Women Quarterly* 18 (2): 133–164.

McCann, N. C., Horn, T. H., Hyle, E. P., and Walensky, R. P. (2020). HIV antiretroviral therapy costs in the United States, 2012–2018. *JAMA* Internal Medicine 180 (4): 601–603.

McKenna, et al. (2017). Human intestinal parasite burden and poor sanitation in rural Alabama. *The American Journal of Tropical Medicine and Hygiene* 97 (5): 1623.

Movement Advancement Project and Center for American Progress. (September 2014). *Paying an Unfair Price: The Financial Penalty for Being LGBT in America.* https://www.lgbtmap.org/unfair-price (accessed 5 May 2022).

National Sexual Violence Resource Center. (2015). Statistics about Sexual Violence. https://www.nsvrc.org/sites/default/files/publications_nsvrc_factsheet_media-packet_statistics-about-sexual-violence_0.pdf (accessed 19 May 2022).

Nettleton, P.H. (2019). She'sa 10, He'sa 2: Playboy cartoons and a culture of male entitlement. In *Race/Gender/Class/Media* (ed. R. Lind) 122–126. Routledge.

New CMSI Study Reveals How Major TV Programs and Newspapers (Mis)Represented Homelessness and Housing Security Issues in 2018. (9 September 2019). Center for Media and Social Impact.

Nietzel, M. (22 February 2021). New from U.S. census Bureau: Number of Americans with a bachelor's degree continues to grow. Forbes.

Okonofua, J.A. and Eberhardt, J.L. (2015). Two strikes: Race and the disciplining of young students. *Psychological science* 26 (5): 617–624.

Parker, T., (Writer/Director), Stone, M., (Writer), and Graden, B., (Writer). (12 March 2008). Tonsil Trouble [series epidsode]. In South Park. South Park Studios.

Pickrell, J. (4 September 2006). Timeline: HIV and AIDS. New Scientist. letter: https://www.pbs.org/wgbh/pages/frontline/aids/docs/francisplea.html.

Pilkington, E. (5 September 2017). Hookworm, a disease of extreme poverty, is thriving in the US south. Why? The Guardian.

Pourriat, E. (2010). Majorité opprimée [Short film].

Prior, R. (28 May 2019). This church turns heads with its political street signs. The messages slam white supremacy, back transgender rights and urge tolerance toward Muslims. CNN.

Rabin, R. C. (2011). *Nearly 1 in 5 women in US survey say they have been sexually assaulted.* The New York Times, 14.

Rank, M.R. and Hirschl, T.A. (2015). The likelihood of experiencing relative poverty over the life course. *PLoS One* 10 (7): e0133513.

Reagan, R. (17 September 1985). The President's News Conference [Speech]. The American Presidency Project.

Reid, M. (2004). Silence + Death [Comic Strip]. mikhaela.net.

Saturday Night Live. (3 December 2017). Welcome to Hell - SNL [Video]. YouTube. www.youtube.com/watch?v=1l26UFQ06eQ

Small, J.L. (2015). Classing sex offenders: How prosecutors and defense attorneys differentiate men accused of sexual assault. *Law & Society Review* 49 (1): 109–141.

Stannard, D.E. (1993). *American Holocaust: The Conquest of the New World.* Oxford University Press.

Stanton, G. (2013). The ten stages of genocide. Genocide Watch.

Status of women in the states. (2011). Institute for Women's Policy Research.

Stein, J. (25 June 2018). The U.N. says 18.5 million Americans are in 'extreme poverty.' Trump's team says just 250,000 are. Washington Post.

TCF Study Finds U.S. Schools Underfunded by Nearly $150 Billion Annually. (22 July 2020). The Century Foundation.

Thomas, L. (2018). Poor Health: Poverty and scarce resources in U.S. cities. https://newsinteractive.post-gazette.com/longform/stories/poorhealth/1/a (accessed 18 May 2022).

Thornton, R. (1987). *American Indian Holocaust and Survival: A Population History since 1492,* Vol. 186. Norman, OK: University of Oklahoma Press.

Trump Apologizes For Impeachment Comment After Learning Disturbing History Of 1918 Lynching Of German American Immigrant Robert Prager. (22 October 2019). The Onion.

United Nations Department of Economic and Social Affairs. (1995). World Summit for Social Development 1995 Agreements; Chapter 2: Eradication of Poverty. https://www.un.org/development/desa/dspd/world-summit-for-social-development-1995/wssd-1995-agreements/pawssd-chapter-2.html (accessed 5 May 2022).

The Vast Majority of Perpetrators Will Not Go to Jail or Prison. (2020). RAINN.

Waldron, L. and Schwencke, K. (10 August 2018). Deadnamed. https://www.propublica.org/article/deadnamed-transgender-black-women-murders-jacksonville-police-investigation (accessed 5 May 22).

World Bank. (2020). COVID-19 to add as many as 150 million extreme poor by 2021. Presss Release No: 2021/024/DEC-GPV.

Weekend Update: Leslie Jones [Video]. (4 May 2014). NBC.

7

Epilogue

The turn of the twenty-first century featured a surge in satirical outlets post-9/11. I regularly attended live tapings of *The Daily Show with Jon Stewart* in 2000 and 2001 because tickets were free and easy to get; acquiring tickets after September 2001 was practically impossible as the show began its meteoric run at the start of the twenty-first century. At the same time, the digital environment saw the rise of *The Onion*, a satirical underground newspaper that had been distributing on college campuses since 1988, startup comedy and satire websites, and prolific user-generated content on social media. Global audiences liked, shared, commented, sampled, and remixed content, which amplified messages and changed meanings with little effort.

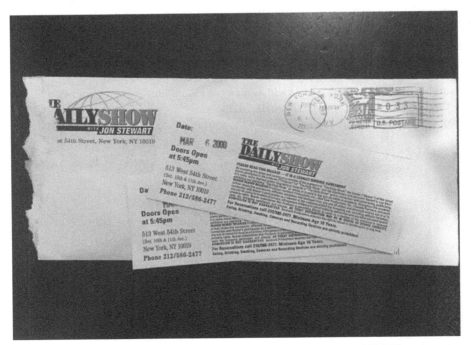

Figure 7.1 I attended 3 live tapings of The Daily Show with Jon Stewart in 2000. When the only impediment to tickets was the speed of the United States Postal Service. Neal Patrick Harris was the guest. *Source*: Charisse L'Pree.

Diversity and Satire: Laughing at Processes of Marginalization, First Edition.
Charisse L'Pree Corsbie-Massay.
© 2023 John Wiley & Sons, Inc. Published 2023 by John Wiley & Sons, Inc.

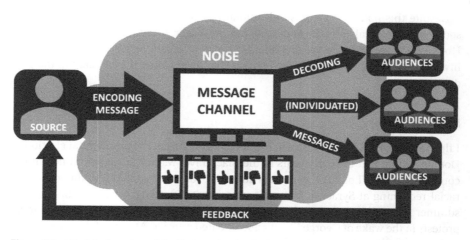

Figure 7.2 Updated version of the Communication Process featured in Chapter 1; Web 2.0 and social media allow audiences to provide feedback directly to media sources, and the cloud of noise has expanded.

To draw on the metaphor of metal ages (e.g., golden, silver, bronze), we are currently living through a "lithium age" of satire. Lithium is the first and lightest alkali metal in the periodic table. Most electronics and digital technologies run on lithium batteries that have short lifespans and must be frequently recharged[1]. Referring to the current satirical environment as the lithium age acknowledges the abundance of satirical content in digital platforms as well as the rapidity of audience reactions online, which seem to be an endless and perpetually rechargeable source of energy. In this environment, audience sentiment and unanticipated outrage can overwhelm producers. Decades of discriminatory content have rendered many unable to detect how they may unwittingly reinforce the marginalization of certain groups. With social media (i.e., Web 2.0), voices that were rendered inaudible can now achieve a groundswell, demanding better, more inclusive content.

Throughout my decade as a college professor instructing aspiring media professionals, one of their most pressing concerns is the fear of being misunderstood and accused of intention when something was a mistake. An inability to effectively convey (encode) your message or audiences' inability to understand (decode) can end the career of a public communicator. The students are afraid of being "canceled." In the case of marginalization satire, cancelation may come from those seeking to maintain the status quo frustrated with jokes at their expense. Or it could come from those seeking to disrupt the status quo frustrated with jokes that repeat historic stereotypes and prejudices even if the jokes were intended to highlight the absurdity of these tendencies.

Satirists are uniquely impacted by this phenomenon given that the content that they create is rooted in obfuscation. As described in the introduction, satirists have historically been forced to hide their critiques to avoid the ire of those in power. They deliver messages with multiple meanings that vary according to the receiver and the context. The inherent polysemy of satire means that it will inevitably be interpreted differently by different audiences, making the satirist uniquely susceptible to the ire of all sides.

---

1 Lithium is also a used as a medication for treating bipolar disorder (Machado-Vieira, Manji, and Zarate Jr. 2009).

Despite this potential for misunderstanding, satire remains an important tool in social and political debates and students are eager to add to this conversation. However, in order to do so, one should aspire to create *responsible* satire, which involves critiquing oneself and the content that one creates at every step in the production process.

Know the History

I first taught Diversity and Satire in the fall of 2016, during the presidential election of Donald Trump and the early years of the Black Lives Matter movement. I taught the course again in fall of 2019, two years after #MeToo went viral and in the midst of a racial reckoning at Syracuse University (Randle 2019). I began writing this book in summer 2020, during COVID-19 lockdowns and international Black Lives Matters protests in the wake of George Floyd's documented murder. At each of these moments, and every moment before, after, and in between, history has been essential to understanding present-day events. The key difference between a satirist and a comedian is that the satirist researches, engages with, and highlights phenomena that may have escaped the awareness of the general audience, whereas the non-satirical comedian makes people laugh without a larger critical goal. Responsible satirists are aware of historical power disparities and how these disparities are upheld. However, operating on common knowledge or grade-school history is insufficient, given that knowledge and the process by which we come to know things are an absurd outcome of our institutions. Therefore, robust historical awareness must be actively fostered. As has been repeated through this book, the satirist must first be a historian, aware of patterns in the past that shape the present.

Last Week Tonight with John Oliver has perfected the process of researching to produce satire (as described in Activity 1.5). Oliver and his team spend a week closely researching a given topic, learning the history that preceded a phenomenon, and synthesizing this information for the viewer before making jokes that highlight social disparities. The result is an artifact that entertains *and* educates; in fact, the show dedicates more minutes to conveying information than it does telling jokes (Terhune and Corsbie-Massay 2020). Oliver and his team model the practice of producing satire, especially given that they frequently satirize topics about which the general audience has little knowledge.

One person could not possibly know everything pertaining to centuries or millennia of discrimination around the world, but public lack of awareness is also a wellspring the responsible satirist may draw from. As a satirical pundit on *The Colbert Report* (2005–2014), Stephen Colbert repeated talking points from the conservative right that were rooted in a lack of knowledge, thereby presenting his character as a joke that underscored widespread societal ignorance.[2] When faced with calls for his cancelation in 2014 (#cancelcolbert) for a screenshot shared on Twitter taken out of context, Stephen Colbert (the real person) took the opportunity to acknowledge the real world racism that the joke was targeting and link users back to the original context (Chen 2014). Responsible satirists must know more than is merely necessary for their artifact and acknowledge when they can learn more.

---

2 As was the case with the lovable bigot described in Chapter 1, viewers interpreted this content in line with their ideological predisposition: conservatives believed that Colbert was a conservative targeting liberals, whereas liberals believed that Colbert was a liberal targeting conservatives (LaMarre, Landreville, and Beam 2009).

Incorporate Others

Satirists seeking to disrupt long-standing social disparities should also confer with others as they develop content, including members of groups whose experiences are being satirized. Although students hate group projects, life - and content creation - is a group project, and engaging with others when crafting messages [it] is important to [consider] the wide array of audience responses. Early iterations of this book were deployed in a satirical writing class taught by Rae Ann Merriweather at Syracuse University; students debated and critiqued their messages, much like a writers room, honing their satirical voices, using the key terms and concepts in the book to describe what worked and what didn't work.

Most of the artifacts cited in this book are the products of a collection of writers, producers, actors, and editors, including *Saturday Night Live, The Onion, The Daily Show* (with Jon Stewart and Trevor Noah), and *Funny or Die*. Although a difference in opinion and interpretation is unavoidable, engaging with diverse creators while generating satire allows scenarios, sketches, and jokes to be proposed, criticized, fine-tuned, or even abandoned (Corsbie-Massay and Green forthcoming). Ideally, this collaborative effort ensures that media producers identify content that may reinforce social disparities before being "canceled" by audiences.

Satirical outlets renowned for their marginalization satire can also suffer from a lack of diversity behind the scenes. In 2019, 91% of showrunners in Hollywood were White and only 13.7% of writers identified as people of color (Hunt 2017). Non-diverse production teams create a difficult working environment for people demanding more diversity and inclusivity. *Saturday Night Live* received criticism for a lack of Black women in the cast and writing staff and auditioned a handful of Black woman in December 2013 in response (de Moraes 2013). According to Wyatt Cenac, the only Black writer on staff at *The Daily Show with Jon Stewart* in 2011, Stewart reportedly became enraged when confronted about a bit that mocked Herman Cain using stereotypical speech patterns of *Amos 'n' Andy's* Kingfish ("Wyatt Cenac" on *WTF with Marc Maron* 2015). During the protests in summer of 2020 in the wake of George Floyd, even *The Onion's* satirical commentary on corporate performative solidarity, was quote tweeted by a former employee to talk about their own hegemonic tendencies that continued to limit margialized voices (see Figure 7.2).

Listen To and Learn From Audiences

The goal of the satirist - as well as the professor - is to draw attention to neglected aspects of reality ideally to change public conversation. I am honored to serve in this privileged position, but few realize the harshness that comes with reading student evaluations. I feel "canceled" at the end of every semester as students take their anger out in the anonymous surveys, often without recognizing the extent to which their comments can make or break an instructor's career (see Selected Negative Teaching Evaluations of Jesus Christ by Amanda Lehr, McSweeney's 2022). However, each negative evaluation is matched by a positive one, and together they inform how to develop materials, messages, and content moving forward.

Therefore, satirists should consider how their content is decoded by segments of the audience, specifically negotiated or oppositional audiences, to ensure that they are not inadvertently contributing to processes of marginalization. Chris Rock retired

Figure 7.3 A dispassionate tweet from a former Onion employee commenting on an Onion post satirizing corporate posts supporting diversity while perpetuating discrimination in their hiring practices; Monahan describes how The Onion perpetuated the same performative diversity that they are criticizing. *Source*: https://twitter.com/momonahan/status/1270095052505780224.

a one of his most famous routies, "N*igg*s vs. Black People" from a 1996 special because it appeared to give racist people "license" to repeat the racial epithet at the heart of the joke (Leung 2005). Being aware of a robust and diverse audience acknowledges that content can be interpreted differently and may help the satirist consider ways to make the artifact more effective.

Dave Chappelle was sharply critiqued for his jokes at the expense of trans people as well as sexual assault victims, the MeToo movement, and non-Black people of color in a series of Netflix specials. Before *The Closer* was released in 2021, thousands of thought pieces, critical essays, and tweets critiquing Chapelle's bigoted jokes from earlier specials had garnered millions of views.[3] However, Chappelle's routine did not appear to evolve. Instead, he increasingly targeted a contingent of his audience by dismissing and mocking their concerns; when accused of punching down, he replied, "'…Punching down?' What the fuck does that mean?" (*The Closer*, 2021). By laughing at marginalized people, he encouraged his fans to ignore long-standing discrimination. Therefore, he is no longer creating satire and instead is reinforcing processes of marginalization, which is and always has been a profitable endeavor (Corsbie-Massay 2019). Prominent comedians, artists, and public figures (e.g., Todd Phillips, J.K. Rowling, Joe Rogan) have decried cancel culture in response to criticism, earning praise and profit from "anti-PC audiences" (Nwanevu 2019; Hopkins 2021).

Lin-Manuel Miranda claims that cancel culture is about "having opinions" (Schulman 2021); Roxane Gay refers to the phenomenon as "consequence culture" (Schwartz 2021); and Seth Rogan implores fellow comedians, "If you've made a joke that's aged terribly, accept it" (Bowden 2021). This can be a challenging task when our default reaction is to defend ourselves and our intentions in the face of criticism, but the ability to respond to criticism affirms the satirist as a cultural commentator. In the face of new information or perspectives, satirists-as-cultural-commentators converse with their critics, integrate new information, and reconsider their earlier work to create better and more effective content. Satirists that refuse to learn inevitably stop creating satire and instead revert to simply telling jokes.

Being a satirist is tough. Social patterns are difficult to observe and even harder to successfully call out and ultimately change. Furthermore, being a satirist in the lithium age takes unique courage and grit. But the history and lessons outlined in this book remain pertinent and applicable for both established satirists and up-and-coming cultural commentators. Digital and social media platforms allow more people to speak, inevitably leading to more diverse conversations about processes of marginalization and more opportunities for satire. By strategically producing satire for these new formats as well as traditional platforms like political cartoons, television, music, and movies, savvy satirists can bend the trajectory of history towards diversity and inclusion.

References

Bowden, J. (25 May 2021). Seth Rogen on cancel culture: 'If you've made a joke that's aged terribly, accept it'. https://thehill.com/blogs/in-the-know/in-the-know/555396-seth-rogen-on-cancel-culture-if-youve-made-a-joke-thats-aged/ (accessed 5 May 2022).
Chen, T. (28 March 2014). Stephen Colbert on the defensive after 'Ching-Chong Ding-Dong' Tweet. https://abcnews.go.com/blogs/headlines/2014/03/stephen-colbert-on-the-defensive-after-ching-chong-ding-dong-tweet (accessed 5 May 2022).

---

3 Both *Sticks and Stones* (2019) and *The Closer* (2021) have low critics scores (35% and 40% respectively) compared to their 99% audience score.

Corsbie-Massay, C.L. (2019). Target vs. Total Market: The paradox of diverse mainstream content. In: *Race/Gender/Class/Media: Considering Diversity Across Audiences, Content, and Producers*, 4e (ed. Lind). Routledge. (accessed on 5 May 2022).

Corsbie-Massay, C.L. and Green, K.N. (forthcoming). Conversations on Race and Entertainment Media. In: *Race/Gender/Class/Media 5.0* (ed. R. Lind). (accessed 5 May 2022).

de Moraes, L. (12 December 2013). UPDATE: 'SNL' to audition black female cast hopefuls monday, pick one for January start. Deadline. https://deadline.com/2013/12/snl-holds-auditions-for-black-female-cast-hopefuls-at-groundlings-651299/ (accessed 5 May 2022).

Hopkins, C. (16 January 2021). Tucker Carlson, Ariel Pink and the cancel culture grift. https://www.mediaite.com/opinion/tucker-carlson-ariel-pink-and-the-cancel-culture-grift/ (accessed 5 May 2022).

Hunt, D. (October 2017). Race in the writers' room: How Hollywood whitewashes the stories that shape America. Color of Change Hollywood. https://hollywood.colorofchange.org/wp-content/uploads/2019/03/COC_Hollywood_Race_Report.pdf (accessed 25 May 2022).

Lehr, A. (2 March 2022). Selected Negative Teaching Evaluations of Jesus Christ. https://www.mcsweeneys.net/articles/selected-negative-teaching-evaluations-of-jesus-christ (accessed 26 July 2022).

Leung, R. (17 February 2005). Rock: Bring on Oscar 'Safety Net.' 60 Minutes. https://www.cbsnews.com/news/rock-bring-on-oscar-safety-net/ (accessed 26 May 2022).

Machado-Vieira, R., Manji, H.K., and Zarate Jr, C.A. (2009). The role of lithium in the treatment of bipolar disorder: Convergent evidence for neurotrophic effects as a unifying hypothesis. *Bipolar Disorders* 11: 92–109. (accessed 5 May 2022).

Monahan, M. [@momonahan]. (8 June 2020). spent a year in the Onion writer's room and it was hugely important that jokes "felt real" to the rest of the (overwhelmingly white, straight, cis, male) room. hard to fathom how many jokes/entire packets have been rejected bc they didn't align with that POV! (but it's a lot). Twitter. https://twitter.com/momonahan/status/1270095052505780224 (accessed 5 May 2022).

Nwanevu, O. (23 September 2019). The "Cancel Culture" Con. https://newrepublic.com/article/155141/cancel-culture-con-dave-chappelle-shane-gillis (accessed 5 May 2022).

Randle, A. (27 November 2019). Racial Slurs, and the 15 Days That Shook Syracuse. https://www.nytimes.com/2019/11/27/nyregion/syracuse-university-racism.html (accessed 26 July 2022).

Schulman, M. (14 November 2021). Lin-Manuel Miranda goes in search of lost time. New Yorker. https://www.newyorker.com/culture/the-new-yorker-interview/lin-manuel-miranda-goes-in-search-of-lost-time (accessed 5 May 2022).

Schwartz, M. (5 March 2021). Roxane gay says cancel culture does not exist. https://www.motherjones.com/media/2021/03/roxane-gay-says-cancel-culture-does-not-exist/ (accessed 5 May 2022).

Terhune, P. and Corsbie-Massay, C.L. (2020). Satirical education or educational satire: Learning and laughing on last week tonight. In: *Laughter, Outrage and Resistance: Post-Trump TV Satire in Political Discourse and Dissent* (ed. L. Henson and S.M. Jankowski), 165–184. New York: Peter Lang Publishing. (accessed 5 May 2022).

Cenac, W. (23 July 2015). WTF with Marc Maron. http://www.wtfpod.com/podcast/episodes/episode_622_-_wyatt_cenac (accessed 5 May 2022).

Appendix A

Satirical Outlet/Artifact	Dates	Type	Included?
Gulliver's Travels	1726	Book	YES
White House Correspondents Dinner	1921 – Present	Live Event	YES
Babbit	1922	Book	YES
Black No More	1931	Book	YES
Animal Farm	1945	Book	YES
Frank Zappa	1955 – 1993	Music	NO
The Twilight Zone	1959 – 1964	Network TV	NO
Myra Breckinridge	1968	Book	NO
Doonesbury	1970 – Present	Comic	NO
Mary Tyler Moore Show	1970 – 1977	Network TV	YES
The Nazi and the Barber	1971	Book	NO
All in the Family	1971 – 1979	Network TV	YES
Blazing Saddles	1974	Movie	NO
Saturday Night Live	1975 – Present	Network TV	YES
"Weird" Al Yankovic	1976 – Present	Music	YES
The Richard Pryor Show	1977	Network TV	NO
MAUS	1980	Graphic Novel	NO
The Handmaid's Tale	1985	Book	NO
The Onion	1988 – Present	Website (Originally Newspaper)	YES
The Simpsons	1989 – Present	Network TV	YES
In Living Color	1990 – 1994	Network TV	NO
Pricilla Queen of the Desert	1994	Movie	NO
She TV	1994	Network TV	YES
Clueless	1995	Movie	NO

Diversity and Satire: Laughing at Processes of Marginalization, First Edition.
Charisse L'Pree Corsbie-Massay.
© 2023 John Wiley & Sons, Inc. Published 2023 by John Wiley & Sons, Inc.

Appendix A

Satirical Outlet/Artifact	Dates	Type	Included?
To: Wong Foo Thanks for Everything Julie Newmar	1995	Movie	NO
The Boondocks (Comic)	1996 – 2006	Comic	NO
The Birdcage	1996	Movie	NO
South Park	1997 – Present	Cable TV	YES
The Daily Show with Jon Stewart	1999 – 2015	Cable TV	YES
Family Guy	1999 – Present	Network TV	YES
College Humor	1999 – Present	Website	YES
The Oblongs	2001 – 2002	Network TV	YES
The Chappelle Show	2003 – 2006	Cable TV	YES
The Boondocks (TV Series)	2005 – 2014	Cable TV	YES
The Colbert Report	2005 – 2014	Cable TV	NO
The Office	2005 – 2013	Network TV	NO
Buzzfeed	2006 – Present	Website	YES
The Hunger Games (Book Franchise)	2008 – 2020	Book	YES
Black Mirror	2011 – Present	Streaming TV	NO
Key & Peele	2012 – 2015	Cable TV	YES
The Hunger Games	2012 – 2023	Movie	NO
Duffle Blog	2012 – Present	Website	NO
Inside Amy Schumer	2013 – 2016	Cable TV	YES
Rick and Morty	2013 – Present	Cable TV	YES
Reductress	2013 – Present	Website	NO
The Nightly Show with Larry Wilmore	2015 – 2016	Cable TV	NO
The Daily Show with Trevor Noah	2015 – Present	Cable TV	YES
The Underground Railroad	2016	Book	NO
Zootopia	2016	Movie	NO
Full Frontal with Samantha Bee	2016 – Present	Cable TV	NO
Funny or Die	2016	Website	YES
Get Out	2017	Movie	NO
A Day in the Life of Marlon Bundo	2018	Book	NO
Sorry to Bother You	2018	Movie	NO
Jojo Rabbit	2019	Movie	NO

Appendix B

ITEM OF PRIVILEGE	CATEGORY(IES)
I have medical insurance.	CLASS/SES
I have dental insurance.	CLASS/SES
I've never had to work the night shift.	CLASS/SES
I have always been able to access and afford childcare.	CLASS/SES
My school system never had to cut programs or classes to save money.	CLASS/SES
There were several honors, advanced placement, or elective classes in my high school.	CLASS/SES
I work in a salaried job.	CLASS/SES
My family and I have never lived below the poverty line.	CLASS/SES
I don't have any student loans.	CLASS/SES
I have never gone to bed hungry.	CLASS/SES
I have never been homeless.	CLASS/SES
My parents pay some of my bills.	CLASS/SES
My parents pay all of my bills.	CLASS/SES
I don't rely on public transportation.	CLASS/SES
I buy new clothes at least once a month.	CLASS/SES
I have never done my taxes myself.	CLASS/SES
I have never felt poor.	CLASS/SES
I have never had to worry about making rent.	CLASS/SES
I have never worked as a waiter, barista, bartender, or salesperson.	CLASS/SES
I have had an unpaid internship.	CLASS/SES
I have had multiple unpaid internships.	CLASS/SES
I went to summer camp.	CLASS/SES
I went to private school.	CLASS/SES
I graduated high school.	CLASS/SES

Diversity and Satire: Laughing at Processes of Marginalization, First Edition.
Charisse L'Pree Corsbie-Massay.
© 2023 John Wiley & Sons, Inc. Published 2023 by John Wiley & Sons, Inc.

Appendix B

ITEM OF PRIVILEGE	CATEGORY(IES)
I went to an elite college.	CLASS/SES
I graduated college.	CLASS/SES
My parents paid (at least some of) my tuition.	CLASS/SES
I had a car in high school.	CLASS/SES
I've never had a roommate.	CLASS/SES
I've always had cable.	CLASS/SES
I have traveled internationally.	CLASS/SES
I travel internationally at least once a year.	CLASS/SES
I studied abroad.	CLASS/SES
I've never skipped a meal to save money.	CLASS/SES
I don't know what "Sallie Mae" is.	CLASS/SES
I spent Spring Breaks abroad.	CLASS/SES
I have frequent flier miles.	CLASS/SES
My parents are both alive.	CLASS/SES
My parents are still married.	CLASS/SES
I am a man.	GENDER
I feel comfortable in the gender I was born as.	GENDER
I still identify as the gender I was born in.	GENDER
I have never tried to change my gender.	GENDER
I have never been denied an opportunity because of my gender.	GENDER
I make more money than my professional counterparts of a different gender.	GENDER
I have never felt unsafe because of my gender.	GENDER
I have never been catcalled.	GENDER
I have never been sexually harassed or assaulted.	GENDER
I have never been raped.	GENDER
I am heterosexual.	SEXUALITY
I have never lied about my sexuality	SEXUALITY
I never had to "come out."	SEXUALITY
I never doubted my parents' acceptance of my sexuality.	SEXUALITY
I have never been called "fag."	SEXUALITY
I have never been called "dyke."	SEXUALITY
I have never been called a "fairy," or any other derogatory slur for homosexuals.	SEXUALITY
I have never tried to hide my sexuality.	SEXUALITY
I am always comfortable with P.D.A. with my partner in public.	SEXUALITY
I have never pretended to be "just friends" with my significant other.	SEXUALITY

ITEM OF PRIVILEGE	CATEGORY(IES)
I have never been ostracized by my religion for my sexual orientation.	SEXUALITY
I have never been told I would "burn in hell" for my sexual orientation.	SEXUALITY
I have never been told that my sexuality is "just a phase."	SEXUALITY
I have never been violently threatened because of my sexuality.	SEXUALITY
My parents are heterosexual.	SEXUALITY
My parents got/can get married without major social or legal hurdles.	SEXUALITY/CLASS/SES/RACE/ABILITY
I am white.	RACE/ETHNICITY
I have never been discriminated against because of my skin color.	RACE/ETHNICITY
I have never been the only person of my race in a room.	RACE/ETHNICITY
I have never been mocked for my accent.	RACE/ETHNICITY
I have never been told I am attractive "for my race."	RACE/ETHNICITY
I have never been a victim of violence because of my race.	RACE/ETHNICITY
I have never been called a racial slur.	RACE/ETHNICITY
I have never been told I "sound white."	RACE/ETHNICITY
A stranger has never asked to touch my hair, or asked if it is real.	RACE/ETHNICITY
I have never lied about my ethnicity as self-defense.	RACE/ETHNICITY
I am not nervous in airport security lines.	RACE/ETHNICITY
I have never heard this statement: "You have been randomly selected for secondary passport control."	RACE/ETHNICITY
I have never been called a terrorist.	RACE/ETHNICITY
I have never been shamed for my religious beliefs.	RELIGION
I have never been violently threatened for my religious beliefs.	RELIGION
I have never been violently attacked for my religious beliefs.	RELIGION
There is a place of worship for my religion in my town.	RELIGION
I have never lied about my religion as self-defense.	RELIGION
All my jobs have been accommodating of my religious practices.	RELIGION
Nobody has ever tried to "save" me for my religious beliefs.	RELIGION
I do not have any physical disabilities.	ABILITY
I do not have any social disabilities.	ABILITY
I do not have any learning disabilities.	ABILITY

ITEM OF PRIVILEGE	CATEGORY(IES)
I have never had an eating disorder.	ABILITY
I have never been depressed.	ABILITY
I have never considered suicide.	ABILITY
I have never attempted suicide.	ABILITY
I have never taken medication for my mental health.	ABILITY
I can afford medication if/when I need it.	ABILITY
I have never been told I'm overweight or "too skinny."	ABILITY
I have never felt overweight or underweight or "too skinny."	ABILITY
I have never been shamed for my body type.	ABILITY
I consider myself to be physically attractive.	ABILITY
I can afford a therapist.	ABILITY
I've used prescription drugs recreationally.	ABILITY
I have never had an addiction.	ABILITY
I have never been cyber-bullied for any of my identities.	INTERSECTIONALITY
I was not bullied as a child for any of my identities.	INTERSECTIONALITY
I have never tried to distance myself from any of my identities.	INTERSECTIONALITY
I have never been self-conscious about any of my identities.	INTERSECTIONALITY
I have never questioned any of my identities.	INTERSECTIONALITY
I feel privileged because of the identities I was born with.	INTERSECTIONALITY

Glossary

acculturation new cultural products that emerge when two groups come into contact that synthesizes the two cultures

achieved identity categories that one chooses to pursue (e.g., occupation)

acknowledged pedigree satire where the content quotes known satirists

allegory a story, poem, or picture that can be interpreted to reveal a hidden meaning, typically a moral or political one

American Dream the national ideology that one can work their way out of the circumstances into which they were born because of the unique opportunities provided to those living in the United States

appreciation the practice of learning about a culture that is not your own with a serious and meticulous interest

appropriation the sampling of cultural artifacts from marginalized/minority groups by the dominant/majority, often without the nuanced context endemic to the artifact being sampled

archetypes recurrent symbols or motifs in literature or art

ascribed identity categories of which one has no control and that have been put upon them by external forms (e.g., race, gender)

asexual individuals people who do experience or express a desire for intimate physical contact but may still engage in intimate emotional relationships

assimilation the adoption of the dominant or majority culture by marginalized or minority individuals

atrocity an extremely wicked or cruel act, typically one involving physical violence or injury

bisexual experiencing intimacy with both men and women (see pansexual)

Blackness the essence and experience of being Black in a majority White society

capitalism an economic system where trade and industry are controlled by private owners for profit rather than by the state, and individual value is associated with resources including land, money, and commodities

cisgender individuals whose gender conforms to the sex assigned to them at birth

class the aggregated categorization of individuals based on socioeconomic status, which can be indicative of social networks and behavioral expectations

colorblindness (ideology) the process of disregarding racial and ethnic characteristics when selecting who will participate in some activity or receive some service

Diversity and Satire: Laughing at Processes of Marginalization, First Edition.
Charisse L'Pree Corsbie-Massay.
© 2023 John Wiley & Sons, Inc. Published 2023 by John Wiley & Sons, Inc.

colorism prejudices against individuals with darker skin tones or for individuals with lighter skin tones

communication process model represents how a sender creates messages with specific meanings (i.e., encode); the message then is transmitted through some channel to a receiver that construes their own meaning from the message (i.e., decode)

content analysis a research method that involves the systematic study of how an issue (or group) is framed across media artifacts

cringe experience a visceral reaction to something embarrassing or awkward

critical race theory past racial discrimination affects current lived experiences

cultural genocide acts and measures undertaken to destroy nations' or ethnic groups' culture through spiritual, national, and cultural destruction (also known as cultural annihilation); it is the elimination of a culture by ignoring or obfuscating cultural meaning

decode to interpret a specific meaning from a message; often independent from the original encoding

demisexual the need for emotional intimacy before physical or sexual intimacy

democracy a system of representative government wherein the whole population or all eligible members can participate

discourse the trends in communication or how a given issue is framed in media content, specifically the angle or perspective from which a story is told

discrimination actions or behaviors that advantage or disadvantage an individual based on their group affiliation

disguised pedigree satire where the content adopts the theme and methods of earlier satirical content

dispassionate commentary straightforward statements about the situation of life that does not deploy humor, irony, exaggeration or ridicule in the process of its critique

dominant receivers audiences who interpret a message as intended by the sender

double bind a situation in which people are confronted with two irreconcilable demands or a choice between two undesirable courses of action

double consciousness a phenomena where [marginalized] people are aware both of who they are and of how the rest of the world sees them and are constantly battling these two states

economic marginalization restricting certain groups from acquiring resources like limiting wages or prohibiting them from certain occupations and opportunities

encode to embed a specific meaning into a message

ethnicity one's cultural upbringing and the social practices of the group in which one was raised

explicit definition satire Satire where the author states the content is satire

extreme poverty (also referred to as absolute or deep poverty) income lower than half the national poverty line listed above according to the UN; income less than $4/day according to USA government

femininity the culturally agreed-upon expectations that come with being categorized as female

feminism the (organized) advocacy of women's rights for political, social, and economic equality; alternatively, the critical dismantling of gendered norms to disrupt their effect on political, economic, and psycho-social disadvantage

feminism; first wave largely defined by the movement for (white) women's suffrage

feminism; fourth wave at the start of the 21st century, intersectional and inclusive focus on unique discrimination against of women of color, queer women, trans women, disabled women, sex workers, and more through digital grassroots campaigns like Black Lives Matter and the MeToo Movements

feminism; second wave the social upheavals of the mid-20th century that focused on the social and economic limitations placed on women, with a focus on equal opportunity

feminism; third wave the "third wave" of feminism refers to advances in the intersectionality of feminism in the late 20th century, spurred by greater global awareness of the plight of women around the world

food deserts urban areas where it is difficult to buy affordable or good quality fresh food

framing (or to frame a message) provide structure that focuses the audience's attention to certain components and away from others

gay an umbrella term to indicate the community of people who identify with sexualities other than heterosexual

gay episodes single episodes of long-running series where a gay character is introduced for the purpose of triggering an emotional and personal epiphany in the main straight character

gender the individual identity (often but not always) associated with one's sex-based category or how we see ourselves and how we show ourselves to others

genderism the belief that that gender is rigid and binary

genocide the systematic eradication of a racial, ethnic, or religious group

hegemonic masculinity socially valued behaviors that allow men to continue to be dominant over women

hegemony the power or dominance that one social group holds over others (Lull 1995); it is also referred to as "asymmetrical interdependence," a strategy for obtaining and maintaining power wherein all groups within the hierarchy adhere to this established power dominance and engage in practices that reinforce this "super structure"

heteronormativity the belief that a long-term monogamous relationship between a man and a woman is the ideal, including the assumption that this relationship status is natural and all other sexualities and relationships are deviant; includes behaviors that are associated with heterosexuality including adopting gendered norms

heterosexual a person whose (binary) category to which they are assigned is associated with their (binary) gendered sense of self as they grow up and are attracted to someone on the other side of this binary association

hidden curriculum the implicit information about social categories embedded in supposedly objective educational spaces

homelessness the state of being without somewhere to sleep at night

homophobia the extreme or irrational fear of or aversion to homosexual people, includes stereotypes, language, attitudes, behaviors, and policies that seek to dehumanize and marginalize people who are not heterosexual and harm gay and queer communities

homophobia (institutional) anti-gay attitudes and behaviors become the basis of policy, often in line with and reinforcing stereotypes

homosexual a person whose binary category as assigned at birth is associated with their binary gender sense of self as they grow and who is attracted to someone on the same side of this binary association

hypodescent a phenomenon where people with any "subordinate" racial group in their heritage are assigned to the subordinate group; the opposite of hyperdescent, which conversely, hyperdescent assigns people with multiple groups to the group that is most superior

ideology a system of ideas and ideals, especially one which forms the basis of policy. Ideology is what we believe and vocalize

income the amount of money that an individual earns by working

income inequality the uneven distribution of income throughout a population

individual discrimination the actions taken by a single individual that favor or harm a person based on their social category (e.g., race, gender, and religion)

individual racism how individuals racialize others, thereby perpetuating racist stereotypes, prejudices, and discrimination to deploy and upload racial hierarchies

institutional discrimination policies within institutions like education and politics that reinforce disparities of social categories (e.g., lack of accessible entrances)

institutional/systemic racism the larger social effects of perpetuating racist stereotypes, prejudices, and discrimination

internalized homophobia the adoption of anti-gay attitudes by gay people

intersex individuals whose anatomy or genetics does not neatly adhere to the categories of male and female

jokes lines that are designed to be funny or to get a laugh

just world phenomenon the tendency to believe that the world is fair and that people get what they deserve.

lesbian women who find intimacy with women

living wage the minimum income necessary for someone to meet their basic needs including food, housing, and clothing

lynching public execution outside of the judicial system

magnification exaggerates or amplifies a singular or relatively small moment to critique a larger social phenomenon; includes amplification or "saying the quiet part out loud"

male entitlement a feature of a patriarchal system wherein (cis gendered) men are expected to have free and unfettered access, often used in reference to women's bodies but can also include geographic and financial access

male gaze the tendency to present women's bodies in a way that is assumed to be desirable to heterosexual men

man the gender expression generally associated with being male

marginalization (to marginalize, to other) to actively exclude, ostracize, alienate, and discriminate against a given group; includes economic marginalization, political marginalization, and social marginalization

marginalization satire satire that critiques this social hierarchy and the processes that maintain it, including the treatment of people who have been historically marginalized. It dissects the social constructs that maintain the marginalization of certain groups by drawing attention to social norms, public memories, and identities

marginalized treated as insignificant or peripheral

marginalized groups groups that have been historically and systematically excluded from participating in society

masculinity the culturally agreed-upon expectations that come with being categorized as male

media literacy the ability to understand the process by which content is produced and distributed and therefore parse deeper meanings associated with a given message or artifact

melting pot a phrase often used to refer to the collection of different cultures of people that all come together in the United States and provide some unique contribution to the larger culture

meritocracy a term used to describe governments or societies where ability determines one's power and status; originated from Michael Young's satirical novel *The Rise of the Meritocracy* (1958)

middle class those earning between double and two-thirds of the median household income— people making between $40,500 and $122,000 yearly

middle passage the perilous transport of millions of enslaved people across the Atlantic Ocean from Africa to the New World (i.e., North America, South American, and the Caribbean) as part of the Atlantic Slave Trade

minimum wage the lowest wage that employers can legally pay employees

misogyny dislike of, contempt for, or ingrained prejudice against women

mocking making fun of someone or something in a cruel way

monogamy the practice of only having one intimate relationship at a time

monosexism the idea that one is either attracted to individuals of the opposite gender (i.e., heterosexual) or of the same gender (i.e., homosexual, gay)

multiculturalism the belief that that cultural and ethnic differences should be celebrated and integrated; the opposite of colorblindness

myth of gay affluence the focus on wealthy white gay men in mainstream media

nature vs. nurture the phrase nature vs. nurture often accompanies debates regarding issues of gender. In this rhetorical argument, nature refers to the gendered behaviors and expectations that are supposedly innate to one's sex category assigned at birth; alternatively, nurture refers to the gendered behaviors and expectations that are nurtured or instilled over time

negotiated receivers audiences who decode the intended message but also engage in alternative interpretations, reading new meaning from a given text that may not have been intended by the sender

noise anything that obstructs or interferes with the encoding, transmission, or decoding of the message

non-binary (see gender-fluid) identifying as both man and woman or neither man nor woman and sometimes moving between these genders

objectification to treat an individual as an object to be desired

one-drop rule the one-drop rule means that anyone with any non-European (read: white) ancestry is automatically categorized as not white

oppositional receivers audiences who decode the message differently from its intended meaning because they do not bring the same body of knowledge to the message as the sender

othering to actively exclude, ostracize, alienate, and discriminate against a given group that is already marginalized

pansexual feeling an attraction – physical or emotional – to people independent of their gender (see bisexual)

parody to imitate the style of a particular writer, artist, or genre with deliberate exaggeration for comic effect

patriarchy a system of society or government in which men hold power and women are largely marginalized

pedigree satire where the content comes from a long line of satirical content or is branded as such (e.g., the White House Correspondents dinner, a traditional satirical venue for decade ensuring that Wilmore's delivery would be primarily interpreted as satire)

phenotype the set of observable characteristics of an individual resulting from the interaction of its genetics with the environment (e.g., hair color, height, muscular structure)

pink collar jobs that have been historically dominated by women (e.g., school teacher, healthcare worker)

pink tax the extra costs associated with products targeted towards women

pluralism/pluralistic a condition or system in which two or more states, groups, principles, sources of authority, etc., coexist

plutocracy a society in which the government is ruled by the wealthy

political marginalization restricting certain groups from participating in civic life through voting restrictions or access to political representation

polygenism the now-defunct theory that different races of humans evolved independently of each other

polysemy the phenomenon in which a message can have multiple meanings

postmodernism a philosophical approach to prior cultural artifacts that involves skepticism, irony, and a general deconstruction of the theories, behaviors, and artifacts that we have largely taken for granted, or accepted as valuable

poverty the state of being extremely poor

poverty line the line at which organized institutions (e.g., government, financial institutions) consider someone as "extremely poor"

prejudice positive or negative (i.e., valanced) opinions or attitudes of an individual or a group

privilege life experiences related to one's social categories that provides unearned statistical advantages in life

processes of marginalization how groups become and continue to be excluded from full and equitable participation in society

punching down any content that targets individuals who are of a lower status on the social hierarchy or disadvantaged groups who do not hold hegemonic power, further disenfranchising the disenfranchised

punching up any content that targets individuals who are of a higher status on the social hierarchy or advantaged groups who hold hegemonic power, further empowering the empowered

race a group of people who have been clustered according to a set of shared characteristics for social, economic, and legal purposes

raced (verb) a characteristic is "raced" when it is used to define whether someone belongs to a given racial category that has been established independent of individual experiences

racial/ethnic signifiers indicators of racial or ethnic categories

racialization (process of) using a singular piece of information (i.e., raced characteristic) to "understand" a whole person

racism the idea or ideology that all members of a given race possess characteristics or abilities specific to that race, especially to distinguish it as inferior or superior to another race or races

rape culture a society where rape and sexual violence are normalized and perpetuated by glorifying sexual violence with positive feedback

rape myths false but persistent beliefs and stereotypes regarding forced sexual intercourse, perpetrators, and their victims

reception theory reception theory states that the interpretation of a message depends on what the user brings to the message

redlining the economic practice of outlining certain areas of a city to indicate the land circumscribed is undesirable or a bad investment

religion a system of ideas and ideals that invokes the sacred through the nature of existence and forms the basis of social policy; also a social group defined by this shared ideology

Religious Freedom Restoration Act (RFRA) established in 1993 to protect religious minorities from being penalized for religious practices that were against federal law

rhetoric language primarily designed to persuade audiences, often in the absence of sincerity

satire the use of humor, irony, exaggeration or ridicule to expose and criticize social and individual absurdity, or something that is ridiculous or wildly unreasonable

satirical artifacts discrete pieces of satirical media content

satirical literacy the ability to access, analyze, evaluate, and even create satirical content that is effective – effective in demonstrating the absurdity of a social phenomenon and encouraging the audience to think differently about their associated social interactions, including seeing non-satirical media more critically

schemas basic narrative outlines or stories that serve as cognitive heuristics, or mental shortcuts (e.g., rags to riches, Cinderella stories, white savior)

scientific racism a pseudoscience that claimed there was evidence for the biological superiority of certain races over others

sex the state of being categorized as male or female, usually at birth

sexism beliefs and historical trends that have afforded greater opportunities and resources for men and relegate women to roles of support and lower income work in a patriarchal society

sexual identity how one personally identifies as an extension of their sexuality

sexual minorities a term used occasionally to indicate that people who identify as gay are in the numerical minority of American

sexual orientation the type of person for whom one feels a sense of sexual attraction

sexual violence sex acts attempted or achieved through violence or coercion, including rape and sex trafficking

sexuality a characteristic and identity associated with how one seeks and receives mature (i.e., adult) intimacy and interpersonal satisfaction, including meeting one's physical and/or emotional needs

sheltered people residing in homeless shelters, transitional housing, hotels and motels paid for charitable organizations

social atrocities cruel acts involving physical violence or injury that impact a society or a social group wherein (1) victims are targeted for their membership in a given social group, (2) the victims are targeted by an organized collective of perpetrators and enablers, and (3) there is a power differential between the perpetrators and the victims of these crimes

social creativity the practice of marginalized groups developing strategies to increase their group's value in response to systematic exclusion or discrimination

social marginalization rhetorically devaluing groups through media (mis)representation and social interactions

socialization learning how to behave in a way that is acceptable to society; also referred to as "hidden curriculum"

socioeconomic status (SES) one's position in a social hierarchy based on objective indicators of economic value (e.g., income and wealth), as well as the potential for monetary value (e.g., education and career)

solipsism the view or theory that the self is the only one that can be known to exist; the psychological tendency to believe that our experiences are the only experiences

statistical discrimination the deployment of observed differences between groups as a rationalization for disparate treatment

suffrage the right to vote

thin ideal the expectation that there is some perfect thin exemplar to which all women should meet, with a small waist and little body fat

toxic masculinity the phenomenon of engaging in behaviors that are detrimental to the health of the individual as well as those around them in order to appear "more manly"

transgender individuals whose gender does not conform to their sex assigned at birth

two-spirit a person who identifies as having both a masculine and a feminine spirit; a term used among Indigenous communities

typecasting represent or regard (a person or their role) as a stereotype

unsheltered people residing in cars, parks, and encampments, or other places not zoned for residential purposes

victimizing the perpetrator framing the long-term well-being of the perpetrator on par with or more important than justice served for their actual victim(s)

wealth the combined value of one's assets, including property and investments

wealth gap the disparity in overall financial worth (including income and assets) between classes

white supremacy an ideology in which white people are believed to be better (e.g., more civilized, more intelligent) than other racial or ethnic groups and characteristics that qualify as European (e.g., light skin, straight hair, narrow features) are perceived as more attractive and desirable

whiteness an ideology that advantages certain ethnic constructs and disadvantages others to maintain a racialized power structure

woman the gender expression generally associated with being female

Index

a

African (of African descent)   74, 79, 121, 124, 129, 144, 147, 167, 169
AIDS (see HIV-AIDS)
All in the Family   20, 21, 40, 83, 84, 101, 118
allegory   3, 18, 27
America   30, 32, 34–35, 38, 56, 58, 67, 76, 81, 104, 117, 127, 131–133, 136, 138–139, 147, 153, 157–158, 167, 172, 174, 183
animation   4–5, 11, 23, 43, 67, 102
anti-discrimination   96, 100, 108–109
anti-gay   95–97, 99–100, 103, 105–108, 114, 116
appropriation   141–144, 146, 167
Archie Bunker   20–21, 39
Asian (of Asian descent)   24, 29, 38, 75, 86, 121, 123–125, 136, 141–142, 144, 149
assault   11, 148, 156–157, 160–162, 171, 174–175, 181
assimilation   124, 141, 144, 149, 167
association   29, 31, 63, 67, 102, 125, 166, 172
atrocity   151–155, 157–164, 169–173

b

Beyoncé   135–136, 149
Bezos, Jeff   47–48, 59
bias   30, 90, 104, 119, 128, 141, 149
bigot   20–21, 100, 102–103, 127, 179
biological   60, 62–63, 68, 92, 117, 119, 133
bisexual   94, 99, 109, 111–114, 116–118, 173
blackface   24, 134
Blackness   90, 94, 130, 132–136, 147
blog   26, 73, 118, 148–149
du Bois, W.E.B   24, 30, 169, 173
Boston   5–7, 10, 25, 149
British   35, 58, 88, 123, 149
Britton, Connie   37, 57
Buzzfeed   21, 29, 35, 62, 118

c

campaign   2, 5, 7, 13, 30, 47, 64
capitalism   14, 34, 40, 48, 58
caricatures   126–127, 155, 167–168
cartoon   1, 4, 10, 46–47, 50, 52, 67, 69, 73, 109, 129, 149, 155, 159, 164–165
casting   70, 75–76, 133, 169
CDC   163, 165, 173
Chappelle, Dave   23–24, 26, 29, 135, 181
Charlie Hebdo   19
cisgender   13, 14, 61, 76, 82, 98–99, 106, 109, 154
class (see socioeconomic status)
Clinton, Hilary   65, 81, 84, 108
CNBC   56–58
Colbert, Stephen   30, 179, 182
colorblindness   138–141, 143–145, 149
Comedy Central   1, 15, 17, 23, 43, 45, 57, 70, 81, 88, 114, 117, 126, 127, 147, 165, 166, 172
communication   22–23, 30, 31, 54, 56, 73, 89, 117, 119, 147, 178
Cooper, Sarah   8, 9, 31, 73

Diversity and Satire: Laughing at Processes of Marginalization, First Edition.
Charisse L'Pree Corsbie-Massay.
© 2023 John Wiley & Sons, Inc. Published 2023 by John Wiley & Sons, Inc.

d

Daily Show, The   1, 8, 9, 30, 43, 45, 81, 104, 117, 127, 147, 162, 166, 176, 179
death   7, 46, 129, 135, 159, 163–165, 172, 175
dehumanization   53, 79, 100, 107, 112, 132–133, 144, 152, 154, 156, 167–168, 171–172
DeGeneres, Ellen   99
democratic   19, 48, 54, 58
discrimination   14, 16–19, 21, 27, 29, 32–33, 37–38, 53, 80, 82, 91, 95–96, 100, 106–109, 111, 115–117, 124, 127, 133–134, 138–141, 145–146, 148–149, 151–152, 154, 166, 171–172, 179–180, 182
diversity   1, 17, 21, 29–30, 32, 54, 60, 75, 77, 91, 93–94, 103, 106, 109, 111, 113–114, 118–119, 120, 128, 133, 135, 139, 144, 147–149, 151, 159, 171, 177, 179–182
Dr. Seuss   154, 173

e

election   8, 15, 26, 54, 81–82, 88, 179
England   77, 122–123, 125, 131
enslaved   38, 137–138, 145, 151, 169–171
entertainment   1, 28, 29, 38–39, 56, 94, 103, 109, 113–114, 119, 182
equality   13, 80, 81, 83, 94, 115–116, 137–138, 140
Eric Cartman   10, 21, 128, 166
ethnicity   68, 120, 123, 125, 133, 145, 172
Europe   32, 35–36, 38, 56, 74, 76, 89, 101, 121–123, 125, 130, 132–134, 138, 155, 167, 174

f

Family Guy   106, 107, 118, 131, 148
femininity   60, 63–66, 68–76, 80, 83, 86–88, 104–105, 152, 161
feminism   71, 80–81, 83, 88–89
feminist   88–90, 109–110
film   30, 64–65, 69, 77, 87, 90, 106–107, 109, 113, 160–161, 175

FOX   42–43, 102, 106, 116–118, 131, 148
Funny or Die   8, 30, 40, 57, 126, 179

g

gay   92, 94–95, 99, 100, 102, 106–107, 109–110, 112–113, 116, 118–119, 143
genderism   76–77, 80–81, 86
genders   61, 76, 87, 92, 94, 96, 99, 111, 161
genocide   25, 125, 135, 143–144, 147–148, 152–153, 157, 167–170, 175
God   48, 54, 75–76, 95, 109, 125
government   3, 5, 11, 13, 19, 40–41, 44–45, 48, 64, 91, 118, 128, 138, 157, 164

h

HBO   29, 94, 117
healthcare   33, 43–44, 65, 106, 159, 166
hegemonic masculinity   64, 73
hegemony   13–18, 21–22, 24, 28, 30–31, 44, 64, 73, 83, 86, 88, 96, 105, 109, 125, 153–154, 170, 181
heteronormative   93, 96, 98–100, 103, 106
heterosexual   14, 67, 69, 77, 91–100, 103–106, 109, 111, 114–115, 118, 163–164
Highet, Gilbert   2–3, 25–27, 30
HIV-AIDS   38, 157, 163–166, 173–175
Hollywood   70, 75, 106, 110, 181, 183
Holocaust   148, 155–156, 172, 175
homeless   25, 47, 59, 114, 117, 152, 157–159, 172, 174
Homer Simpson   21, 49, 104
homophobia   96–97, 99–101, 103–108, 111, 114, 116–118, 127, 163–164, 173
homosexual (see gay)
Huey Freeman   10–13
humanity   11, 17, 25, 61–62, 76, 124, 139, 152–154, 169, 172

i

ideology 13–14, 16–17, 21, 34, 39, 86–87, 89, 96, 115, 125, 127, 130–131, 133, 135, 138–139, 144, 149, 152–153, 167,169
immigrant 18, 122, 135, 141, 147
income 32–33, 41–42, 44, 46–48, 50–51, 54–56, 68, 114, 157–159
Indigenous (of Indigenous descent) 38, 74, 108, 121, 123–125, 130, 136, 145, 151, 153, 160, 167–169
inequality 33, 42, 46, 54, 57, 81, 83, 137, 147
institutionalized discrimination 7, 13, 17, 32, 35, 39, 41–42, 54, 86, 91, 96, 100, 106–108, 127, 140, 153, 159, 166
interpersonal 5, 60, 68, 74–75, 77, 80, 91–92, 100, 109, 111, 160, 171
intersectionality 1, 25, 36–37, 67, 74, 81–82, 84, 110, 113
intersex 62, 79, 88, 96
irony 1–2, 4, 7, 27, 35–36, 40, 44, 50, 102–103, 106

j

Jesus Christ 27, 95, 181, 183
journalism 7, 30, 83, 100, 109, 119
justice 1, 14, 83, 117–118, 129, 148, 154, 162

k

Key & Peele 15–16, 30, 97, 114, 117, 137

l

leadership 3, 13, 24, 62, 69, 73–74, 81, 88, 138, 163–164
Lear, Norman 20–22, 30, 118
lesbian (see gay)
LGBTQ 14, 89, 99, 109, 111–114, 117–118, 166, 174
London 30–31, 89, 123
low-income 38, 43, 54, 58, 152, 166

m

magazine 15, 19, 23, 30, 99, 170, 173
magnification 3, 5, 7, 27

Mandvi, Assaf 126
marginalization satire 1, 12–17, 19, 20–25, 28, 32, 45, 53, 60, 64, 68, 79, 83–86, 91, 100, 111, 113, 115, 120, 139, 151–153, 156, 164, 167, 171–172, 177–178, 181–182
marriage 37, 89, 91, 94, 105, 115–116, 132, 143
Married with Children 40
mascots 144, 167–168, 173
masculinity 60, 64–69, 73, 76–77, 80, 83, 86–88, 102, 104–105, 109, 161
Mexico 8, 30, 38, 76, 144, 172
middle-class 40, 45, 51–53, 82, 109, 158
millennials 35, 56–57, 118, 133, 138–139
movie (see film)
Murphy, Eddie 134
music 8, 11, 30, 56, 69–70, 72, 107, 134–135, 143, 145, 155, 182
Muslim (of Muslim faith) 19, 30, 125–126, 138, 145
myth 90, 112, 114, 147, 160, 174

n

NBC 36, 41, 57–58, 66, 77, 116, 134–135, 155, 169, 176
newspapers 49, 159, 174
Noah, Trevor 8–9, 30, 104–105, 117, 180
non-binary 14, 61–63, 76–77, 79–80, 91, 94, 96, 99–100
NPR 89, 124, 148

o

Obama, Barack 2–3, 128, 148
Onion, The 7, 26, 29, 33–34, 47, 49–50, 58–59, 79, 86, 88, 157, 173, 175, 177, 180, 183
oppression 32, 95, 103, 114, 118, 155
Orwell, George 3

p

pandemic 8–9, 48, 57, 65, 159, 163–164, 166
pansexual 94, 99, 111
parody 2–5, 8, 15, 26–27, 31, 44, 70, 75, 77–78, 85, 88, 89, 106, 111, 126, 134, 155, 165, 168

platforms   54, 113, 116, 178, 182
police   10, 63, 128–129, 132, 137, 147–148, 160–161
poverty   15, 31, 35, 37–42, 46–48, 54–58, 114, 116, 128, 149, 156–159, 165, 169, 171, 173–175
prejudice   16–18, 20–21, 27–30, 32–33, 53, 68, 78, 80, 91, 97, 100, 116, 119, 124, 140, 127, 133, 140, 142, 145, 152, 166, 171–172, 178
prison   30, 118, 161–162, 175
privilege   35, 46–47, 55, 64, 112, 130, 146–147, 163, 171
psychology   20, 30, 44–45, 58, 60, 64, 88–89, 91–92, 118, 120, 124, 147–149, 174–175

r

race   10, 16, 27, 31, 35, 38, 74, 95, 109, 121, 123, 125, 127–129, 132–133, 135–141, 144, 146–149, 152, 167, 179, 181, 183
racism   15–16, 30–31, 120, 123–124, 126–130, 133–134, 138–149, 163, 167, 172–174, 179, 181
rape   8, 25, 153, 160–162, 170–174
Reagan, Ronald   163–165, 175
religion   12–14, 27, 35, 68, 83, 98, 108–109, 113, 115, 125–127, 139, 145–146, 152–153
Romney, Mitt   47, 50–52, 56–57, 59

s

Saturday Night Live (SNL)   36, 66, 89, 136, 149, 156, 175, 182
Schumer, Amy   70
segregation   34, 45, 129
socioeconomic status (SES)   12–13, 25, 27, 32–38, 40, 42–48, 50–56, 58, 64, 67–68, 74, 86, 113–114, 118, 129, 137, 157–159, 163
sex   12, 37, 60–63, 67, 76–77, 82, 87–88, 91, 98–99, 103, 105–106, 111, 140, 160, 164, 175
sexism   37–38, 56, 70, 73, 76, 81, 86, 163, 169
sexual orientation (see sexuality)

sexuality   30, 91, 94–97, 100, 107, 109, 111, 113, 117–118
Simpsons, The   1, 21–22, 29, 40, 51, 53, 102–104, 117–118
sitcom   20, 51, 67, 99, 126–127
slave (see enslaved)
slavery   25, 109, 137, 144, 152, 157, 167–170, 173
socialization   34, 60, 62–63, 69, 83, 99
solipsism   44–45, 49, 54, 96, 115
South Park   17, 18, 21, 31, 79, 165, 174
sports   15, 64–65, 79, 88, 104, 144, 167–168
standards   11, 52, 74, 138
Stanford University   15, 161–162, 174
Stanton, Gregory   152–153, 155, 175
stereotype   16–18, 21, 23–24, 27–28, 29, 33, 40, 43, 54, 66, 75, 83, 88, 98, 105, 116, 123, 125–126, 142, 146, 152, 159, 168, 181
Stewart, Jon   43, 45, 57, 81, 127, 147, 162, 166, 176, 179
suffrage   14, 80, 82
Swift, Johnathan   3
Sykes, Wanda   94, 98, 117, 140

t

tax   35, 42, 44–46, 50–51, 70, 91, 115
television   1–2, 15, 22, 25, 29–30, 40, 45–46, 51, 56, 69–70, 83, 100, 109, 113, 117–118, 148–149, 159–160, 174, 182
transgender   13, 61, 63, 76–77, 79–80, 82, 88–89, 94, 96, 99–100, 116–118, 151, 154, 156, 172, 174–175, 181
Trudeau, Garry   12, 19, 31
Trump, Donald   5–10, 25–26, 30, 46, 58, 65, 173, 175, 179
Twitter   21, 29, 54, 58, 70, 88, 179–180, 183

u

University of California, Los Angeles (UCLA)   116–117, 141
upper-class   13, 45, 53, 67, 82, 109, 162
user-generated content (UGC)   1, 54, 79, 97, 111, 133, 177

w

war   25, 35, 118, 124–125, 138, 152, 158
welfare   30, 33, 41–44, 108
white supremacy   14, 16, 130, 133, 175
Wilmore, Larry   2, 127
working-class   16, 20, 39–40, 50–51, 54, 67, 82, 174

y

Yankovic, "Weird" Al   4–5, 13, 31
Young-White, Jaboukie   104–105, 117
YouTube   29–31, 57–58, 75, 88–90, 96, 111, 117, 119, 121, 141–142, 147–149, 173, 175